"Comprehensive and easy to read, this career guide is perfect for anyone just about to hit the job market. Its insights helped me realize that **A GREAT NONPROFIT JOB IS WITHIN REACH**."

— John Pham, Baruch College, Class of 2008

MORE PRAISE FOR *The Nonprofit Career Guide . . .*

"An exceptionally clear and engaging tour of the nonprofit sector. *The Nonprofit Career Guide* explains the types of jobs available, how to prepare for them, and how to land the job you want. Interviews featuring nonprofit staff and leaders add the touch of reality that makes this book such a valuable tool."

— Russell A. Cargo, PhD, Director, Nonprofit and Civil Society Program, Virginia Tech Institute for Policy and Governance

"I highly recommend Shelly Cryer's book to any student or young grad who wants to make a difference in the world. If you're looking for resources, insight, or advice, you can find everything you need in *The Nonprofit Career Guide.*"

— Sheila J. Curran, Executive Director, Duke University Career Center, and coauthor of *Smart Moves for Liberal Arts Grads: Finding a Path to Your Perfect Career*

"This book is a gem and an absolutely essential resource for anyone considering a career in the not-for-profit sector! It offers keen insights into the community and the myriad of exciting and interesting career opportunities to be found. Anyone interested in challenging work, professional growth, and making a difference will be even more inspired after consulting this guide."

— Carole Dickert-Scherr, Vice President, Human Resources, PBS

"The candid advice from Shelly Cryer and other experts make this book an invaluable guide for anyone who wants to land a job that makes a difference."

— Kimberly Hendler, Executive Director, Princeton Project 55, and Young Nonprofit Professionals Network National Board Member

"What a tremendous resource—a must read for new students! *The Nonprofit Career Guide* is a thoughtful and insightful journey into the exciting and personally rewarding career opportunities in the nonprofit sector."

> – William L. Pollard, PhD, Vice President, National Association of State Universities and Land-Grant Colleges (NASULGC)

"Finding a job in the nonprofit sector just got easier. This book is a comprehensive tool for anyone seeking a job in the nonprofit sector *and* for those of us who advise others on how to obtain one. It has important information about key trends, an overview of the subsectors and job opportunities of the sector, and a summary of research that will dispel the myths about these jobs. It is a must for any career counselor or life coach's office."

> – Terri Barreiro, Director, Donald McNeely Center for Entrepreneurship, Saint John's University and the College of Saint Benedict in central Minnesota

"*The Nonprofit Career Guide* details all the decisions and steps to finding the right job with the right organization. It provides practical advice and offers a pathway for making a career of making a difference."

> – Bill Bentley, President & CEO, Voices for America's Children

"Whether you are 22 or 62, if you are looking for work in a nonprofit, this book is a useful tool. Shelly Cryer not only gives you a step-by-step guide to matching your skills with the nonprofit of your dreams, but along the way she is a terrific salesperson for the value and meaning of working in the nonprofit sector. I'll recommend this book to all my students."

> – Peter Brinckerhoff, nonprofit consultant and author of *Generations*

"What a useful overview of career opportunities in the nonprofit sector and of the sector itself!"

> – Irv Katz, President & CEO, National Human Services Assembly

"Thanks to Shelly Cryer, we have the perfect road map for the future leaders of the nonprofit sector, who will benefit from the map and the quality counsel she offers."

> – Robert F. Long, Director, Greater Battle Creek Programming and Senior Program Officer, W. K. Kellogg Foundation

"This book is the most comprehensive piece yet on the nonprofit sector. It is a must for the neophyte job seeker to the most experienced nonprofit professional."

> – John D. Welty, President, California State University, Fresno

THE NONPROFIT CAREER GUIDE

how to land a job that **makes a difference**

SHELLY CRYER

FIELDSTONE
ALLIANCE

SAINT PAUL
MINNESOTA

Fieldstone Alliance is committed to strengthening the performance of the nonprofit sector. Through the synergy of its consulting, training, publishing, and research and demonstration projects, Fieldstone Alliance provides solutions to issues facing nonprofits, funders, and the communities they serve. Fieldstone Alliance was formerly Wilder Publishing and Wilder Consulting departments of the Amherst H. Wilder Foundation. If you would like more information about Fieldstone Alliance and our services, please contact

800-274-6024
www.FieldstoneAlliance.org

For more information on American Humanics, please see pages 281–282 at the back of this book.

Edited by Vincent Hyman
Designed by Bruce Kreps Design
Manufactured in the USA
First printing, May 2008

**Library of Congress
Cataloging-in-Publication Data**

Cryer, Shelly, 1968-
  The nonprofit career guide : how to land a job that makes a difference / by Shelly Cryer.
     p. cm.
  ISBN 978-0-940069-59-6
  1. Nonprofit organizations--Vocational guidance. 2. Nonprofit organizations--Employees. I. Title.
  HD2769.15.C79 2008
  650.14--dc22

                2008006880

Photo credits:

Cover images from Getty Images, iStock, and Veer

p 13   Sigrid Estrada
p 25   Martin Lueders, Insight Photos, courtesy of the Corporation for National and Community Service
p 31   Keu Stone
p 48   Courtesy of the Skoll Foundation
p 60   Courtesy of SAM public relations
p 78   Jennifer Coate, March of Dimes
p 119   Catherine Gaffney
p 140   Gloria Baker
p 146   Daniel G. McCarthy
p 174   Kea Taylor, Imagine Photography (2007)
p 208   John Pelikan
p 241   Kansas State University photographic services
p 252   Fond Memories (2007)
p 283   Alden Ford

All photo portraits were provided by the subject and used with permission.

DEDICATION

My parents did little teaching—they offered their daughters great freedom and showed unconditional support for our explorations. But there were two lessons that I learned, undisputedly, by way of my parents' example. My father taught me to ask questions. My mother taught me to listen to answers. Add to this mix a quite extraordinary sister who, from as early as I can remember, taught me to think critically about what I was told (and to have fun).

It is thanks to this base that I have found such rewarding work in the nonprofit sector. The best organizations provide ample space for people with curious and creative minds who want to make the world a better place. Because of my family, I like to be around such people. And although this is a modest book, it may be my only one, and so it is to my father, mother, and sister that I dedicate it.

But it got written because of Michael and Hannon, and the sweet and supportive music they made while I typed. Thank you.

Shelly Cryer
April 2008

CONTENTS

LIST OF PROFILES

ACKNOWLEDGMENTS

My deep appreciation goes to Courtney Herren Gardner, who as a student at William Jewell College worked at American Humanics to help me develop the vision for this book and plan its content. She conducted thorough research, drafted text, and provided leadership in organizing our approach. Courtney also contributed good humor and smart thinking and was such a pleasure to work with that this book truly launched on the right foot.

Special thanks to Kelly Nuxoll, for her adept researching and writing of the "Spotlight on . . ." sections on the nonprofit subsectors. Kelly is a freelance writer and editor who has worked in seven of the nonprofit subsectors, including arts, education, politics, and international aid.

Thank you to the nonprofit sector leaders who offered personal insights and inspiration in the profiles found throughout this book. Thank you, as well, to the other experts who contributed juicy tips and substantive information through their sidebars. They represent admirably the talent, skills, and passion for mission that fuel the sector and enable its organizations to succeed.

Thanks to James Yin for his assistance with the sample job descriptions.

Thank you to Jamie Darrah, an American Humanics NextGen Leader scholarship recipient from the City University of New York, Baruch College, for her helpful research and marketing ideas.

Continued thanks to Melissa Witham and Cathy Crimmins-Lechowicz who made invaluable contributions to this project as star research assistants during its initial phase at New York University's Wagner Graduate School of Public Service. Now professionals in the nonprofit sector, their contributions to the sector continue and expand.

Thank you to the UPS Foundation for most generous support of American Humanics' Initiative for Nonprofit Sector Careers, of which this book is one project. Thanks also to the other grantmakers that have supported the initiative, including the W.K. Kellogg Foundation, Ewing Marion Kauffman Foundation, and William Randolph Hearst Foundation.

Consulting editor Vince Hyman brought to this project deep knowledge of the nonprofit sector, great editing skills, and encouragement. As importantly, Kirsten Nielsen's management of this project was excellent. Fieldstone Alliance's Carol Lukas first helped establish the relationship with American Humanics and she, Vince, Kirsten, Becky Andrews, and their colleagues make a wonderful team of collaborators. Their fine editing, design, and marketing contributed enormously to the quality of this book.

Thank you to Richard Potter and all American Humanics staff for their good ideas and contributions to the field. Special appreciation goes to AH president Kala Stroup, who responded with alacrity to the idea for a national Nonprofit Sector Workforce Coalition to help build the pipeline of talent into the sector. She and AH's board of directors and staff devoted resources and energy to this initiative for a good much greater than any one organization. Their work has collaboration as its underpinning and is a model for the sector.

Kala also has been unfailingly supportive of my writing, and accommodating when I temporarily abandoned the project to birth a baby before a book. I am grateful that after my time in the sector, I was affiliated with American Humanics when I wanted to find a way to balance a happy personal life with a meaningful professional life. I hope this book is better for that—I know my life is.

---

your input is appreciated

careerguide@humanics.org

Fieldstone Alliance, American Humanics, and the author hope to update this guide regularly. We welcome your input on its content, as well as specific resources that should be included or deleted. Those who submit recommendations for our updates will be entered in a raffle to receive free copies of the revised book. Send your comments via e-mail to careerguide@humanics.org.

Thank you in advance for your feedback.

PREFACE

What if the nonprofit sector needed a résumé? Could you put one together? Probably not—because it would be impossible to create a document that captured the entire scope and value of nonprofit organizations' contributions to society.

If the résumé only focused on the opening decade of the twenty-first century—a decade representing a mere "blip" in the history of nonprofit organizations—it still would be hard to decide which world events to highlight or nonprofit sector responses to cite.

Iraq. Darfur. Congo. September 11th.

Hurricane Katrina. The Asian tsunamis. Earthquakes in Iran and Kashmir.

Pollution. Peak oil. Deforestation.

SARS. HIV/AIDS. Malaria. Tuberculosis.

From delivering water and food to refugees displaced by civil war to mobilizing people around global climate change, every day of every year, the nonprofit sector operates as a major player in world affairs.

But just as critically, the nonprofit sector offers vital services in even the smallest of communities. It is responsible for summer camps, after-school programs, food banks, and libraries. It runs blood banks, Audubon centers, and museums.

The nonprofit sector addresses problems we've struggled with for centuries—violence, famine, natural disasters. But it is also dynamic and evolving, and takes on issues and opportunities we couldn't have dreamed of even a decade ago.

It speaks for the people when the government is absent . . . or mistaken.

It protects our oceans and forests and the creatures that live in them. It produces and preserves art. It builds homes. It feeds. It explores; it educates. It upholds laws and defends basic rights. It thinks, it writes, and it teaches how to read. It ministers. It heals.

It steps in to offer assistance when a tragedy is of such epic proportion that it shakes a nation. And, just as willingly, it extends a hand when only one life is in need.

Of course, "it"—this diverse, dynamic, and absolutely vital nonprofit sector—is nothing if not its people. In the United States, it is 12.9 million paid workers and the equivalent of 4.7 million full-time volunteers committed to their communities and engaged in their work. That's almost 18 million people who get to go to bed each night with the knowledge that during their days, they work to make a difference.

Because you picked up this book, it's likely that you, too, have heard the "call to serve." The leaders running organizations that make up the nonprofit sector—hungry for talented and committed individuals—hope you will heed that call. And I hope that this book will help connect you to the job you have dreamed of—a job that will be the beginning of a long and rewarding career in the nonprofit sector.

introduction

WELCOME JOB SEEKERS

FINDING A GREAT JOB AND BUILDING A CAREER IN THE NONPROFIT SECTOR

For most people in the nonprofit sector, their work is not just a "job." It is part of a life of meaning that depends, in no small part, on building a career that makes an impact for good.

Nonprofit organizations attract individuals who want to make a difference. Leaders at the best organizations continually cultivate a pipeline of new workers who bring skills, experiences, and passion for an issue to their teams. Great leaders and their effective organizations nurture talent, provide opportunity, and make good use of these, their most valuable human resources.

In the best cases, an organization's newest recruits have landed jobs that fuel their commitment to

the work and launch a long and rewarding career in the nonprofit sector. Many of these workers will switch organizations and some may spend time working in business or government. But their fundamental commitment to service—to doing work that contributes to positive social change—was established early in their career, with a great job at a well-run, professional nonprofit organization.

Too often, however, individuals interested in a career of public service find it difficult to land a great first job. Nonprofit organizations can seem difficult to break into, plum jobs appear scarce and are given to more experienced professionals, decision makers are hard to reach, and human resources departments are frequently understaffed (or don't exist). Career development professionals and other individuals who job seekers go to for guidance are often uninformed about work in the nonprofit sector. Good advice is hard to find.

Hence this book, written to provide up-to-date information and advice for the nonprofit sector job seeker.

This book offers concrete data on the size and scope of the nonprofit sector and the types of organizations that comprise it. It provides a *sense* of what it feels like to work at a nonprofit organization. It details recommendations on how to gain and communicate the skills and experiences that will make you an attractive candidate to a prospective employer. And then it offers specific strategies for how to find suitable openings, get your application noticed, and land a job.

But this book is dedicated to more than just helping the nonprofit sector job seeker land a job. First and foremost, it seeks to help you identify and secure a *great* job at a *good* organization filled with *professional* staff members whom you will be happy to call your colleagues. The job you find should match your interest areas and make good use of your talents. You can and should be discriminating, and this book will help you conduct a search that leads to identifying an appropriate professional home in the nonprofit sector.

Second, this book is dedicated to helping you find a job that, ideally, will launch a long and rewarding *career*. This is the path you embark on that is bigger than any one job. It is about establishing a professional life that reflects who you are and what you care about. A rewarding career means finding and following your calling, and being fulfilled financially, intellectually, and emotionally. It is about devoting your days—and perhaps occasional evenings—to work that matters so that when you go to bed at night, you feel good about what you have done.

The right first couple of jobs and the career they lead to will result in the ultimate professional gift. Make yourself lucky enough to be able to look back on your life after ten, twenty, or even forty years of various jobs and say, "I loved my work. I am happy with my choices. I am proud of what I contributed."

This Book Is Written For . . . You

The people who work in the nonprofit sector are as varied as the organizations that comprise it. There is a place for everyone—from salespeople, scientists, and computer technicians to teachers, writers, and even bakers. Your interest areas and skill sets should not limit your consideration of a nonprofit sector job; they should simply be used to direct you to the one most appropriate for you.

Furthermore, the best nonprofit leaders want to recruit new talent representing the full diversity of the populations their organizations serve. The best organizations are hungry for fresh perspectives and innovative thinking that will contribute to strategies and programs to advance their missions. The diversity of race, ethnicity, religion, economic background, and sexual orientation that you bring to an organization will provide this fresh perspective. This diversity will be viewed as an asset by savvy leaders working to make their organizations succeed in the decades ahead.

No matter who you are or what you want to do, if you're interested in the nonprofit sector as a place of employment—and if you've prepared yourself appropriately—there is a job for you.

This book is written for anyone interested in a nonprofit sector career. It will help job seekers who know precisely the type of organization they want to work for and job they want to do. For these individuals, this book will help you find and land the right job and parlay it into a great career.

This book also will help job seekers who have less direction, but who know generally that they want to be part of an organization that emphasizes its mission more than a financial bottom line. For these individuals hoping to "make a difference" in the work you do but grappling with where to look, the book will help you narrow your focus and direct your search.

The book provides information, advice, and specific strategies suitable for anyone, at any point in his or her career. Some of the material is targeted to individuals entering the workforce for the first time, with their education still under way or just recently completed. However, the majority of the book is appropriate for all nonprofit sector job seekers of any age or level of experience.

The book also provides critical information for career advisors—guidance counselors, career counselors, academic advisors, and placement directors, to name just a few. If you provide career advice to students or young or midlevel professionals, this book will deepen your understanding of the nonprofit sector as a place of employment and help you better serve individuals interested in public service. If you teach classes covering the nonprofit sector, this book serves as a practical tool to help your students grasp the power of the sector and career opportunities it offers.

What's Inside

This book is a true handbook. It was designed for job seekers who want to read it cover to cover, but it works just as well for "flip-through" readers who want to pick and choose the information they need. Regardless of your approach, you should know what's inside so that you can make the best use of the material ahead.

Chapter 1: Understanding the Nonprofit Sector

Chapter 1 helps you understand what the nonprofit sector is all about. It presents the most current data available to explain the size and scope of the sector, the range of organizations that comprise it, and the work that these groups perform and services they provide. It also covers the culture of nonprofit organizations and what it "feels" like to work at one. The chapter addresses the vital role nonprofit organizations play in our society and recent trends that affect its workforce, and describes how those trends are relevant to the job seeker.

a note on sidebars

Throughout this book you will find sidebars (or boxed information), often contributed by experts in the field. In brief text format, these sections cover a range of subjects relevant to the nonprofit job seeker—from compensation in the nonprofit sector to why to avoid cell phones in your outreach efforts. The sidebars are designed so that they stand out from the text, but are connected to the bigger issues discussed in the main body of the chapters where they appear. You might want to flip through the book just to skim all of the sidebars. But make sure you spend time with the boxes—and accompanying main text—most relevant to you.

Chapter 2: Spotlight on Key Nonprofit Subsectors

Chapter 2 focuses in on nine key subsectors that most nonprofit organizations can be classified into. These nonprofit categories include organizations that focus on

- arts, culture, and humanities
- education
- environment and animals
- health
- human services
- international, foreign affairs
- public or societal benefit
- religion-related
- mutual/membership benefit

For each category, the book provides an overview of the work of this subsector and specifics on the types of organizations in it. It offers a brief history of the field and key trends. Each section concludes with a few bullets on current statistics relevant to the subsector, such as its funding streams, size relative to the sector overall, and growth and workforce needs. Readers will also find boxes featuring a few key websites specific to careers and job opportunities in that field.

Chapter 3: Jobs in the Nonprofit Sector

Chapter 3 discusses the range of job functions in the nonprofit sector. It describes positions that exist in business and government as well as at nonprofit organizations, and describes what they look like and work they are responsible for when based at a nonprofit. The chapter also covers jobs that are unique to nonprofit organizations, such as fundraising and development jobs.

The book covers jobs in five categories of responsibility (and also details key subcategories in each):

- senior management (including executive director and associate director positions)

- programs and service delivery (including advocacy, counseling and direct social services, education and training, and research and policy positions)

- administration, human resources, and finance (including accounting and finance, operations, clerical and data entry, human resources, information technology, sales and telemarketing, and customer service positions)

- development and fundraising (including annual fund, grant writing and administration, major gifts, planned giving, and special events positions)

- communications (including editing, writing, and publications; graphic design; marketing and advertising; media relations; and web development and design positions)

——— *profiles* ———

Throughout the book are profiles of nineteen real people working in the nonprofit sector. These two-page spreads focus on nonprofit sector professionals who represent a range of experiences, skills, and education levels and who perform very different jobs. Some have spent their careers in the nonprofit sector, others have transitioned from business or government to their current nonprofit home. Some are very senior managers or executive directors, others are early- or mid-career professionals.

The individuals profiled work at organizations that are very different as well. Their groups represent a range of missions and budget sizes, and they employ different strategies to advance their work. Some groups are based in small towns, others in major metropolitan areas. Some employ hundreds of staff members, others just a handful.

All of these individuals responded to the same set of questions; their different answers offer insight into the real people and actual jobs at nonprofit organizations. They also offer career advice—within the profiles you'll find tips on what they look for in recruiting staff, their perspective on who excels in their type of work, and some concrete resources if you're interested in their field.

The profiles demonstrate the breadth of opportunity in the nonprofit sector and the variety of career paths a nonprofit professional can follow. Hopefully, they will inspire as much as instruct.

Chapter 3 also covers consulting work in the nonprofit sector, both as a solo practitioner and as a member of a consulting firm that specializes in nonprofit organization clients.

The second part of Chapter 3 provides sample job descriptions. These are fictional job descriptions at fictional organizations that were developed from actual postings. They offer the job seeker a sense of the types of jobs available and the skills and experience required. Determine which job postings sound interesting and appropriate for you, and as you're reading the book, think about how you can apply the information to a job search strategy geared toward those positions.

Throughout Chapter 3 readers will find notes connecting a job function description to a related sidebar, profile, or sample job description. If you are interested in research work, for example, in the section that describes research positions you will be directed to a profile of a researcher, as well as a sample job description that describes one type of research position.

Chapter 4: Preparing for a Career in the Nonprofit Sector

Chapters 4 and 5 cover the nuts and bolts of landing a job and building a career in the nonprofit sector. Chapter 4 focuses on the preparation you can do, both in terms of the mental preparation of understanding who you are and establishing direction for what you want to do professionally, as well as the practical preparation achieved through academic programs, internships, volunteering, networking, and other activities.

Job seekers often ignore how important it is to do the first piece—know thyself (probably because it is the $64 million question that many people wrestle with for a lifetime). Chapter 4 encourages you to explore these framing questions:

- What are the issues you care about?
- What type of work have you done and enjoyed?
- What are you good at?
- How do you want to live?
- How do these beliefs and experiences point toward what you might like to do?

The chapter uses these questions to offer advice on how to direct your search. This direction can make all the difference to how successful your search is and how rewarding you find your career.

Chapter 4 then goes on to discuss a range of opportunities that will help you build knowledge, develop skills, and gain experience to support your career goals. In the process, you also are likely to refine even further your ideas about the work you would like to do and organizations you would like to work for. The chapter covers opportunities for the student and recent graduate—as well as the professional hoping to transition into the sector—including

- educational tracks

- certificate programs
- advanced degrees
- volunteering
- interning
- other extracurricular activities
- mentoring
- professional development opportunities
- year of service programs

Once prepared to launch your career, you're now ready to land that job, so move on to Chapter 5.

Chapter 5: Landing a Great Job in the Nonprofit Sector

Chapter 4 helped you sharpen your focus on what you want to do. Chapter 5 provides concrete tips to help you land a great job. The chapter discusses the professionalism and other characteristics you should demonstrate as you approach your job search. It then concentrates on why and how to use seven key tools in your outreach efforts. You'll learn about

- sound research
- effective networking
- targeted search strategies
- persuasive cover letters
- a stellar résumé
- deal-closing interviews
- appropriate follow-up and negotiation

Effectively employing these tools will help you stay up to date and informed about your field and work that is available in it, build networks of contacts who can support your career and give you a "leg up" in the job search, identify positions and organizations that are appropriate for you, and then get your application noticed once you apply for a position. Interviewing advice and tips for appropriate follow-up will help you seal the deal and negotiate the offer you deserve.

Appendix: Resources

In the back of the book you'll find additional resources to help you in your nonprofit sector job search and career development efforts. The Resources section features some top books, websites, and organizations related to nonprofit sector careers. The lists are not exhaustive. Indeed, a major emphasis of the advice in this book is that you will need to conduct your own research around the issues and organizations you care about and want to explore professionally. Ideally, you will create a targeted mini library of resources and websites you consult regularly that are specific to your individual professional goals and qualifications.

Embarking on the Search

As with so many resources, this book is only as useful as the reader makes it. Finding a job is difficult work. Building a career requires extra energy and commitment. And landing a *great* job and establishing a meaningful *career* in the nonprofit sector takes even more perseverance and dedication.

This book provides valuable advice, resources, and career-building strategies to help you find great work at a nonprofit organization. But only *you* can apply the information so that it benefits your life and advances your career goals. Mentally prepare yourself for the work ahead and the research and networking you will have to do. Remind yourself that even the best of candidates faces rejection and disappointments. A certain amount of luck plays a part—a last minute decision to attend a party where you meet your future boss; or an internship at an organization that lands a new grant and must quickly expand programs, and taps you for a newly created full-time position. But as Gregg Behr says in his interview ("Working at a Foundation," pages 95–97), you can "make yourself lucky," and this book should help.

Give yourself plenty of time for your search. Be deliberate but also flexible in your actions. Solicit additional advice and heed the best of it. Apply the strategies and outreach efforts you read about that make sense to you. Revisit sections of the book that you find particularly helpful.

Be true to your own personality and style, but if reserved, push yourself to be as extroverted as possible during the process, even if it doesn't come naturally to you. Finding a job depends on believing in yourself, that you are worthy of help from the people in your network, and that you have something valuable to offer a position and an organization. It also depends on your ability to communicate these beliefs. Humility is a virtue, but false modesty serves no one and certainly not your career aspirations.

Be discriminating in your job search and committed to finding a stellar job. You won't be in your first positions forever, but the choices you make early on will influence your career. Assess both the quality of the positions you are considering as well as the organizations where they are based. Be realistic about the level of responsibility and the compensation package you deserve, and then try to achieve them. At the same time, be flexible and open to unexpected opportunities and be willing to compromise and take risks when appropriate.

End the search process being able to tell yourself you did everything possible to land the best job for you. And then go on to do everything in your power to make your new job as interesting and rewarding as possible. And above all, have fun. Build a career where you find joy in your work, feel good about the organization and mission you are contributing to, and are inspired by your colleagues.

one

UNDERSTANDING THE
nonprofit SECTOR

"And Lettuce Is Nonanimal" ... What Is the "Nonprofit Sector"?

The extraordinarily diverse and dynamic non-profit sector is defined, alas, by what it is not. Scholar Roger Lohmann pokes fun at the nonprofit sector's naming dilemma with his retort, "And lettuce is nonanimal."[1] Indeed!

But what is the nonprofit sector?

The nonprofit sector of the U.S. economy goes by many names: the independent sector, the voluntary sector, the third sector, the nongovernmental sector, or the nonprofit (or not-for-profit) sector. But each is, in a sense, a misnomer.

Independent? Nonprofit organizations do not exist independently of the other sectors; in fact, the collaborations among the three sectors—government, for-profit companies, and nonprofit organizations—are growing stronger and more vital every year. Nonprofits are interdependent, not independent.

Voluntary? Many nonprofit organizations certainly rely on volunteers, but they are not entirely sustained by them, and the overwhelming majority of organizations are run by paid, professional staff members.

Third? Nonprofit organizations do not come "after" public and private entities; many people would want to rank the sector "first."

Nongovernmental? A term used more often in international development, nonprofit organizations are indeed "nongovernmental organizations" (NGOs), although many partner with government agencies. Of course, this is more defining in the negative—and it could be argued that businesses are also "nongovernmental" since they are not part of government.

Nonprofit? While nonprofit organizations do not report to shareholders and do not have profits as their goal, they must make money to survive; they have rent and salaries to pay and programs and services to fund, and they can make a *surplus,* or profit. However, unlike business profits, nonprofit surpluses are used to improve programs and services rather than enrich individuals.

Since none of the sector's names is ideal, we'll stick with its most common label—the nonprofit sector—and throughout this book, we will help you understand what the sector *is,* rather than what it is not.

This chapter begins by exploring the scope of the nonprofit sector, the nature of the work its organizations perform, and key aspects concerning the organizational culture of nonprofits. The chapter answers the following questions:

- What is a nonprofit organization?
- Why do we need the nonprofit sector?
- What is the size and scope of the sector?
- What does it feel like to work at a nonprofit organization?

A sidebar by Marcia Avner covers the vital advocacy role that many nonprofit organizations play.

A piece by David Eisner addresses just how heavily the nonprofit sector—and our country—depends on volunteers. His thoughts serve as a reminder both that volunteering is excellent experience for a nonprofit sector career and that many nonprofit sector professionals will need to know how to manage volunteers as part of their work. Maureen Curley tackles the important question of maintaining a healthy work-life balance in the nonprofit sector.

The second part of the chapter addresses key nonprofit sector trends and their implications for the job seeker. From the growing leadership needs of nonprofit organizations to increasing collaborations among nonprofits, government, and business, all of the trends point to new types of positions and advancement opportunities now open to individuals pursuing nonprofit sector careers. But they also point to the need for excellent preparation and careful attention on cultivating your leadership ability.

What Is a Nonprofit Organization?

The simplest distinction between nonprofit organizations and other organizations is found in the Internal Revenue Code. Under U.S. tax law, nonprofit organizations are not required to pay taxes and, according to Section 501(c), the gifts received by qualified nonprofit organizations are also tax deductible.

From the government's perspective, most non-profit organizations fall into the more specific tax status of 501(c)(3) "public charities." The code says that an organization may be classified this way, "if it is organized and operated exclusively for one or more of the following purposes: religious, charitable, scientific, testing for public safety, literary, educational, or prevention of cruelty to children or animals."[2] Most arts, education, health care, and human services organizations, as well as religious congregations, fall into this category—although congregations are not required to register with the IRS.[3] Private foundations also are included in this category.

In addition to the public charities and private foundations that fall into the 501(c)(3) category, the Bureau of Labor Statistics estimates that there are close to half a million other nonprofit organizations in the United States. These include social and recreational clubs, trade associations, labor unions, and veterans associations. Advocacy and lobbying organizations are nonprofit organizations that fall under the 501(c)(4) category. Money given to these organizations is not tax deductible. However, it's important to understand that a 501(c)(3) organization can engage in lobbying activities (see Marcia Avner's sidebar, "Encouraging Advocacy," pages 16–17). Chapter 2 discusses the various subsectors comprising the nonprofit sector.

But what determines whether organizations are qualified to benefit from the tax breaks awarded to nonprofit organizations? Nonprofit organizations must have something more fundamentally similar than just the numbers and letters in their IRS classifications. Indeed, nonprofit organizations do share other characteristics. In general, they are mission driven, rather than profit driven; they exist to serve a public benefit; they value volunteerism and altruism; they are governed by a board of directors; and they tend to be flexible and autonomous.

Nonprofit organizations are mission driven; revenue is not the end in itself. Unlike their friends in the business or for-profit sector, non-profit organizations do not pay dividends to stockholders or any other individuals or groups. Rather, for nonprofit organizations, revenue is a means to an end—a means to pursue the organization's mission. It is worth noting, though, that government agencies are similar in this respect. However, whereas government agencies obtain revenue through taxation, nonprofit organizations, which are self-governing, must generate their own revenue by other means. These means include contracts with government organizations, fundraising, fees for goods and services, and grants from various types of foundations.

Nonprofit organizations serve the public. Nonprofits exist to serve some public benefit; they raise revenue to serve the good of the public. "Public" can be broadly or narrowly defined, resulting in two main categories of nonprofit organizations: member serving (organizations that serve a small section of the public) and public serving (organizations that serve the broader public). The extent to which the public is served creates a second "bottom line" for nonprofit organizations. If the performance of for-profit businesses is determined by the financial bottom line, then nonprofits are doubly charged to perform at a high standard—meeting both financial obligations and public service obligations. This two-part measurement of success can make nonprofit organizations seem confusing to people who have spent the majority of their working lives in profit-making ventures.

Nonprofit organizations highly value volunteerism and altruism. On a slightly more abstract level, certain core values are essential to and promoted by nonprofit organizations. Among these are altruism and volunteerism. In addition to the mission orientation of nonprofit organizations, evidence of these values in the sector is found in organizations' governance and the volunteer power found across the sector. Not only are governing boards volunteer powered, but so are many other aspects of nonprofits. In fact, the organization Independent Sector estimated volunteer time to be worth $18.77 per hour in 2006.[4]

Nonprofit organizations are governed by a board of directors. All nonprofit organizations are required to have a board of directors (see Susan Meier's interview, "Serving on a Board of Directors," pages 198–200). Individuals volunteer to govern the organization because they are committed to its work. Board members ensure that the organization carries out its mission and hire and fire the executive director. They often bring functional- or issue-area expertise to the board, are usually influential in their communities, and play a vital role in fundraising.

Nonprofit organizations are flexible and autonomous. While nonprofit organizations may collaborate with other nonprofit organizations, government, or for-profit enterprises, their leading strengths include their autonomy and flexibility. Nonprofit organizations are free (and indeed expected) to respond to social needs as they arise. Government can be notoriously slow to innovate: businesses are always accountable to their shareholders and bottom line. Nonprofit organizations, on the other hand, are only required to serve their mission. They understand and monitor issues relevant to their work and can respond to developments in the field.

The nonprofit sector is not simply an indescribable amalgamation of everything that cannot be categorized in the other sectors. Rather, in some respects, the nonprofit sector boasts of having the best attributes of the two other sectors—it operates privately to serve the public, creating a unique condition of competition tempered by cooperation and fueled by a charitable spirit.

NAME CHANGE, PLEASE
THE CASE FOR "SOCIAL PROFIT" ORGANIZATIONS

by **Claire Gaudiani**

Clinical Professor • Heyman Center for Philanthropy • New York University • www.scps.nyu.edu

Nonprofit should be nonexistent—the term "nonprofit," that is. What could be more profitable than the sector of our economy that has brought the world polio vaccines, commercial aviation, radar, penicillin, and private higher education? What has created more growth in our economy over the past three centuries than the millions of private scholarships that have educated generations of sons and daughters of the less than wealthy?

Charitable organizations are committed to profit. They invest time and dollars. They have taken great risks too, all in the pursuit of profit: *social* profit, change for the better. We should unite around this name for our sector of the economy and abandon all references to nonprofit. This term diminishes the inputs and the outputs of our millions of donors, volunteers, and entrepreneurs.

With courage and clarity, leaders in our sector must take the first steps and refer to ourselves positively as social profits. We must invite our donors to invest in our social profit-making ventures, and, like any venture, feel comfortable describing the risks and possibilities.

Management guru Peter Drucker says, "The nonprofit organization exists to bring about a change in individuals and in society."[5] To achieve this, the organizations in this category need to remain creative and entrepreneurial. If we achieve Drucker's vision, we create social profit. To continue calling the sector nonprofit is non-sense. ∎

Claire Gaudiani served for thirteen years as president of Connecticut College where she was also professor of French. She holds PhD, MA, and BA degrees in French literature. Claire is the author of *The Greater Good: How Philanthropy Drives the American Economy and Can Save Capitalism* (New York: Henry Holt/New York Times Books, 2003).

MARC MORIAL
President and CEO

Age: 49

Education: BA, economics; JD

Years at current organization: 5

Years in current position: 5

First job out of college: Associate in a law firm

First job in nonprofit sector: Current position

National Urban League
www.nul.org

Mission: The National Urban League is the nation's oldest and largest community-based movement devoted to empowering African Americans to enter the economic and social mainstream. More than one hundred local affiliates provide direct services to more than two million people through programs, advocacy, and research.

Operating budget: $47 million

Number of employees: 100

Number of employees who report to you: 6, the senior vice presidents for affiliate services, programs, development, marketing and communications, and finance; and executive director, National Urban League Policy Institute

Q & A

Q: Informally, describe your career track.
A: I worked throughout school in a range of part-time jobs—from staffing a mail room to serving as an academic department's program associate. After I graduated from law school, I worked at a law firm for two years and then ran my own practice for ten years. But I come from a family where public service and the obligation to "give back" was drilled into my DNA. So while I was

practicing law I ran for and got elected to the Louisiana State Senate. Later I decided to run for mayor of New Orleans, was elected, and served two 4-year terms. Afterwards, I was back at a law firm when I received a call from a headhunter, inviting me to interview for this job.

Q: What do you know now that you wish you had known when you were first job hunting?

A: I had student loans, and I made some early decisions based on money. I wish I had explored certain opportunities regardless of the financial sacrifice.

Q: Describe a representative work day.

A: I am responsible for leading my organization—for setting our direction, and for overseeing fundraising, public communications, human resources, and the management of our national network of affiliates. I travel about 40 percent of my time and a typical day on the road involves meetings with corporate CEOs and elected officials, conducting interviews, and giving a public speech. If I am at my office, I'll spend time on e-mails and try to get through dozens of phone calls to funders, partners, and other leaders in the field. I also will hold meetings with members of my senior team.

Q: What misconceptions do people have about your job? What's the reality?

A: People believe that this organization is flush with money. In fact, we're financially stable but run a tight ship. The other misconception is that we're an all-purpose organization that can be all things to all people. We can't—we have a mission and a mandate to focus on certain work.

Q: What do you love about your work?

A: Nonprofit organizations offer the excitement of making a difference, and the satisfaction of knowing that your work is relevant to something greater than a bottom line. You have the chance to effect change in people's lives, and this is empowering. I like the variety of work my job offers. I enjoy trying to make this organization run well and strategizing with my colleagues about our programs. But what I am most passionate about is fulfilling our mission and trying to make a difference.

Q: What advice would you give to someone interested in a career similar to yours?

A: You don't have to spend your career in one sector. If you frame it correctly, experience in corporate America or government can be applied effectively to nonprofit sector employment.

Q: What resources might help someone interested in your field and job function?

A: To lead an organization, you need experience being in charge. You can gain this through jobs, volunteering, serving on community boards, or participating in alumni associations, for example. Immerse yourself in issues you care about. Throw yourself into your community and be an example for others. Make your voice heard. And listen.

Q: What do you look for when hiring a new employee?

A: I look for stellar communication skills, enthusiasm for our mission, an honest understanding of teamwork, problem-solving skills, and a can-do attitude of wanting to overcome obstacles.

ENCOURAGING ADVOCACY

by Marcia Avner

Public Policy Director • Minnesota Council of Nonprofits • www.mncn.org

Public policy is the set of decisions made at the federal, state, and local levels about how we as citizens will care for one another, as well as our communities, nation, and planet. Nonprofit organizations play a powerful and vital role in shaping the public dialogue about policy priorities. They do this through advocacy—educating and organizing key audiences around an issue and pushing for a specific policy or programmatic solution.

Nonprofit advocacy is absolutely legal, if poorly understood. All groups are free to educate and advocate as much as they like. Furthermore, federal law makes it explicit that 501(c)(3) organizations are entitled to engage in both direct lobbying (contacting legislative officials in person) and grassroots lobbying (influencing public opinion to eventually affect legislative action). The extent to which a 501(c)(3) can lobby is determined either by its expenditures or a test concerning how "substantial" the activities are.[6]

Through advocacy, nonprofit organizations bring to the table real experience, expertise, and stories. Nonprofits offer decision makers in elected or appointed positions more complete information than they would otherwise have. Nonprofits provide the perspective and experience of scholars, researchers, community leaders, and, perhaps most important, the constituents their organizations serve—individuals directly affected by the policy decisions made.

Imagine how priorities, regulations, and budgets at all levels of government might look without the work of nonprofit organizations that advance their programmatic and service goals through advocacy. Whether health care, the environment, taxes, unemployment, or war, nonprofit organizations influence all issues and every aspect of American life. Here are a few examples that don't even begin to scratch the surface of the policy impact nonprofit organizations have had:

- Environmental organizations helped educate and mobilize citizens around clean air and clean water concerns and played a major role in establishing a cornerstone of environment legislation, the Clean Water Act. More recently, they actively promoted sound energy policy.

- Consumer advocacy organizations worked to implement and enhance seat belt and air-bag requirements in automobiles, remove Red Dye #2 from the market, compensate victims of asbestos poisoning, improve food labeling, and explore the impact of genetically modified foods.

- Lesbian and gay rights organizations almost single-handedly forced government to confront the HIV/AIDS crisis, invest in research, shorten the drug approval process, and educate the public about the health crisis.

- Women's rights organizations mobilized to secure suffrage for women; minority and women's rights organizations spearheaded a civil rights movement that led to the Civil Rights Act and other legislation and policies bringing fundamental rights to all Americans.

- Advocates for people with disabilities—and the nonprofit organizations they created—established the movement leading to passage and implementation of the Americans with Disabilities Act.

- Child care, health care, and affordable housing organizations keep the needs of their constituencies alive in a period of debate about whether government should play a role in meeting essential needs for families and children.

In all of these efforts, nonprofit organizations advocate on behalf of certain people, around specific issues. They educate elected officials, other national thought leaders, and the media. In many campaigns, the organizations form alliances and coalitions with other groups, businesses, and government agencies to support shared policy objectives and demonstrate a community's support for their proposed solutions. Part of their work involves lobbying—the advocacy tactic that specifically tries to influence legislation. But perhaps most important, nonprofit organizations serve as vehicles for democracy, providing a means for people to participate in the decisions affecting their lives. And that is advocacy at its core. ■

In addition to her work with the Minnesota Council of Nonprofits, Marcia teaches at the Center on Advocacy and Political Leadership at the University of Minnesota–Duluth. She serves on the boards of the Center for Lobbying in the Public Interest and the *Nonprofit Quarterly*. Marcia is the author of *The Lobbying and Advocacy Handbook for Nonprofit Organizations* (Saint Paul, MN: Fieldstone Alliance, 2002).

Why Do We Need the Nonprofit Sector?

The hidden figures (such as the value of volunteer hours) and vast array of intangible contributions scattered across the statistical reflections of the nonprofit sector make underestimating the role of the sector an easy thing to do. However, it would be difficult to exaggerate the impact that the nonprofit sector plays in the United States. In a nation dedicated "to promote the general welfare" as the preamble to our Constitution states, nonprofit organizations play an indispensable role.

Nonprofit organizations support and strengthen nearly all arenas of social, political, and economic life from education to advocacy to the arts and, within each of these areas, provide a variety of services to the public. They operate on the international, national, and local levels. Generally, nonprofit organizations serve the public by meeting a need in society or working to eliminate the cause of the need—or working toward both of these goals at once.

As an example, consider the vast arena of health, and the specific issue of breast cancer. National nonprofit organizations focus on breast cancer research, supporting scientists looking for new treatments. Other organizations specialize in educating women about the value of early detection, by publishing and disseminating materials and maintaining comprehensive websites on the disease. Some are membership organizations of physicians and surgeons with cancer expertise who

---

to learn more about the nonprofit sector

One of the best and most up-to-date sources of data about the nonprofit sector is *The Nonprofit Almanac 2008* (by Kennard T. Wing, Thomas H. Pollak, Amy Blackwood, and Linda M. Lampkin, published by The Urban Institute Press). Request it at your library or order your own copy at www.urban.org.

For more details on the nonprofit sector workforce, read the report *Employment in America's Charities: A Profile*, by Lester M. Salamon and S. Wojciech Sokolowski (Baltimore: Johns Hopkins Center for Civil Society Studies, December 2006). It's also available at the following URL: www.jhu.edu/~ccss/research/pdf/Employment%20in%20Americas%20Charities.pdf.

---

come together to share knowledge and collaborate on research. Other membership organizations unite breast cancer survivors to lobby government for increased public spending on breast cancer research. Still other organizations operate solely to support women who have faced the disease, perhaps providing money and services to low-income breast cancer survivors in particular. A local nonprofit organization may have as its mission the operation of a mobile mammogram van that visits women in a specific community. The same community may have a nonprofit hospital where a woman with breast cancer is treated, as well as a community foundation that has chosen breast cancer as one of its core program areas.

Nonprofit organizations are active in every area of the breast cancer arena at the local, regional, national, and international levels. These groups perform a wide range of work—from direct services, lobbying and advocacy, research, and organizing members, to making charitable gifts. While some organizations may receive government support and collaborate with public and for-profit agencies, nonprofit organizations address needs not covered—or not adequately covered—by government or the private sector.

The Size and Scope of the Nonprofit Sector

The nonprofit sector is enormous. The United States is home to approximately 1.4 million nonprofit organizations that are registered with the IRS. Of these, just fewer than one-third had gross receipts large enough to require that they report to the IRS. In 2005, these "reporting organizations" had $1.6 trillion in revenue and $3.4 trillion in assets.

The sector accounts for 5 percent of gross domestic product (GDP) of the U.S. economy, 8 percent of wages and salaries, and 10 percent of employment. In addition, 29 percent of Americans volunteer through formal organizations. Nonprofit organizations receive $260 billion in donations.[7]

The Urban Institute estimates that in 2005, paid employment in the nonprofit sector was 12.9 million. The sector enlists the support of the equivalent of more than 4.7 million full-time volunteers, representing a total of more than 17.6 million workers.[8]

Researchers estimate that in 2006 nonprofit wages plus the value of volunteer time was almost $713 billion. According to World Bank data for the same year, if the nonprofit sector were a country, this would put it just shy of Australia in terms of GDP. Based on wages paid only, the sector would push out the Netherlands to be the sixteenth largest economy in the world.[9]

For the nonprofit sector job seeker, the size and scope of the sector mean that a great breadth of organization types and employment opportunities exist in the sector. Nonprofit employment—like overall U.S. employment—tends to be concentrated in the Middle Atlantic, South Atlantic, and East North Central (surrounding Indiana and Illinois) regions. Metropolitan areas experiencing the top level of growth of new charities (with percentage increase) include

- Atlanta (new charities up 23 percent)
- Las Vegas (up almost 21 percent)
- Orlando (up 20 percent)
- Houston (up just more than 19 percent)
- Miami/Ft. Lauderdale (up almost 19 percent)
- Nashville (up almost 18 percent)[10]

But the sector's size suggests you are apt to be able find a healthy nonprofit organization working in the field and geographic region where you would like to work.

The nonprofit sector is growing. Between 1995 and 2005, the number of organizations registered with the IRS grew by more than 27 percent. However, the number of public charities—those classified as 501(c)(3) as described above—grew at a rate greater than 50 percent over ten years. More than one hundred new nonprofit organizations file with the IRS every day.

The sector's finances are also increasing, and faster than the rest of the U.S. economy. The U.S. GDP increased by approximately 35 percent from 1995 to 2005 after adjusting for inflation. The nonprofit sector's major financial measures each increased by at least 54 percent over the same period. The nonprofit sector as a whole had total assets increase by more than 77 percent.

Given the expansion of the nonprofit sector, it is no surprise that employment in the sector is growing as well. From 1998 to 2005, employment in the sector grew by 16 percent—three times faster than the rest of the economy.

For the nonprofit sector job seeker, the fact that the nonprofit sector is growing faster than the rest of the economy suggests that employment and leadership positions in it will develop more quickly than elsewhere. It's a great time to consider a nonprofit sector career, and opportunities are likely to increase.

---

overview of the U.S. *nonprofit sector, 2004–2005*

501(c)(3) public charities

Public charities	845,233
Reporting public charities	299,033
Revenue	$1,050 billion
Assets	$1,819 billion

501(c)(3) private foundations

Private foundations	103,880
Reporting private foundations	75,478
Revenue	$61 billion
Assets	$455 billion

Other nonprofit organizations

Nonprofits	464,595
Reporting nonprofits	112,471
Revenue	$250 billion
Assets	$692 billion

Giving

Annual, from private sources	$260 billion
From individuals and households	$199 billion
As a percent of annual income	1.9%
Average, from households that itemize deductions	$3,576
Average, from households that do not itemize deductions	$551

Volunteering

Volunteers	65 million

Source: Pollack and Blackwood, *The Nonprofit Sector in Brief, 2007.*

Most nonprofit organizations are small. The majority of reporting public charities—almost 74 percent—are small organizations with expenses less than $500,000. Although these groups dominate the sector in terms of number of organizations, they don't dominate financially. The behemoths of the sector—public charities with more than $500 million in revenue—account for fewer than 0.1 percent of organizations but more than 27 percent of the sector's assets and revenue.

As a nonprofit sector job hunter, it's important to consider the size and institutional capacity of organizations dominating the sector (more about

---

the top twenty largest nonprofit organizations

In its "NPT 100," *The NonProfit Times* annually ranks the one hundred largest nonprofit organizations—those that generated the most income in a given fiscal year. Making the top twenty for 2007 were

1.	American Red Cross	
2.	YMCA of the USA	
3.	United Jewish Communities	
4.	Catholic Charities USA	
5.	The Salvation Army	
6.	Goodwill Industries International	
7.	Memorial Sloan-Kettering Cancer Center	
8.	Boys & Girls Clubs of America	
9.	Habitat for Humanity International	
10.	Boy Scouts of America	

11. American Cancer Society
12. The Nature Conservancy
13. National Easter Seal Society
14. World Vision
15. Planned Parenthood Federation of America
16. Gifts In Kind International
17. AmeriCares Foundation
18. Food For The Poor
19. Volunteers of America
20. Girl Scouts of the USA

Note: The 2007 edition of the NPT 100 reflects financial data from the fiscal year ending 2006. To qualify for the list, an organization must receive at least 10 percent of its total revenue from public support. As such, many hospitals are not included. In addition, the NPT 100 does not include the United Way—despite its $4 billion in assets—because the researchers want to avoid counting dollars more than once. They consider United Way largely to be a "pass-through" agency that redirects contributions to other charities or causes.

Source: "The 2007 NonProfit Times Top 100: An In-Depth Study of America's Largest Nonprofits," *The NonProfit Times* (November 1, 2007); available at www.nptimes.com/07Nov/071101SR.pdf (accessed January 9, 2008).

this in Chapter 4). However, the majority of non-profit organizations are small, both in terms of budget and staff size—so it is more likely that you will work for one of the many small nonprofits at some point in your nonprofit career. Most groups will not have an individual assigned to human resources. And of those organizations that do, for the majority the function is not dedicated exclusively to HR work.

As such, when applying for jobs at smaller organizations, job candidates should recognize that recruitment probably is being handled by a program or executive director juggling many other responsibilities. Staff members directing a job search may not have been trained in professional human resources processes. If you suspect a prospective employer has limited HR capacity, consider doing more follow-up than you might normally believe is appropriate. For example, you might ask references to make calls on your behalf if your application is being seriously considered, even if they haven't received a call. (These and similar issues are covered in Chapter 5.)

Fees for services and goods are the dominant source of revenue for reporting public charities, and account for more than 70 percent of gross receipts. This income is generated by Medicare and Medicaid reimbursements and other patient payments for hospital care, tuition fees at colleges and universities, theater tickets, or, nominally, the sales of goods at places such as thrift or museum shops. Other revenue sources for the sector include private contributions (just more than

12 percent), government grants (9 percent), and investment income (just more than 5 percent), as well as other income.

The lifeblood of the sector: contributions of time and money

To understand the nonprofit sector, you have to understand something about the role of volunteers and the nature of charitable giving in the United States. Individuals' contributions of time and money are indeed the lifeblood of the sector.

Volunteers are vital to nonprofit organizations. They serve on boards of directors, administer programs, staff offices, perform administrative duties, raise funds, and organize special events. They drive vans for senior citizens, pick up trash, and provide counseling for at-risk teens. Think of any work within the nonprofit sector, and you can bet volunteers play an important role.

A significant slice of the American population volunteers: in 2005, the Bureau of Labor Statistics reported that more than one in four Americans (just under 29 percent) volunteered through a formal organization. This represents a small increase over the 2002 rate of just more than 27 percent. Among different demographic groups, blacks or African Americans had the greatest increase in volunteering, with an increase of approximately 3 percent. In terms of age, people between the ages of 35 and 44 are most likely to report that they volunteered, with more than 34 percent indicating they had in 2005.

Every nonprofit sector professional must understand the contribution volunteers make in advancing an organization's mission and delivering its services. Your work is apt to depend on volunteer labor, and you may even be expected to recruit or manage volunteers. And of course, volunteering yourself is a great way to learn more about the nonprofit sector and increase your network—both before you start working and even after you have a job with a nonprofit organization.

Charitable giving in the United States set a new record in 2006. *Giving USA*, an annual study of philanthropy in the nation, estimated it at more than $295 billion, a 1 percent increase over 2005 when adjusted for inflation.[11] The increase is noteworthy given that 2005 charitable donations were particularly high because of disaster relief giving, especially for victims of Hurricane Katrina and the Asian tsunamis.

Highlights of 2006 giving included Warren Buffett's $1.9 billion contribution—the first installment of his promised $31 billion gift to four foundations over twenty years. The bulk of the Buffett donation will go to the Bill & Melinda Gates Foundation, which expects to double its giving to $3.2 billion by 2009, and is expected to eventually have $60 billion in assets. In addition, at least twenty-one individuals gave more than $100 million to charity in 2006.

While contributions from individuals are always the largest source of donations (and accounted

charitable contributions by subsector

Type of charity	% of charitable contributions
Religion-related	32.8
Education	13.9
Human services	10.0
United Ways and other community causes	7.3
Health care	6.9
Arts, culture, humanities	4.2
Environment, animals	2.2
International and foreign affairs	3.8

Source: Giving USA, as reported in Holly Hall, "Donations by Americans reached $295 billion in 2006," *Chronicle of Philanthropy* (June 28, 2007), available at http://www.philanthropy.com/free/articles/v19/i18/18002701.htm (accessed January 11, 2008).

for more than 75 percent of giving in 2006, or 83 percent when including bequests), "mega gifts" such as Buffet's account for a little more than 1 percent of the total. The vast majority of philanthropic giving comes from normal citizens: 65 percent of households with incomes lower than $100,000 gave to charity.

However, contributions from Americans of more modest means did not increase in 2006 as mega

THE VOLUNTEERING IMPERATIVE

by David Eisner

Chief Executive Officer • Corporation for National and Community Service • www.nationalservice.gov

September 11, 2001, and the hurricanes of 2005 have forever changed the way Americans think about service and volunteering. While our country has a long history of protecting and supporting the less fortunate, these tragedies catapulted the "call to serve" from something once thought of as "nice" to now understood as profoundly "necessary."

Volunteering is critical both in responding to unexpected disasters as well as in addressing the ongoing social and economic challenges so many people face that are disasters in their own right. Consider that in the United States 37 million people live in poverty; 3.5 million people are homeless; and 15 million youth and children have no caring mentor to guide them. The statistics are overwhelming and have a very human face.

No government initiative, no nonprofit organization, no business venture can tackle our social ills without one key resource—ordinary citizens who have made a commitment to give back to their communities and country. The difference volunteers make cannot be overstated.

Take one example. On any given day, 10.3 million children in the United States have one or both parents in prison. Seventy percent of these children will end up in prison themselves unless we do something. And yet a simple intervention can cut this risk in half—when one person agrees to mentor one child for one hour each week. Simple, and yet life changing.

Take another example, this time in a specific community. In Madison, Wisconsin, in the late 1990s, African American students were six times as likely as white students to fail third grade literacy tests. When five hundred volunteer tutors led by fifteen AmeriCorps VISTA (Volunteers in Service to America) members took on the challenge, they virtually erased that performance gap. These volunteers cared about the faces behind an alarming and unacceptable statistic, stepped in, and changed these children's lives.

Citizen engagement is the single most powerful intervention in solving many of the toughest challenges our communities face: illiteracy, homelessness, gangs, crime, high school dropouts, hunger, poverty, and the divide between the haves and the have-nots. In every case, the most effective action a community can take is to mobilize its people. In many communities, members of AmeriCorps, Senior Corps, VISTA, National

Civilian Community Corps (NCCC), and Learn and Serve America—all national service programs of the Corporation for National and Community Service—are helping fellow citizens to address critical needs.

The nonprofit sector and the people it serves depend on volunteers. Together with our nation's nonprofit and faith-based organizations, we believe we can increase the number of American adult volunteers to 75 million by the year 2010, and make their service experiences positive ones. If we succeed in reaching these numbers and deepening each community's commitment to engaging citizens, there's no telling what America can achieve in the years ahead. ∎

The Corporation for National and Community Service is the nation's largest grantmaker supporting service and volunteering. Through its Senior Corps, AmeriCorps, and Learn and Serve America programs, the Corporation provides opportunities for Americans of all ages and backgrounds to express their patriotism while addressing critical community needs. Previously, David Eisner was an executive with AOL and AOL Time Warner, where he oversaw the AOL Foundation.

gifts did. Donors faced the challenge of increased fuel costs, rising consumer debt, and poor local economies in many regions. For organizations— usually smaller organizations—whose core support comes from many small donations rather than a few large gifts, this change can have a dire impact.

A large percentage of private philanthropy is directed to religious organizations, which received approximately 36 percent of charitable gifts. It's important to note, however, that religious giving is only an estimate because congregations are not required to file annual returns with the IRS. Education comes next, receiving approximately 15 percent of gifts. See the sidebar text "Charitable Contributions by Subsector," page 23, for the ranking of the subsectors vis-à-vis charitable receipts.

The Foundation Center tracks foundation giving, which was estimated at $40.7 billion in 2006 and reflected a greater than 8 percent increase over 2005 when adjusted for inflation. The increase is connected to the rise in the stock market, as foundations make grants relative to the value of their assets. Researchers also attribute the increase to two other trends—more "pass-through" foundations dedicated to distributing all of their assets each year, and the increased number of pharmaceutical foundations. Nearly 9 percent of foundation giving in 2005 came from the operating foundations of twelve pharmaceutical companies dedicated to distributing medications to needy individuals. Corporate giving overall in 2006 was estimated at $13.8 billion.[12]

JAMIE ROACH
Manager of Major Grants

Age: 26

Education: BA, psychology

Years at current organization: 5

Years in current position: 4

First job out of college: Intern at an arts and counseling organization

First job in nonprofit sector: Intern at an affordable housing organization

Harvesters
The Community Food Network
www.harvesters.org

Mission: Harvesters is the community's response to hunger. By providing food we give sustenance and hope to those in need. We also work toward long-term solutions through nutrition education, hunger awareness, and advocacy.

Operating budget: $5 million

Number of employees: 56

Number of employees who report to you: 1, prospect and grant research coordinator

Q & A

Q: Informally, describe your career track.
A: Along with my degree in psychology, I earned the American Humanics Nonprofit Management Certification. As a part of the certification process, my first several jobs were internships. My first noninternship position after college was with my current employer, Harvesters.

Q: What do you know now that you wish you had known when you were first job hunting?
A: Sometimes it's worth it just to get your foot in the door with an entry-level or temporary position. These positions afford you the opportunity to show your employer what you can do.

Q: Describe a representative work day.

A: I manage donor relationships with individual, corporate, foundation, religious, and government funders. I write and manage proposals, and cultivate prospects. On any given day, I will have a list of proposals or reports I'm working on. Those are typically interspersed with taking donors or potential donors on tours of Harvesters' facility, meeting with a committee about one of Harvesters' programs, attending grant information sessions, and setting up meetings with donors. And don't forget about "other duties as assigned," which can mean stuffing thank-you letters or doing inventory in the warehouse.

Q: What misconceptions do people have about your job? What's the reality?

A: People often react negatively to grant writing, saying, "So, you write grants all day?" There is much more to major gift fundraising than writing proposals: it's about relationship building, finding creative connections, and developing strategies. The key is to be passionate about your cause or organization. You are just giving people the opportunity to make a difference!

Q: What do you love about your work?

A: I love working for something that makes a difference in the community. Even on bad days, I go home knowing that because of the efforts my colleagues and I have made, someone will receive a meal today. It's incredible to experience the generosity of individuals and organizations.

Q: What advice would you give to someone interested in a career similar to yours?

A: Gain experience writing proposals (that, hopefully, are successfully funded) and forming relationships any way you can. This can help you get your foot in the door with an organization. And any familiarity with fund development is a plus—from organizing a food drive to helping with a fundraiser for an organization where you volunteer. For the nonprofit sector in general, nothing beats internships, volunteering, and networking within the sector.

Q: What resources might help someone interested in your field and job function?

A: America's Second Harvest has great information on hunger (www.secondharvest.org). Harvesters provides information about hunger here in Kansas City (www.harvesters.org). (My favorite feature is a family budget calculator that shows how difficult it can be to make ends meet on a limited income.) For information on development and grantwriting, explore the Association of Fundraising Professionals (www.afpnet.org), and the Foundation Center (www.fdncenter.org).

Q: What do you look for when hiring a new employee?

A: I look for a passion for the mission, social services, and nonprofits in general. Excellent written and verbal communication and computer skills are a must. Many things can be taught, but excitement for the work of the organization is an essential requirement.

Organizational Culture in the Nonprofit Sector

What does it *feel* like to work at a nonprofit organization? Regardless of your job title or the issue you are working on, what will your days be like? What's the *vibe* around the lunch table, the *attitude* at the water cooler, the *climate* during staff meetings? What kind of energy and support can you expect from your coworkers, what kind of relationship will you have with your boss?

The nonprofit sector is extraordinarily diverse and its organizations have dramatically different structures, missions, and approaches to their work. In addition, the nonprofit organization leaders who direct these "ships" (and have great control over the climate at the office) do so by exhibiting a full range of management styles. It's impossible to predict what your nonprofit sector work experience will be like. However, research on nonprofit sector organizational culture suggests that certain commonalities do exist—and that there are things to watch out for, and to seek.

A study by New York University researcher Paul Light suggests that as compared to the federal government and private sector, the nonprofit sector has the healthiest workforce in the United States.[13] Nonprofit organization employees care about their work and have the type of work that talented people want. They are more likely than government or business workers to say that the people they work with are open to new ideas, willing to help their colleagues learn new skills, and are concerned about their organization's mission. They also find their work stimulating and presenting long-term opportunity. However, nonprofit sector employees do report a shortage of resources, high levels of stress, and overwhelming workloads.

Nonprofit practitioners and consultants Mike Allison and Jude Kaye depict a similar nonprofit environment in their summary of key characteristics of the small and midsize organizations that comprise the majority of the sector.[14] They identify three key attributes of these groups that affect organizational culture: a passion for mission, an atmosphere of "scarcity," and a bias toward informality, participation, and consensus.

Having a passion for mission means nonprofit organizations are often filled with people who are driven and deeply committed. It creates an atmosphere of creativity, high energy, and urgency that can be invigorating but also can lead to burnout (see Maureen Curley's advice on this topic, "Maintaining a Work-Life Balance in the Nonprofit Sector," pages 30–31). Leaders who focus too heavily on mission can communicate to their teams that they don't value good management. On the other hand, leaders who balance their own passion with sound, professional practices end up cultivating passion in others and are tremendously inspiring to work with.

The atmosphere of scarcity refers to the fact that many nonprofit organization leaders and staff members feel that they don't have sufficient resources to accomplish necessary work. One result is that staff members can be pressured to work long hours with inadequate tools and support, because managers are either unable or unwilling to allocate additional funds to a project. At the best organizations, however, the recognition that resources—both financial and human—are precious leads to efficient practices, streamlined programs, and a clear sense of priorities.

The bias toward informality, participation, and consensus speaks to the lack of formal hierarchy in many organizations. Many leaders talk about their organizations and staff as their "families" and pride themselves on the friendly and supportive work environment they create. The participatory climate means that many nonprofit sector employees feel as if they are part of a team and that new opportunities are always open to them. But it also can be connected to blurry job descriptions and an expectation that everyone will multitask. Decision making can be slow if leaders overemphasize consensus.

Again, no two nonprofit organizations are alike. And many of the characteristics just described apply mostly to smaller organizations. Many large organizations—and a certain share of smaller ones—have work environments that feel remarkably similar to a for-profit business operation.

(And undoubtedly many businesses—especially small ones or family-owned establishments—are run with what some people would say is a nonprofit organization "spirit.") It simply depends on the organization, its resources, and, especially, its leaders. As a job seeker, you want to learn as much as possible about the culture of the organizations where you are considering working.

Key Trends in the Nonprofit Sector

Major changes are taking place in the world and many of them at an amazing rate. To respond to these developments, the nonprofit sector is evolving quickly as well. Studies appear regularly that address new trends in the nonprofit sector or changes in the way nonprofit organizations operate to fulfill their missions. It would be impossible to capture all of these developments, but a few key ones are particularly relevant to the nonprofit sector job seeker. These include

- the growing leadership needs of nonprofit organizations

- attention to nonprofit sector compensation

- active recruitment of a diverse workforce

- increasing collaborations among nonprofits, government, and business

- a surge in social entrepreneurship

- increased accountability and oversight of nonprofit organizations

MAINTAINING A WORK-LIFE BALANCE IN THE NONPROFIT SECTOR

by **Maureen Curley**

President • Campus Compact • www.compact.org

The concept of "burnout" is all too often associated with careers in the nonprofit sector. But this shouldn't—and doesn't have to—happen to you. The best nonprofit organizations recognize that good employees are their lifeblood, and want them to be happy and to stick around.

Yes, days can be long and workloads can be daunting when you are passionate about an issue. In addition, work can fluctuate throughout the year. Annual fundraising events or seasonal services such as summer camps usually bring with them periods of some longer days. But when the volume of work is consistently too high, then there is a problem.

Every worker should be able to have a long, successful career in the nonprofit sector while maintaining a healthy personal life. The trick is to set balance as a priority and commit yourself to achieving it. And the best time to do this is at the launch of your career. Good habits are hard to break.

Here are some basic tenets of establishing a healthy work-life balance from my perspective as a manager as well as a worker:

- **Select your employer carefully.** In researching a prospective employer, learn as much as you can about the organizational culture and leadership style. It probably isn't necessary to talk about your commitment to your personal life in an interview, but do find out whether there's an unhealthy expectation that people work late into the night, every night. Determine whether staff members are happy.

- **Establish clear boundaries.** If you approach your work with professionalism, good humor, and a team spirit, your colleagues are unlikely to begrudge you not coming in on Saturdays. If your boundaries are reasonable, you don't need to offer apologies or personal explanations for your choices. Promise yourself when you will leave the office and the amount of work you will take home. Be open to some exceptions, but otherwise honor your priorities.

- **Work hard, but efficiently.** If you can't seem to get your work done, make sure that you are managing your time well. Are you clear on your priorities and how to approach your "to-do" list? Are you wasting time on optional items or, worse, the Internet? Do you help meetings to move along at a nice pace and steer the conversation away from personal updates? Are you a good manager of support staff, delegating tasks appropriately?

- **If you're burning the midnight oil, be honest about why.** Do you care even less about your personal life than your employer does? Have friends or family suggested you might be a workaholic? Tackle the tough questions about how you're spending time and whether you're using work to avoid bigger and more complex personal issues.

- **If your job is too big for one person, say something.** If your position is simply bigger than you are, you're not helping yourself, your organization, or the issue you care about if you keep quiet with that information. Schedule a formal meeting with your manager, detail your perspective clearly and without undo emotion, present proposals for a solution, and then hear what your manager suggests. If you've proven yourself to your organization, its leadership is apt to value your insights and want to prevent you from burning out. ∎

Campus Compact is a national coalition of more than a thousand college and university presidents—representing some five million students—who are committed to fulfilling the civic purposes of higher education. Maureen Curley previously served as executive director of the Massachusetts Service Alliance, the state Commission on Community Service and Volunteerism; and as chief relationship officer at Bridgestar, a Boston-based network of nonprofit leaders.

The following section provides some details on these nonprofit sector trends, especially in the context of employment in the sector.

Nonprofit organization leadership needs = Advancement opportunities

The "Size and Scope of the Nonprofit Sector" discussion earlier in this chapter (see pages 19–29) presented some statistics on the sector's employment, its sizeable share of the U.S. economy, and its dramatic expansion. People interested in rapid career movement may find it in the large, vital, and evolving nonprofit sector with its pronounced leadership needs.

Opportunities abound, not only because of the sector's growth, but also because many of its Baby Boomer leaders are expected to retire. Nonprofit organizations are hungry for talent, both for entry-level workers and to build their "bench strength"—the talent in their ranks prepared to assume leadership positions. A number of recent studies estimate the nonprofit sector's forthcoming leadership needs:

- The Bridgespan Group released *The Nonprofit Sector's Leadership Deficit* in 2006. The study found that over the next decade, "organizations will need to attract and develop some 640,000 new senior managers—the equivalent of 2.4 times the number currently employed." By 2016, almost 80,000 new executives per year will be in demand (in contrast to 56,000 needed in 2006).[15]

- *Daring to Lead 2006: A National Study of Nonprofit Executive Leadership* by CompassPoint Nonprofit Services found that 75 percent of responding executives planned to leave their posts within five years (and smaller organizations are more likely to experience transitions than larger organizations). Although the majority of those planning to leave their positions said they expected to stay within the sector, the pipeline of talent will be tested. CompassPoint found that "bench strength, diversity, and competitive compensation are critical factors in finding future leaders."[16]

- An earlier study by the Annie E. Casey Foundation, *Nonprofit Executive Leadership and Transition Survey 2004*, found that of 2,200 executives surveyed, 65 percent planned to leave their positions by 2010. This study also pointed to the lack of leadership diversity: 84 percent of executives are white, 10 percent are African American, and 4 percent are Hispanic/Latino.[17]

- The United Way of New York City offers one local example. It estimated that 45 percent of current executive directors of New York City nonprofit organizations planned to retire within five years of the survey.[18]

This scholarship bodes well for professionals looking for employment and leadership opportunities at nonprofit organizations. Visionary nonprofit organizations are paying attention to the talent wars not only for today's frontline workers, but because they know these "new recruits" will be tomorrow's sector leaders.

Attention to nonprofit sector compensation = Livable salary

The nonprofit sector is famous for low salaries. And there's no denying that too many nonprofit sector employees are overworked and underpaid. However, researcher Lester Salamon attributes low salaries more to the field of work that nonprofit organizations perform than the fact of being nonprofit. (See "Wages in the Nonprofit Sector," page 35.) Plus, benefits in the sector may be better than assumed. Respondents to the Annie E. Casey Foundation's *Nonprofit Executive Leadership and Transition Survey* said of their organizations that 64 percent offer retirement benefits to which the organization contributes, 79 percent offer employer-paid health insurance, and 73 percent offer retirement benefits.

In addition, as the talent wars escalate and nonprofit organizations acknowledge the competition they face from business and government recruiters, many leaders are voluntarily conducting compensation studies and adjusting salaries for entry-level and junior professionals. Job candidates also shouldn't be surprised to hear about less traditional perks that a recruiting organization can offer—from flexible work hours or job sharing to valuable professional development opportunities and special work assignments.

Not surprisingly, the larger organizations tend to pay higher salaries to top staff, and these organizations also showed higher increases in compensation, according to the *2007 GuideStar Nonprofit Compensation Report*.[19] As one example, Table 1 (below) shows median salaries for the top program position by organization budget size.

TABLE 1:
Median Compensation for Top Program Position, by Organization's Budget Size

Organization's Budget	Median Compensation
less than $250,000	$29,981
$250,001–$500,000	$47,967
$500,001–$1,000,000	$61,350
$1,000,001–$2,500,000	$63,450
$2,500,001–$5,000,000	$68,154
$5,000,001–$10,000,000	$75,085
$10,000,001–$25,000,000	$86,146
$25,000,001–$50,000,000	$102,550

Health and science organizations—fields that require specialized knowledge and tend to be associated with larger organizations—have the highest median salaries overall. Where are the lowest salaries found? Food, religion, housing, animal-related, and youth development organizations rank at the bottom (see Tables 2 and 3, page 34).

TABLE 2:
**Five Program Areas with *Highest*
Overall Median Compensation, 2005**

Program Area	Median Compensation
Science and Technology Research Institutes, Services	$125,947
Health—General and Rehabilitative	$117,459
Medical Research	$112,914
Social Science Research Institutes, Services	$110,513
Mutual/Membership Benefit	$109,667

TABLE 3:
**Five Program Areas with *Lowest*[20]
Overall Median Compensation, 2005**

Program Area	Median Compensation
Religion	$67,021
Food, Agriculture, and Nutrition	$67,274
Housing, Shelter	$73,399
Animal Related	$74,975
Youth Development	$75,000

As a job seeker, think carefully about your bottom-line salary and benefits requirements. If you're paying off student loans and other debt,

factor that in. Consider Robert Shireman's tips on how to approach debt ("Don't Let Debt Deter You," pages 36–37). Conduct careful research on salaries in your field, and refer to James Weinberg's interview on compensation ("Compensation in the Nonprofit Sector," pages 177–179) and Deepak Malhotra's on negotiation ("Negotiating with Aplomb," pages 256–260).

women's wages and leadership at nonprofits

Women dominate employment in the nonprofit sector, and in certain subsectors—such as health—the data are particularly pronounced. However, nonprofit sector compensation for women continues to lag behind men when considering comparable positions at similar organizations, according to the *2007 GuideStar Nonprofit Compensation Report*. The compensation deficit ranges from 7.4 percent at organizations with budgets between $500 thousand and $1 million, to 25.2 percent at organizations larger than $50 million. Furthermore, women hold 50 percent of CEO positions at organizations with expenses of $1 million or less, but represent only 34 percent of CEOs at larger organizations. Some gaps are shrinking: women CEOs at organizations with expenses greater that $25 million received a higher median compensation increase than men. Results are mixed for smaller organizations.

WAGES IN THE NONPROFIT SECTOR

by **Lester M. Salamon**

Director • Center for Civil Society Studies • Johns Hopkins Institute for Policy Studies • www.jhu.edu/~ccss

In 2004, nonprofit organizations pumped $322 billion in wages into the American economy. Average weekly wages for nonprofit sector workers varied from a high of $752 in hospitals to a low of $390 in social assistance organizations.

While the average wage among nonprofit workers is lower than the average wage among for-profit workers, this difference is because nonprofits are more heavily concentrated in fields offering lower wages. In fields where both nonprofits and for-profits operate, however, the nonprofits actually have higher average wages than their for-profit counterparts. For example, average wages among nonprofit hospital workers are 7 percent higher than they are among for-profit hospital workers. For museum workers, nonprofit wages are 15 percent higher; for social assistance workers, they are 25 percent higher.

The overall lower average wage for nonprofit sector workers is thus an industry phenomenon, not a sector phenomenon. For education, social services, residential care, and day care, nonprofit wages actually exceed for-profit wages, often by a substantial margin. In some respects, nonprofit organizations are the more generous employers. It may be that for-profits are able to operate in these fields at a profit because their compensation levels are below the already low nonprofit levels. ∎

Lester M. Salamon is a pioneer in the empirical study of the nonprofit sector in the United States. His 1982 book, *The Federal Budget and the Nonprofit Sector* (Washington, DC: Urban Institute Press), was the first to document the scale of the American nonprofit sector and the extent of government support to it. Lester's *America's Nonprofit Sector: A Primer* (New York: Foundation Center, 1992) is a standard text on the nonprofit sector in universities across the country.

DON'T LET DEBT DETER YOU

by **Robert Shireman**

Executive Director • Project on Student Debt • www.projectonstudentdebt.org

Most college graduates borrowed money to get through school, and the prospect of paying back all those loans can be daunting. But don't rule out pursuing a career in the nonprofit sector just because of those debts. Consider these facts:

FACT: You're not alone. By the time they graduate, two-thirds (66.4 percent) of students at four-year colleges have student-loan debt, including nearly two-thirds (62 percent) of public university graduates. Three-quarters (74.5 percent) of new college graduates who take jobs with nonprofit organizations have student-loan debt.

FACT: The nonprofit sector doesn't necessarily pay less than for-profit employment. Nonprofit employees receive about the same pay as their for-profit counterparts who do the same type of work. Nonprofit industries do tend to offer lower pay on average, but this is because of the field of work, not because the employer is a nonprofit organization. In fact, nonprofit sector workers in hospitals, nursing or personal care facilities, and social services earn as much or more than their for-profit counterparts.

FACT: If most of your loans are federal (such as Stafford or Perkins loans), you are in luck: there is now a sliding-scale payment option. In 2007, President George W. Bush signed into law a policy called "Income Based Repayment," designed to make repaying loans easier for graduates pursuing jobs with lower salaries. It does this by pegging the monthly payments to the borrower's income, family size, and total amount borrowed. For a single college graduate earning a salary of $30,000, loan payments are capped at 8 percent of income; with an income of $40,000, they are capped at 10 percent of income. In other words, if you have federal loans, you need not worry that the loan payments will overwhelm your ability to repay. And if the payment caps end up stretching your payments to twenty-five years, any remaining debt is canceled.

FACT: There's even better news for public service professionals with federal student loans. A new public service loan forgiveness program will discharge all of your remaining federal loan debt after ten years of repayment and full-time employment in public service. Public service

Active recruitment of diverse workforce = Your background is valued

Nonprofit organizations need and want diverse new workers, and many organizations are committed to cultivating such individuals so they are positioned to lead their organizations in the years ahead.

Nonprofit organizations based in the United States serve an extraordinarily and increasingly diverse population. In 2007, the U.S. Census Bureau reported that the nation's minority population reached 100.7 million, representing one in three U.S. residents. This makes the American minority population larger than the population of all but eleven countries worldwide. The U.S. Hispanic population topped 44 million, the African American population topped 40 million, and the Native Hawaiian and Other Pacific Islander group hit the one million mark. Four states and the District of Columbia are already "majority-minority" populations.[21]

By 2040, the U.S. Census Bureau predicts that ethnic minorities—encompassing African Americans, Hispanics, and Asian Americans—will represent more than half of the U.S. population. Diversity in the American labor pool is increasing as well. By 2010, demographers expect that almost half of all the nation's new workers will be individuals traditionally classified as "minorities."

jobs include government, public safety and law enforcement, and public services in health, education, early childhood education, child care, social work, and for individuals with disabilities or the elderly, as well as public interest legal services, among others.

If you have student debt, you should find a career that will allow you to pay it off. Luckily, the nonprofit sector provides ample opportunities to do so. Whether you find a career in teaching, nursing, or environmental preservation, you can manage your student debt while making a difference through public service. ■

Robert Shireman's program works to raise awareness of the role loans play in making college possible and advances cost-effective solutions that expand educational opportunity. Robert previously served as an education policy advisor at the White House National Economic Council and in the U.S. Senate. He holds a BA in economics and MAs in education and public administration.

Research suggests that employment and governance structures in the nonprofit sector are not keeping pace with the racial and ethnic diversity of our country.

Based on the most recent data available, the sector is approximately 81 percent white, 10 percent African American, 5 percent Latino, 3 percent other, and 1 percent Asian or Pacific Islander. A 2002 Independent Sector study indicates that the nonprofit sector employs a greater proportion of African Americans and smaller proportion of Latinos than do the public and private sectors. Variation exists within nonprofit subsectors. For example, African Americans represent 16 percent of the health services, social services, and legal services subsectors; and Latinos represent 6.7 percent of the arts and culture subsector.

Approximately 68 percent of the nonprofit sector's workforce are women; however, men are disproportionately represented in upper-level management positions. (See "Women's Wages and Leadership at Nonprofits," page 34.)

Nonprofit organizations' governing boards are more homogenous than the sector's overall workforce. A 2007 study by the Urban Institute found that 86 percent of board members are white, non-Hispanic; 7 percent are African American or black; 3.5 percent are Hispanic/Latino; and the balance are from other ethnic groups. Fifty-one percent of boards are exclusively white, non-Hispanic. Only 7 percent of board members are under age 36. (The study did not explore the socioeconomic diversity of board members, since data on income and wealth were not available. Similarly, there is little information on the socioeconomic diversity of the nonprofit sector workforce.)[22]

These figures are discouraging but also reveal the leadership opportunities available for women, people of color, and other job seekers from traditionally underrepresented or inadequately represented populations. Many nonprofit sector leaders believe that the sector has a moral imperative to serve as an example in recruiting, retaining, and promoting to leadership positions individuals representing the full spectrum of American society. Simply put, because nonprofit organizations are mission driven and exist for a public benefit, they should value diversity and set the standard for workplace inclusiveness. And barely half of nonprofit organizations (53 percent) surveyed recently said they were satisfied with their ability to recruit qualified minorities.[23] These respondents point to a clear demand: they see a need to create a diverse workforce that they are unable to fill.

Forward-looking leaders in the sector know that their organizations can't create the best programs, deliver the most appropriate services, or properly reach their target audiences unless their staff members reflect the full range of people they're dedicated to serving. As Frances Hesselbein, the leader of the Girl Scouts of the USA in the late 1970s and 1980s, said, "A successful journey involves developing a richly diverse organization to reflect the diversity of the community, so that we may respond 'yes' to the critical question: 'When they look at us, can they find themselves?'"[24]

Finally, individuals on the front line of efforts to recruit and retain talent recognize that for nonprofit organizations to compete effectively in our country's escalating talent wars, they must be able to access the full labor pool. As the U.S. Census Bureau estimates, in just a few years 50 percent of new workers will be "minorities." These individuals bring with them the skills, talent, experiences, perspectives, and commitment to mission that nonprofit sector organizations need.

Leaders of the healthiest nonprofit organizations are eager to recruit staff, board members, and volunteers who represent racial and ethnic diversity as well as all socioeconomic backgrounds, religions, sexual orientations, and physical abilities. The healthiest nonprofit organizations don't just stop with their diversity "head count"—they integrate the perspectives of their diverse staff members into how they develop and implement their programs and engage with their different constituencies.

The most inclusive organizations make their commitment to diversity explicit, and communicate this commitment through their most senior leaders. With every vacancy, these organizations work to recruit the most diverse applicant pool possible. With every hire, they assess the representation of their workforce. With every promotion, they consider how well their leadership represents the people they serve. And with every retirement or resignation, they see an opportunity to do even better.

Although many organizations have limited recruitment resources, organizations that are committed to building a diverse staff recruit talent from nontraditional sources. They tap professional associations whose members are people from diverse communities, they post job announcements on websites and in newspapers that attract very specific audiences, and they make explicit when asking for word-of-mouth referrals that they are seeking candidates who will represent all of their constituents. But mostly, these organizations lead (and recruit) by example. Their leadership—including their board members—reflect the organization's commitment to building a truly representative workforce.

Increasing collaborations with government and business = Sector-cutting skills wanted

The social, political, and economic changes to our country and world have inspired—and at times forced—changes to the work of businesses, government, and nonprofit organizations, as well as the relationships among them. Consider just a few of the many developments that have marked the start of the twenty-first century:

- The radically changing demographics of the American population—its aging and increasingly diverse population—brings the need for new and expanded services for a wider range of people.

- The escalating influence of the Internet and other technological advances are the engine of a new information economy that is more accessible to more people. They shrink the world while underscoring that the divide between rich and poor is at a historic high.

- The global economy is bringing countries closer together through trade and, for the first time, touching and connecting once-isolated rural communities.

- Global warming is expected to increase the frequency and magnitude of natural disasters, which are having a more devastating impact on people's lives because of political conflict, public health crises, and failed food and water distribution systems.

With rising and changing needs both at home and abroad, government—pressured to operate more efficiently and to limit taxes—is reducing support from areas historically under its purview. National problems are increasingly in the hands of local and state systems. Public functions are thrust upon the private sector, making businesses and nonprofit organizations more accountable and more competitive as they work to fill the gap in services. Businesses—always looking for new markets and expanded profits—find promise in social venture collaborations, both to address public problems and build their reputation among consumers. Nonprofit organizations look for new partnerships and funding opportunities to do their work, and businesses are showing interest.

As a result, competition as well as collaboration is increasing among nonprofit organizations, business, and government. The result can be innovative and effective programs, and exciting new opportunities for the nonprofit practitioner. Take, for example, the case of the female condom in Zimbabwe (see sidebar, page 41).

This trend toward collaboration and innovative program design makes it an exciting time for the nonprofit sector job seeker. Nonprofit organizations testing such initiatives are recruiting staff with new skills and perspectives. They need individuals who understand how to secure government funds and work with public officials, as well as how to craft programs that serve business interests. They often are looking for professionals with an entrepreneurial acumen, some business knowledge, and a flair for creative marketing and strategic coalition building. (All this, while also being an expert on the issue.)

---

government, business, and nonprofit collaboration: the case of the female condom in Zimbabwe

The Players: U.S. Agency for International Development (USAID) [*government*]; Population Services International (PSI)/Zimbabwe [*nonprofit*]; Female Health Company, Zimbabwean hair salons [*businesses*].

The Problem: In Zimbabwe, the HIV/AIDS epidemic hits women even harder than men. Approximately 21 percent of Zimbabwean women ages 15 to 49 are HIV-positive, compared with 14.5 percent of men. In 1996, 20,000 Zimbabwean women petitioned Parliament to make the female condom available—a barrier method developed by the Female Health Company that provides dual protection against unintended pregnancy and sexually transmitted infections, including HIV. But four years into the campaign promoting the female condom, studies showed that awareness of and access to the life-saving product was limited.

The Program: With financial support from USAID, project design and implementation from PSI/Zimbabwe, and partnership with the Female Health Company and local Zimbabwean hair salons, an innovative social marketing campaign to promote the female condom was born. The "hair salon initiative" trained hairdressers (frequented by 97 percent of Zimbabwean women at least monthly) to discuss the benefits of using the female condom, demonstrate correct use to their clients, and sell the product. Access to, awareness of, and sales of the female condom skyrocketed, and it could not have happened without each partner's involvement.

Note: For more information on this campaign and similar collaborations in the public health arena, visit www.psi.org/aidsmark/index.html.

41

ANDREA BROWNE-PHILLIPS
Research Associate, FIELD and MicroTest

Age: 30

Education: BA, international economics; graduate certificate, international business management

Years at current organization: 3

Years in current position: 3

First job out of college: Research assistant, The Aspen Institute

First job in nonprofit sector: As above

The Aspen Institute
Economic Opportunities Program

www.aspeninstitute.org

Mission: The mission of The Aspen Institute is to foster enlightened leadership and open-minded dialogue. The microenterprise Fund for Innovation, Effectiveness, Learning and Dissemination (FIELD) began in 1998 to identify, develop, and disseminate best practices in the microenterprise field, and to educate funders, policymakers, and others about microenterprise as an antipoverty strategy.

Operating budget: $17 million

Number of employees: 162

Number of employees who report to you: 1, MicroTest Program intern

Q & A

Q: Informally, describe your career track.
A: My intuitive passion is for education, international development, and balancing the scale of socioeconomic inequality both at home and abroad. My work in the international communications industry opened my eyes to some of the disparities that exist. My work with MTV Networks and the Caribbean Sport Television Network provided a context and framework for learning. My

current position allows me to tie my experience, knowledge, and passion together because I am not only researching issues that are of interest to me, but I am also directly involved with practitioners who work in the microenterprise sector.

Q: What do you know now that you wish you had known when you were first job hunting?

A: I now understand how my extracurricular activities allowed me to develop my management, communication, and team-building skills while in college. It is important to gain experience and then communicate this experience to potential employers so they understand your strengths and skills and all you can bring to an organization.

Q: Describe a representative work day.

A: I work on providing more than ninety small-business consulting programs and nonprofit loan funds with the training and technical assistance they need. On a daily basis, I prepare materials for presentations, training, and publications, and collect and verify self-audits from our members. My ongoing projects include maintaining our databases and client records, conducting data analyses, and contributing to Aspen Institute publications and websites.

Q: What misconceptions do people have about your job? What's the reality?

A: One major misconception is that I do statistics all the time. However, my current portfolio gives me room to develop my self-management skills, professional management style, and knowledge and understanding of the industry. I also have direct access to seasoned researchers on interesting policy issues. To me, this unlimited access to balanced information and perspectives is exciting and refreshing.

Q: What do you love about your work?

A: Externally, I love the interaction with the programs across the nation. Internally, I appreciate the flexibility to develop and implement practices to help improve the operation and efficacy of the program. I also appreciate the networking opportunities, professional exposure, and hands-on learning environment that I have at a non-profit organization.

Q: What advice would you give to someone interested in a career similar to yours?

A: Volunteer, research, ask questions, and strategize. I have my dreams, and I have my goals. The closer I get to closing the gap between the two is the closer I get to what I consider to be success. My plan and strategy are not fixed but flexible and customized.

Q: What resources might help someone interested in your field and job function?

A: For information on the microenterprise field, I would start with The Aspen Institute's own websites: www.aspeninstitute.org, www.microtest.org, and www.fieldus.org.

Q: What do you look for when hiring a new employee?

A: The desire to learn and grow.

BE BOLD
CREATE A CAREER WITH IMPACT

by **Cheryl L. Dorsey**, President
and **Lara Galinsky**, Vice President of
Strategy and Communications
Echoing Green • www.echoinggreen.org

"The urge to live a life of meaning is one of our most elemental desires as human beings. We *want* to make a difference in the world; we *need* to leave our footprint in the sands of time to mark our existence. By honoring the beliefs and values we hold dear, we allow ourselves to live lives that matter.

" . . . This includes decisions about your career, because your career is more than just a job. It is a way of leaving your footprint." ∎

From *Be Bold: Create a Career with Impact,* by Cheryl L. Dorsey, Lara Galinsky, Don Cheadle, and John Prendergast (New York: Echoing Green, 2006). The book tells the story of twelve nonprofit sector leaders who are also Echoing Green Fellows and whose careers have had tremendous impact. More information is available at www.bebold.org.

Surge in social entrepreneurship = Support for new initiatives available

Triggered, in part, by the need to expand services on sometimes shrinking budgets and increased competition from business (as mentioned previously), nonprofit organizations are developing innovative strategies and applying fundamentally entrepreneurial principles to effect social change. Some call this social entrepreneurship.

Definitions of *social entrepreneurship* generally fall in two categories: one focuses on a more general strategy to develop innovative responses to social needs; the other focuses more specifically on generating earned income for social purposes. The earned income strategy might be connected to the organization's mission, or may be totally independent and designed solely to generate revenue. Strategies can include fees for service, the sale of products, rents, or licensing and cause-related marketing activities. (See Timothy J. McClimon's piece, "What Is Cause-related Marketing, and Who Does It?" page 140.)

Most experts agree that social entrepreneurs operate in the business, government, and nonprofit worlds. Their *approach* is often more important than the structures in which they work. They might tackle issues as individuals, in teams, or through new or existing organizations. A selection of some leading nonprofits focusing on supporting social entrepreneurship—as well as their basic definition of the approach—includes the following organizations:

- **Ashoka** defines social entrepreneurs as "individuals with innovative solutions to society's most pressing social problems. They are ambitious and persistent, tackling major social issues and offering new ideas for wide-scale change." (www.ashoka.org)

- **Echoing Green** identifies emerging social entrepreneurs as "visionary leaders with bold ideas for social change." They "work to address deeply rooted social, economic, and political inequities to ensure equal access and help all individuals reach their potential." (www.echoinggreen.org)

- **Ewing Marion Kauffman Foundation** focuses on entrepreneurs (not social entrepreneurs specifically) and defines them as "Americans who have the desire and the ability to build and sustain innovative enterprises." Their enterprises "leverage technology and other inputs that have the potential for a national impact with special attention to high-growth opportunities." (www.kauffman.org)

- **Omidyar Network** invests in both for-profit and nonprofit efforts that "leverage market-based, collaborative approaches in order to unleash human potential on a global scale." (www.omidyar.net)

- **Schwab Foundation for Social Entrepreneurship** also invests in both business and nonprofit ventures led by someone who is a "pragmatic visionary who achieves large-scale, systemic, and sustainable social change through a new invention, a different approach, a more rigorous application of known technologies or strategies, or a combination of these." (www.schwabfound.org)

- **Skoll Foundation** says, "Motivated by altruism and a profound desire to promote the growth of equitable civil societies, social entrepreneurs pioneer innovative, effective, sustainable approaches to meet the needs of the marginalized, the disadvantaged and the disenfranchised." (www.skollfoundation.org)

The spirit of social entrepreneurship is something that many nonprofit organizations embrace. If you consider yourself a social entrepreneur, you don't necessarily need to create a new venture in order to advance your ideas for change. It may be one possible path (see thoughts from Ethan Hutt and Aaron Tang, "Thinking of Starting Your Own Nonprofit?" pages 105–107), but you also may find that your ambition, creativity, resourcefulness, and bold vision for how to reshape society has a home in an existing nonprofit organization.

THE SEVEN HABITS OF HIGHLY SUCCESSFUL SOCIAL ENTREPRENEURS

by Jeff Skoll

Founding President • eBay

Social entrepreneurs are people who apply rigorous discipline to social problems. They use many business tools and apply them to the social sector. Their work is characterized by innovation, empowerment, and lasting change. The difference is that their bottom line is not in profits earned but in lives, communities, and societies transformed. In short, social entrepreneurs are people who believe in and act on the unshakable conviction that individuals, acting alone or together, can truly make a difference in the world.

1. Social entrepreneurs demonstrate a profound sense of hearing loss.

Social entrepreneurs are incapable of understanding the words "it can't be done." Indeed, these words seem to be the social entrepreneur's rallying call. In the early 1970s, Gloria de Souza, an Indian schoolteacher who was one of the first elected Fellows of Ashoka (www.ashoka.org), tried to innovate teaching by stressing experiential learning instead of rote memorization. She spent five years enduring constant "no's" from her colleagues until she managed to convince them to change. Her persistence paid off. By the late 1980s, her early education model became the standard for every first-, second-, and third-grader in India. That's a persistence that has morphed into unshakable resolve and gritty determination.

2. Social entrepreneurs are "A" students who are not afraid to get "F's."

Social entrepreneurs are not afraid to risk failure. Nick Moon and Martin Fisher of KickStart (www.kickstart.org) spent a decade in Kenya inventing one product after another that didn't quite catch on. But each insight eventually led to their low-cost, human-powered irrigation pumps that have helped start more than 45,000 new businesses in Kenya, Tanzania, and Mali, driving almost 1 percent of gross domestic product in Kenya alone.

3. Social entrepreneurs know when to boil the clothes.

When Florence Nightingale first arrived in Turkey during the Crimean War, she found thousands of sick and wounded soldiers lying in dirty, flea-infested clothing. She realized the simple solution to getting them well was to boil their clothes in water. In three months, she helped cut the death rate in British army hospitals in Scutari from 43 percent to 2 percent. That kind of practical genius is everywhere among social entrepreneurs.

4. Social entrepreneurs inhabit zones of lesser gravity.

An astronaut on the moon can jump six times higher than on earth because of the lesser force of gravity. Somehow, social entrepreneurs replicate that effect and do more with less than anybody thinks possible. Muhammad Yunus, founder of the Grameen Bank (www.grameen-info.org) and winner of the 2006 Nobel Peace Prize, has lifted more than 70 million people out of poverty, all starting with a few dollars from his own pocket.

5. Social entrepreneurs have a knack for making molehills out of mountains.

Social entrepreneurs can take big, seemingly intractable problems and make them feel manageable. Maybe you don't feel you can protect the environment on your own, but you can create a lending model that helps farmers transition to green production, as William Foote has done through Root Capital in Latin America (www.ecologicfinance.org), improving management of more than 75,000 acres.

6. Social entrepreneurs have X-ray vision.

Some people look at the half of humanity who lives on a dollar or less a day and see only poverty and squalor. Social entrepreneurs see talent and potential. Luis Szarán was the eighth child of struggling farmers when he was "discovered" by a prominent musician and given the opportunity to study with master teachers in Europe. Luis founded Sonidos de la Tierra in Paraguay (www.sonidosdelatierra.org.py) to give similar opportunities to other children, because, he says, "Young people who play Mozart by day do not break windows at night." In the midst of oppressive poverty, Sonidos de la Tierra has helped residents of one hundred communities establish philharmonic societies. That's X-ray vision, indeed.

7. Social entrepreneurs are all pyromaniacs at heart.

It's impossible for social entrepreneurs to talk about their work without setting a room on fire. A great American abolitionist named Wendell Phillips was once asked why he got so fired up when he talked about the issue of

(continued on page 48)

47

(continued from page 47)

slavery. He replied, "I am on fire because I've got mountains of ice to melt." Whether the ice you've got to melt is poverty or hunger or child labor or whether it means standing up for human rights—to me, social entrepreneurs are the real heroes in our world today, and they are setting the world on fire.

Social entrepreneurs are rebels. They are rebelling against one of the worst ideas that has ever gripped mankind—namely, that the problems surrounding us are so big that ordinary men and women can't make a difference. Social entrepreneurs prove every day that one person and one idea can make a difference. ∎

Jeff Skoll created the Skoll Foundation in 1999, which takes an entrepreneurial approach to philanthropy by investing in, connecting, and celebrating the world's most promising social entrepreneurs to effect lasting, positive social change worldwide. One initiative of the foundation is Social Edge, a global online community where social entrepreneurs and other practitioners of the social sector connect to network, learn, inspire one another, and share resources (www.socialedge.org).

Increased accountability and oversight of nonprofits = Strong managers and effective leaders needed

The Sarbanes-Oxley Act of 2002 focused on corporate America but had significant implications for the nonprofit sector as well. The federal legislation was developed in response to the massive corporate fraud scandals of Enron, Arthur Anderson, WorldCom, Tyco, and other companies that were attributed to lack of adequate accounting and reporting mechanisms, especially vis-à-vis board oversight, executive compensation, and conflict of interest of auditing firms and within the securities industry.

The nonprofit sector faced its own scandals—from the use of 9/11 funds by the American Red Cross and excessive executive compensation at the Smithsonian Institution to allegations of conservation tax abuses by the Nature Conservancy. Even though there were only a few high profile cases of abuse, the news stories shook the sector. For many nonprofit sector leaders, Sarbanes-Oxley is a wake-up call on accountability, transparency, and the vital role of the board of directors. In corporate America, the scandals hurt shareholders and the U.S. economy. In the nonprofit sector, the scandals shook the public trust (see Diana Aviv's piece, "Maintaining the Public Trust," pages 49–50).

MAINTAINING THE PUBLIC TRUST

by **Diana Aviv**

President and CEO • Independent Sector • www.independentsector.org

The ability of America's nonprofit community to enrich lives and solve problems depends on maintaining the public's trust. Only then will organizations continue to receive the support they need to fulfill their incredible variety of missions.

To build this trust, charities and foundations must show that they are responsible stewards of the public's generosity. A key part of this effort is the Panel on the Nonprofit Sector, convened by Independent Sector in 2004 at the encouragement of the leaders of the U.S. Senate Finance Committee. The panel brought together thousands of people from across the nonprofit community to examine how to strengthen the accountability of charitable organizations. At the heart of its work is the idea of balance, of providing oversight that deters and punishes those who would use non-profits for personal benefit while safeguarding the independence that enables organizations to find innovative, effective ways to improve lives.

The panel issued two reports that together contained more than 150 recommendations for action by Congress, the Internal Revenue Service, and charitable organizations in areas such as increased IRS funding, clearer laws on certain forms of giving, principles for setting executive compensation, and improved functioning of boards. The charitable reforms in the Pension Protection Act of 2006 incorporated many of the recommendations requiring Congressional action.

Most recently, the panel focused on how charities and foundations can improve their own standards of practice. In 2007, drawing on existing systems and standards for ethical, transparent operations for organizations in specific program or geographic areas, the panel developed *Principles for Good Governance and Effective Practice: A Guide for Charities and Foundations*. Its thirty-three principles are designed to establish common guidelines that organizations of all types, areas, and sizes can aspire to in order to strengthen their effectiveness and accountability.

High ethical standards are only a start to maintaining the public trust. Charities and foundations must also operate programs that improve lives, then communicate those achievements to

(continued on page 50)

(continued from page 49)

staff, board members, donors, volunteers, service recipients, and public officials. Only by constantly demonstrating their central role in communities will nonprofit organizations receive the support that enables them to fulfill their vital roles: nurturing spiritual and creative aspirations, caring for vulnerable people, protecting our natural and cultural heritage, and spreading democracy. Producing those results requires both strong ethics and effective practices. ▪

Independent Sector is a nonprofit, nonpartisan coalition of approximately 575 charities, foundations, and corporate philanthropy programs dedicated to advancing the common good by strengthening the charitable community. Immediately prior to joining Independent Sector in 2003, Diana served as vice president for public policy and director of the Washington Action Office of United Jewish Communities.

Increased accountability and oversight mean that many nonprofit organizations are getting their houses in order. The nonprofit sector job seeker will find leaders dedicating additional resources to accounting and other financial and administrative functions, paying closer attention to board development and oversight, and rethinking the fairness of their compensation packages. Applicants who have at least some knowledge of accounting and finance, understand and communicate their commitment to the ethical standards organizations must meet, and demonstrate good leadership and a strong moral center will be increasingly coveted in the years ahead.

In a Nutshell . . .

This chapter described what the nonprofit sector is. It discussed the broad characteristics of organizations in the sector and the work they perform. Key data communicated the size and scope of the sector, its rapid growth, and the opportunities for employment (and long-term careers) that it holds. The chapter addressed some of the perceived challenges of nonprofit sector work, including long days and low salaries, and tried to separate some myths from reality. You learned a bit about what it feels like to work at a nonprofit organization—information you may already know from your own volunteer, internship, or employment experiences in the sector. Finally, the chapter described some key trends that nonprofit organizations are a part of, and their implications for the nonprofit sector job seeker.

Some of the information may inspire you, some of it may serve as a reality check. Ideally, you can apply all of it to your own experience and knowledge of nonprofit organizations and your field of work.

If at this point you need more direction about where you might fit within the sector, the next chapter is for you. Chapter 2 describes the key nonprofit subsectors and the work that organizations in them perform. Turn the page to see what field is of greatest interest to you, and is most likely to tap into your skills and expertise.

t w o

SPOTLIGHT ON KEY
nonprofit SUBSECTORS

With 1.4 million nonprofit organizations in the United States, the nonprofit sector covers a massive breadth of organizational purposes (or missions) and approaches. To get a handle on the overwhelming scope of work, this chapter drills into nine key nonprofit subsectors and the work that organizations in them perform.

The nine nonprofit subsectors are based on the National Taxonomy of Exempt Entities—Core Codes (see "NTEE-CC: Classifying Organizations of the Nonprofit Sector," page 55). They include

- arts, culture, and humanities
- education
- environment and animals
- health
- human services
- international and foreign affairs
- public or societal benefit
- religion-related
- mutual/membership benefit

Each subsector discussion[25] covers a basic description of the field's key issues and the types of organizations that operate in it. It provides a history of the subsector, key trends, and relevant facts and figures. Each section also includes recommendations on a few websites specific to jobs in that subsector.

Keep in mind that within the defined subsectors, a wide variety of organizations and organizational missions are represented. The classification system reflects only the tip of the iceberg when it comes to the diversity of organizations within the sector, but it is a convenient way to get started on exploring the nonprofit sector.

Certain groups of nonprofit organizations—including hospitals, churches, and colleges and universities—are not explored in detail in this book. These very distinct subsectors have their own specialized resources. People interested in careers in health, religion, and education should use materials dedicated to those fields in combination with this book.

In addition, the organizational categories described in the following pages—while providing a vital framework—do not necessarily convey what an organization actually does and who it actually serves. The National Center for Charitable Statistics is working to classify organizations by *types of programs,* through its Nonprofit Program Classification (NPC). As you think about different organizations in a given sector, you'll want to consider not only their mission, but also their approach and the activities they undertake to advance that mission. The NPC system classifies activities, including

- direct service
- advocacy
- awards and competitions
- capacity building
- communications and public education
- fundraising and financial support
- licensure and certification programs
- management, administrative, and technical support
- membership programs
- professional development and training
- research and public policy analysis
- volunteer programs

When thinking about how you want to create a meaningful and rewarding career in the nonprofit sector, consider both an organization's mission and its program activities. And, of course, you will also want to weigh its size (both staff and budget), history, location, funding sources, and staff and board leadership.

NTEE-CC: classifying organizations
of the nonprofit sector

One of the best resources for learning about the types of organizations working in the nonprofit sector is the National Center for Charitable Statistics (NCCS). This national clearinghouse for data on the nonprofit sector in the United States is a program of the Center on Nonprofits and Philanthropy at the Urban Institute. The NCCS's website offers a wonderful portal into the size and scope of the nonprofit sector. The Urban Institute also publishes *The Nonprofit Almanac 2008* (referenced extensively in Chapter 1).

The NCCS classifies organizations by organizational purpose using codes from the National Taxonomy of Exempt Entities (NTEE) system.

The NTEE-Core Codes (NTEE-CC) is a modified version of the NTEE that corresponds well with various government classifications, including IRS classifications. The NTEE system divides the universe of nonprofit organizations into nine broad categories, plus a tenth for "unknown" in cases when an organization does not provide sufficient information to be classified. It further refines the categories into twenty-six major groups (that you can explore online) with additional subclassifications. These nine categories are a useful framework for exploring the work of the nonprofit sector, and are the key subsectors discussed in this book.

Note: Visit the website of the National Center for Charitable Statistics (www.nccs.urban.org) for more information on the classification system and data on the nonprofit sector.

Spotlight on Arts, Culture, and Humanities

The arts, culture, and humanities subsector is only a small slice of the nonprofit sector pie; however, it includes some of the most prominent organizations in the country: for example, the Smithsonian museums in Washington, DC; New York's Lincoln Center; the Chicago Symphony Orchestra; and public television.

Organizations in this subsector can play several roles. Many serve as entertainment; going to a museum or listening to a performance can be a leisure activity. They are also educational; often, organizations in this sector explicitly teach. At the same time, they perform a valuable function by housing artifacts important to our heritage and inviting the public to interact with them. Organizations in this subsector are apt to describe their mission as some combination of entertainment, education, preservation, or information dissemination.

The arts, culture, and humanities subsector can be broken into five categories:

- museums, including art, children's, history, natural history, science, and zoos
- venues, including opera houses, concert halls, and theaters
- performance groups, including dance, ballet, theater, music, symphony orchestras, opera, music groups, and bands
- councils, conservatories, and historical societies
- distribution channels, including public radio and television, recording companies, and artist management firms

The work

In addition to its mission, the funding source of the organization also affects its work. For instance, most museums generate some revenue from ticket sales, gift shop sales, or intellectual property. But these activities rarely provide enough revenue to balance the operating budget. Additional revenue from endowments and charitable contributions is necessary to subsidize the museum's mission. As a result, marketing, entrepreneurship, and donor cultivation may be as much a part of the organization's business model as programming. Other roles might include audience development, maintaining facilities, and managing volunteers.

In contrast to museums, humanities funding comes almost entirely from local, state, or federal government. Additionally, humanities organizations are often part of universities; as a result, they may benefit from fairly reliable funding streams, but have the challenge of demonstrating that their work has a broad interest and value worthy of its place in the civic and intellectual community. Roles in these organizations also may include grant writing and stewardship, researching and editing publications, and creating databases or digital records of materials.

National Endowment for the Arts—a snapshot

The National Endowment for the Arts is the official arts organization of the U.S. government. The NEA is "dedicated to supporting excellence in the arts, both new and established; bringing the arts to all Americans; and providing leadership in arts education."

- The NEA is the largest annual funder of the arts in the United States, and is largely credited with making the arts accessible to people outside of just the major cities.

- Since its founding, the NEA has awarded more than 124,000 grants totaling more than $3.9 billion to individuals, arts organizations, and state agencies.

- NEA funding helped launch the Sundance Film Festival, Steppenwolf Theatre Company, and Minnesota Public Radio's *A Prairie Home Companion*.

- After steadily increasing appropriations during its first thirty years, the federal government slashed NEA funding from $162 million in 1995 to $99.5 million in 1996, and continued cuts through 2000.

- Since 2001, funding has increased, but it has not yet returned even to 1995 levels. In 2007, the NEA received $124.5 million in appropriations (representing about 1 percent of total arts philanthropy).

Source: Mission statement and data are from the NEA's website at www.nea.gov.

History and trends

From its emergence in the nineteenth century, the arts, culture, and humanities sector has been associated with an elite audience and philanthropists with a specific vision—for instance, Paul Mellon, who helped fund the National Gallery of Art, or William Vanderbilt, who cofounded the Metropolitan Opera.

In the second half of the twentieth century, the sector opened to a broader public. In 1965, the federal government established the National Endowment for the Arts (see box at left) and the National Endowment for the Humanities. City and state governments also often contribute, and benefactors may include businesses, families, and smaller-dollar donors. On one hand, the democratization of the sector, not to mention its place in the federal budget, allowed more people to participate; on the other hand, it inspired controversy about the purpose of public art.

The controversy became particularly heated from the mid-1980s to the mid-1990s. Some citizens objected especially to National Endowment for the Arts (NEA)-funded artists, most notably Robert Mapplethorpe, whose photographs of male nudes during the height of the AIDS crisis were celebrated by some as works of art with social significance and denounced by others as obscene. Partly in response to the furor, in 1996 the U.S. government cut NEA funding almost in half. Although the federal budget has steadily increased NEA funding since 2001, the sector continues to seek a balance between advancing original work, delivering quantifiable results (e.g., attendance numbers), and satisfying a civic mission. Just what constitutes "civic mission" has become more complicated as the U.S. population becomes more culturally diverse.

Today, the subsector faces a number of challenges and opportunities from decreased arts and humanities education in schools and hot competition for funding to doors that are opening thanks to demands for new technology and the departure of many organization leaders.

Professionals in this sector will likely find themselves introducing the arts and humanities to young audiences, some of whom may be being exposed to the field for the first time. New professionals may also be surprised at this sector's focus on business and social concerns, as organizations strive to compete in a commercial market and meet public accountability standards. As researcher Margaret Wyszomirski describes vis-à-vis museums, a trend in this subsector is to be more outward focused and deliver "social enterprise that is accessible, unpretentious, and lively."[26] Many organizations are working to develop an online presence. Although digital capabilities represent new avenues for creativity and opportunities to disseminate, they can also be expensive and require additional staff and skills. Finally, especially high rates of executive transition at many

arts organizations suggest that both turmoil and leadership opportunities exist in this subsector.

For people considering careers in this subsector, the arts, culture, and humanities remain engaging fields that can delight audiences and comment on national and international issues. As the work becomes increasingly complex, business, technological, and political savvy are also important factors for success. People who can bridge the esoteric and the pragmatic have the potential to lead the sector into its next era.

arts jobs sites

In addition to the general nonprofit jobs websites listed in the Appendix, check out these sites for arts-related jobs:

ArtJobOnline (membership required)
www.artjob.org

Art Search
www.artsearch.us

Americans for the Arts
www.artsusa.org

International Society for the Performing Arts Foundation
www.ispa.org

American Association of Museums
museumcareers.aam-us.org

facts and figures: arts, culture, and humanities

- Arts, culture, and humanities organizations represent 11.5 percent of all reporting public charities in the United States (but only approximately 2 percent of expenses and 4 percent of assets).

- Arts organizations create an estimated 5.7 million full-time equivalent jobs.[*]

- Of organizations in this subsector, 41 percent classify themselves as "other": they are arts services, arts education, and media and communications organizations, or arts agencies and councils.

- About 35 percent of the organizations focus on performing arts.

- Museums account for the smallest number of reporting public charities in the arts, culture, and humanities subsector, but they hold almost 40 percent of the subsector's total assets.

- Arts, culture, and humanities organizations reported more than $27 billion in total revenue in 2005.

- Private contributions (from individuals, foundations, corporations, and other public charities) account for approximately 41 percent of total revenue in this subsector. That ranks this subsector third in terms of dependence on private contributions—behind international and foreign affairs and environment and animals.

- Nonprofit arts contribute an estimated $37 billion to the economy annually.[†]

- In 2006, donations to arts, culture, and humanities organizations were $12.5 billion, or up more than 6 percent. This subsector had the highest growth rate in charitable giving (along with educational institutions).[‡] However, between 2000 and 2005, corporate giving to the arts dropped 65 percent.[§]

- The subsector's charitable giving growth rate has been approximately 5 percent over the past decade.[**]

Sources: Unless noted, all data are from *Nonprofit Almanac 2008.*

[*] Americans for the Arts, "Study Shows $166 Billion in Economic Activity," press release, May 22, 2007.

[†] National Endowment for the Arts, "NEA At A Glance," available at www.nea.gov/about/Facts/AtAGlance.html (accessed January 11, 2008).

[‡] *Giving USA (2006),* as reported in Hall, "Donations by Americans reached $295-billion in 2006."

[§] Americans for the Arts, *The Future of Private Sector Giving to the Arts in America* (2006), 7.

[**] *Giving USA (2006),* as reported in Hall, "Donations by Americans reached $295-billion in 2006."

Erika Lindsay
Public Relations Associate

Age: 31

Education: BA, literature

Years at current organization: 9

Years in current position: 4

First job out of college: Current position

First job in nonprofit sector: Current position

Seattle Art Museum

www.seattleartmuseum.org

Mission: The Seattle Art Museum (SAM) provides a welcoming place for people to connect with art and to consider its relationship to their lives. SAM collects and exhibits objects from across time and across cultures, exploring the dynamic connections between past and present.

Operating budget: $18.3 million

Number of employees: 200

Number of employees who report to you: 2, community campaign public relations coordinator and a community campaign outreach coordinator

Q & A

Q: Informally, describe your career track.
A: During college I interned in public relations at a historical museum in Maryland and at the Smithsonian Institution. These experiences helped me land a position at SAM when I graduated.

Q: What do you know now that you wish you had known when you were first job hunting?
A: You need to approach your job hunt as a job in itself. It pays to explore as many organizations and positions as possible. Be thoughtful about your choice.

Q: Describe a representative work day.

A: I coordinate public relations efforts for the opening of the Olympic Sculpture Park, Seattle Art Museum, and Seattle Asian Art Museum, and I provide support to the communications manager in coordinating internal and external communication. My days involve responding to press requests for images or information, collecting information from various sources for a press release, and planning future PR strategies or events to familiarize people with SAM. I am on the phone a lot "pitching" story ideas, arranging interviews for our experts on staff, and responding to requests for information. I am also in front of the computer writing press materials. We keep staff up to date on the latest news concerning the museum, our messages, and what is released to the press.

Q: What misconceptions do people have about your job? What's the reality?

A: People don't really understand the nature of media work and how television, radio, newspaper, and magazine stories are created. They also don't tend to understand what public relations is all about, and that I don't work directly with the public! Also, that I can't just pick up the phone and get anything placed in a news outlet.

Q: What do you love about your work?

A: I love art and I am happy to be able to work at a museum that is run so professionally. I love that nothing stays the same and that there is always something new to work on so it's never monotonous. Staff here are wonderful and we make the work as fun as possible.

Q: What advice would you give to someone interested in a career similar to yours?

A: Hone all of your communication skills and create a portfolio of first-rate writing samples and press materials (such as press releases, media advisories, public service announcements, and so forth) that you can show prospective employers. Even offer to create some for an organization where you volunteer so that you have samples to share. Learn about the business of news and be able to demonstrate that you are organized, articulate, and tenacious!

Q: What resources might help someone interested in your field and job function?

A: For someone interested in working at a museum, *The Official Museum Directory* and the American Association of Museums (www.aam-us. org) are great resources. The Public Relations Society of American (www.prsa.org) can provide some initial information on my job function.

Q: What do you look for when hiring a new employee?

A: I look for enthusiasm, a solid work ethic, and experience. Writing skills are important, but so are strategic planning, the ability to work well under pressure, and initiative. The Seattle Art Museum is a fast-paced environment and to excel here you need drive and passion.

Spotlight on Education

As a means to prepare a capable workforce and informed citizens, the education subsector plays a critical role in our nation's economy and democracy. Its scope is vast: it reaches people of all ages, from young children to the elderly. It also draws from a broad range of funding sources, including government grants and subsidized loans, tuition, contracts, endowments, philanthropic gifts, revenue from intellectual capital and educational products, and tax-exempt status.

Areas in the education subsector include

- early childhood, elementary, and secondary schools, including child care, research, government-funded public schools, nonprofit private schools, and charter schools

- higher education, including community colleges, four-year colleges and universities, graduate schools, professional programs, and executive training

- supplemental programs, including academic and nonacademic programs, workforce development programs, career centers, community-based organizations, and agencies formed by government funding

- educational materials, including textbooks, curricula software, games and toys, and tours

- groups and libraries, including sororities and fraternities, alumni associations, and parent–teacher groups

The work

Perhaps the most obvious work in the education subsector is as a teacher. To comply with government regulations, K–12 public schools require teachers to pass a state certification test. Most private schools do not have this requirement, and requirements for charter schools vary by state. Teaching at colleges and universities usually requires BA and MA degrees, and often a PhD.

Beyond developing an expertise in a subject or grade area, people seeking careers in schools can also work as therapists, counselors, administrators (such as principals and deans), administrative staff, public relations officials, admissions and financial aid officers, fundraisers, and financial and strategic planners. In short, any role that contributes to the educational purpose or to the operation of a school is a potential career avenue for professionals in the sector.

Outside of schools, professionals may find roles in areas not necessarily addressed by traditional K–16 education. For instance, you might work as a tutor, a program officer in a nonprofit organization addressing disparity in access to education, a researcher studying the effects of early childhood development on academic achievement, an employee for a state department of education, or a trainer in a career center that prepares welfare recipients for employment.

Increasingly, many education nonprofits team up with community and commercial organizations to provide products or knowledge to meet the needs of local businesses or to help advance medicine and technology. Professionals with business, science, or creative skills may find roles in these emerging partnerships. In addition, many educational institutions have recently embarked on ambitious capital campaigns, so fundraising and development professionals will find themselves in particularly high demand in this subsector.

History and trends

Public school education, which Thomas Jefferson described as available to all children to equip them with basic skills for work and citizenship, remains a fundamental right. However, the focus of K–12 public school changed as the United States moved from a mostly agrarian nation of farmers, to an industrial nation, to a world superpower in the information age.

Partly in response to a desire to keep the United States globally competitive, Congress passed the No Child Left Behind (NCLB) law in 2001. To receive federal funding, NCLB requires K–12 public schools to demonstrate that the overwhelming majority of their students can pass standardized tests, especially in math and reading. The legislation reflects an overall trend of

tying education funding to specific outcomes. As a result, professionals will most likely find that "accountability" is an important topic in their organization.

In addition, many communities in the late twentieth and early twenty-first centuries tried to increase the choices families have of where to send children to school. One solution is the charter school movement, which allows communities to use public money to create small, often experimental schools with a test run of five years. Another proposed solution to improve the effectiveness of education is to turn management of K–12 schools over to private organizations.

These solutions are controversial, as they blur the distinctions between public and private resources. The debate is further complicated by philanthropies' increasing involvement in education, most notably the Gates Foundation. As a result of these shifts, many new professionals may find themselves considering issues of fairness, effectiveness, and the civic and social roles of K–12 schools.

The history of U.S. higher education is somewhat different. Beginning with the founding of Harvard in 1636, many early colleges and universities were designed to train religious clergy. Through the nineteenth and twentieth centuries, higher education institutions expanded to encompass the liberal arts, vocational and agricultural training, and research. They flourished especially at the end of World War II, when the G.I. Bill allowed many veterans to attend college. At the beginning of the twenty-first century, steady changes in technology and innovations contribute to an influx of adult learners and midcareer professionals.

Competition among private and public schools remains a key issue in higher education, with the latter schools making up the bulk of the sector. As a related issue (since it has financial as well as academic implications), many institutions also grapple with whether to conduct research for its own sake or for a practical application. For education-sector professionals, the trend toward diversifying higher education offerings may suggest new opportunities for creative marketing, online course offerings, revenue from intellectual and other property, and supplemental services.

education jobs sites

In addition to the general nonprofit jobs websites listed in the Appendix, check out these sites for education-related jobs:

Academic360.com
www.academic360.com

Academic Careers Online
www.academiccareers.com

Agent K–12
www.agentk-12.org

The Chronicle of Higher Education
www.chronicle.com

HigherEdJobs.com
www.higheredjobs.com

There also is a wealth of specialized resources on careers in education. Look for the ones that address your particular interest area. For example, Teach for America (www.teachforamerica.org) places teachers in low-income communities. In 2006, they recruited 2,426 new members and had a "corps" of 4,400 recent graduates working nationwide.

facts and figures: education

- Education public charities numbered 57,991 in 2005 and accounted for almost 19 percent of all charities.

- Nearly 30,000 new education organizations were awarded charity status between 1999 and 2004. More than half were groups that support education (such as remedial reading) or were parent-teacher, adult education, or scholarship and financial aid organizations.*

- Charter schools were the fastest growing group in the education subsector between 1999 and 2004, skyrocketing from 11 registered charter schools (1999) to 640 (2003).†

- This subsector reported $188 billion in revenue in 2005.

- Tuition payments and other fees for services account for just about 56 percent of education revenue, ranking it second (behind health) as the subsector most dependent on this type of revenue source.

- Private contributions account for approximately 15 percent of revenue, making it one of the subsectors least dependent on contributions.

- Elementary and secondary education organizations account for 20 percent of all organizations in this subsector.

- Colleges, universities, and other higher education organizations account for fewer than 4 percent of education reporting charities, but account for nearly 74 percent of total assets.

- In 2006, donations to education organizations increased by $41 billion, up more than 6 percent. This subsector had the highest growth rate in charitable giving (along with arts organizations).‡

Sources: Unless noted, all data are from *Nonprofit Almanac 2008*.

* Harvey Lipman, "Religion and Education Groups Grew the Most," *Chronicle of Philanthropy* (January 6, 2005).

† Ibid.

‡ *Giving USA (2006)*, as reported in Hall, "Donations by Americans reached $295-billion in 2006."

YVONNE FORMAN
Executive Director

Age: 61

Education: BA, French; MFA, sculpture

Years at current organization: 9

Years in current position: 6

First job out of college: Assistant to a dietician at a hospital

First job in nonprofit sector: Taught in a youth center for migrant children

PAX
Program of Academic Exchange

www.pax.org

Mission: PAX is a nonprofit educational organization that promotes and arranges international student exchange to foster the positive development of the world's young people and to support international peace, friendship, and cross-cultural understanding.

Operating budget: $3 million

Number of employees: 23

Number of employees who report to you: 13 people report to me directly, including the director of operations, director of finance, and regional directors

Q&A

Q: Informally, describe your career track.
A: After teaching in and directing day care centers, working as an artist, and after beginning a family, I entered the world of cultural exchange by finding host families for J-1 visa exchange visitors and supervising their placements. Over time I moved into the position of regional director, managing local coordinators throughout a geographic region. Nine years ago, I joined PAX as director of student services. Two years later I agreed to direct the day-to-day operations as executive director.

Q: What do you know now that you wish you had known when you were first job hunting?
A: I know now that behind all mission-driven ventures lies the need for smart, well-informed business practices. I knew this to some extent when I first began job hunting, but did not fully appreciate the critical importance of marketing and sales skills and solid business acumen to the success of a nonprofit venture.

Q: Describe a representative work day.
A: I oversee day-to-day operations. I manage staff, communicate with overseas partners (who identify and screen exchange students coming to the United States), develop programs, engage in strategic planning, and ensure that the organization is in full compliance with regulations, goals, and objectives. On a typical day, I might spend several hours in face-to-face meetings (planning, consulting, interviewing, staff meetings, hosting visitors, etc.), a couple of hours answering e-mail (internal and external), and perhaps the rest of the time developing program materials (creating incentives for finding host families, revising forms, generating newsletters, etc.) and supervising their production.

Q: What misconceptions do people have about your job? What's the reality?
A: The expectation is that my job is easy going, relaxed. People have no idea how complex and demanding the job is, and how much is at stake. Despite the simple concept and lofty mission, it is a challenging sales business to find host families for 1,000 exchange students from 40 countries every year, and then to supervise them. But the reality is worth it—through this program, high school students from other countries become "ambassadors" and are building respect for and an appreciation of differences and similarities between cultures. I work hard, but am glad to be part of my organization's mission.

Q: What do you love about your work?
A: I believe deeply in PAX's mission as a way to foster mutual respect among different people of the world. And I like the variety of work I have throughout the day and that I am always learning.

Q: What advice would you give to someone interested in a career similar to yours?
A: Find a cause you believe in and prepare to work hard and work smart. Your reward will come in the form of seeing the difference your contribution is making.

Q: What resources might help someone interested in your field and job function?
A: For information on student exchange: Council on Standards for International Educational Travel (www.csiet.org), the Alliance for International and Cultural Exchange (www.alliance-exchange. org), and the U.S. Department of State (www. state.gov/youthandeducation). For information on managing and leading people, I'd recommend: *Primal Leadership* by Daniel Goleman, *Selling the Invisible* by Harry Beckwith, and *Seven Habits of Highly Effective People* by Stephen Covey.[27]

Q: What do you look for when hiring a new employee?
A: When I'm looking for a new recruit, I seek someone who shares a passion for PAX's mission, has the appropriate skill set(s) for the position, and demonstrates a solid and appropriate employment history.

Spotlight on Environment and Animals

Nonprofit organizations dedicated to the environment and animals largely seek to raise public awareness and improve public policy to protect and beautify the environment. Many of the older and better established environmental groups—including the Nature Conservancy, the Sierra Club, and Greenpeace—are well known to most Americans. However, numerous small nonprofit organizations advocating for earth-friendly practices and animal welfare also contribute to the environmental movement.

The work of the environment and animal-related subsector covers

- environmental protection, including pollution prevention, recycling, and conservation of water, land, energy, and forests

- parks and gardens, including botanical gardens and garden clubs

- environmental education, including outdoor survival programs

- animal welfare, including wildlife preservation and protection, protection of endangered species, bird sanctuaries, wildlife refuges, veterinary services, zoos, and zoological societies

The work

Most environmental and animal nonprofit organizations are involved in advocacy of one kind or another—influencing individuals, businesses, or public policy to effect widespread change.

Nonprofit organizations achieve influence most commonly through persuasive research and communications, lobbying, and developing relationships with members of other groups. A professional in this field may work as a researcher, especially in investigating the science or economics behind environmental themes. Writers, public affairs officers, marketers, curriculum developers, and educators translate the research into compelling messages and deliver it to key audiences.

Professionals in this subsector may also be effective as lobbyists, policy experts who can make recommendations to elected officials, or lawyers who can press for resolution of an issue by pursuing litigation. Negotiators often play an important role in developing coalitions among like-minded organizations or in finding an appropriate solution for organizations with potentially competing interests.

Membership coordinators are particularly important in this subsector, which draws significant influence from the number of individuals who financially and politically support its work. As with any nonprofit, fundraisers and marketing professionals are also important; environmental and animal nonprofits usually draw revenue from a combination of foundation money, corporations, major donors, membership subscription fees, and sales of products.

At gardens, sanctuaries, zoos, and similar organizations, a great deal of work connects directly to the facility. Positions range from an animal curator (who is responsible for a certain portion of an institution's collection) to a registrar (who maintains computer records on the collection and oversees licenses to hold or transport animals). Veterinarians, technicians, researchers, conservationists, biologists, and (surprise!) zoologists are employed by animal-related organizations such as zoos or aquariums.

Finally, professionals in this subsector may find new avenues partnering with businesses, especially with skyrocketing interests in going "green" and sustainability (see "The New 'Green-Collar' Workforce," at right). Strategic thinkers with an appreciation both for business and environmental needs may find a place helping for-profit institutions build nature-friendly practices into their work, not only meeting the minimal green requirements but also making eco-positive and sustainable contributions over time.

the new "green-collar" workforce

One of the hottest new trends in the environmental movement has given birth to a "green-collar" economy. This refers to jobs created to develop clean, renewable energy products and services. Some people also include organic farming and green building practices here. Congressman Jay Inslee (D-Wash.) estimates that a successful clean energy movement could create three million new jobs, especially in the areas of research, technology, and manufacturing. Proposed federal legislation (e.g., the Green Jobs Act) would support the creation of green jobs. Not all of these jobs will be in the nonprofit sector, of course, but many will be. And it is the next generation of nonprofit sector leadership who will create and advance the green movement.

History and trends

Concern for the environment and animals began to develop as a movement around the end of the nineteenth century in the United States. It gained momentum in the 1970s, when the American public became increasingly concerned about the predicted population boom, not to mention nuclear war and other human impacts on the environment. In the 1990s, the number of nonprofit organizations dedicated to the environment and animals more than doubled.

The increased number of organizations, coupled with the steady rise in membership and dollars for environmental causes, allowed the sector to extend its influence. Many environmental and animal issues now often transcend national boundaries and are considered international concerns. The sector also enjoys the benefit of a good deal of financial support and a fairly positive reputation—as sustaining life on earth is generally considered a worthwhile cause.

However, the increase in environmental and animal groups also means that the field risks becoming crowded and redundant. One solution, especially popular through the 1990s, is to develop coalitions, not only among other nonprofit organizations, but also with businesses and community groups.

Another response to the increase in competition for resources and attention is for large organizations to create local chapters. Since the multiple smaller offices require more staff, many nonprofit organizations hope to offset the cost of salaries with improved technology and grassroots efforts.

As a result, professionals will likely be charged with finding new solutions to organizational and advocacy efforts, but at the same time face increasingly complex and expensive environmental challenges.

environment and animals jobs sites

In addition to the general nonprofit jobs websites listed in the Appendix, check out these sites for environmental and animal-related jobs:

Association of Zoos and Aquariums
www.aza.org/joblistings

EcoEmploy.com
www.ecoemploy.com

Environmental Career Opportunities
www.ecojobs.com

EnvironmentalCareer.com
www.environmentalcareer.com

EnvironmentalJobs.com
www.environmentaljobs.com

facts and figures: environment and animals

- Environment and animal-related organizations accounted for more than 4 percent of all public charities in 2005.

- This subsector reported almost $12 billion in total revenue in 2005.

- Private contributions account for 48 percent of total revenue for this subsector, making it the second-most dependent subsector on private contributions (behind international and foreign affairs).

- Fees for services and goods (e.g., admission and educational program fees) account for 25 percent of environment and animal-related organizations' revenue.

- In 2006, donations to this subsector decreased by more than 1 percent.[*]

- In 2005, donations to this subsector increased by 14 percent, probably because of concern about global warming and experiencing more storms as severe as Hurricane Katrina. (Fundraisers expect this interest to continue in the years ahead.) The subsector has grown at a rate of more than 7 percent over the past decade.[†]

- The sector's largest environmental organization—the Nature Conservancy—employs more than 2,500 people. But a growing number of employment opportunities are found at the grassroots level.

Sources: Unless noted, all data are from *Nonprofit Almanac 2008.*

[*] *Giving USA (2006)*, as reported in Hall, "Donations by Americans reached $295-billion in 2006."

[†] Ibid.

LISA DARDY McGEE

National Parks & Forests Program Director

Age: 33

Education: BA, anthropology/art history
double major, minor in women's studies; JD

Years at current organization: 3

Years in current position: 3

First job out of college: Park ranger
(naturalist) in Grand Teton National Park

First job in nonprofit sector: Outreach
intern for a local conservation organization

Wyoming Outdoor Council

www.wyomingoutdoorcouncil.org

Mission: The mission of the Wyoming Outdoor Council is to protect Wyoming's environment and quality of life for future generations.

Operating budget: $690,000

Number of employees: 9

Number of employees who report to you: None

Q & A

Q: Informally, describe your career track.
A: I've always loved the outdoors and nature. During college I worked for the national parks in the summer—scooping ice cream in the Grand Canyon first, and then as a ranger intern in Yellowstone. After graduating, I took a seasonal ranger position in Grand Teton National Park. I worked three summers there and pieced together off-season work in Jackson, Wyoming. I then decided to attend law school, with a focus in environmental law. During law school, I served as a research assistant for a water law professor and as a legal intern for the Wyoming Outdoor Council. Upon graduation, I took a one-year judicial clerkship in

Alaska. Close to the end of that year, my current position became open at the Wyoming Outdoor Council, and I came to work here.

Q: What do you know now that you wish you had known when you were first job hunting?
A: I wish I had spent more time identifying my expectations for a position. During the job search, think through what you want—in an organization, a supervisor, the work environment, a job function, and so forth—and have good questions prepared to help you learn about those things.

Q: Describe a representative work day.
A: I am one of three attorneys on staff, and I work on issues facing the national parks and forests in Wyoming. I spend a lot of time on research, writing, strategy, and outreach. I frequently submit comments to public land management agencies regarding proposed actions as part of the National Environmental Policy Act (NEPA) process. On any given day I may have meetings with partner organizations to determine the next steps in a campaign. I might draft a press release, write an editorial, or speak to a reporter to help get our messages out. I may meet with an elected official. There are times when I have to work on my program budget or other administrative tasks. And every day involves receiving and responding to a huge number of e-mails.

Q: What misconceptions do people have about your job? What's the reality?
A: When family friends ask what I do, my parents often say, "Lisa is saving the land." It's true that I'm working to protect special places in Wyoming and to keep our air and water clean and our wildlife healthy. However, the misperception is that on a daily basis I am successfully saving the land. In fact, these issues take years to resolve—and we don't always see the result we'd hoped for.

Q: What do you love about your work?
A: I have been deeply influenced by the wild places in Wyoming where I've backpacked, skied, or floated, and I am happy to know that the work I do helps protect these special areas. Having a sense of pride in the work I do is important to me.

Q: What advice would you give to someone interested in a career similar to yours?
A: Volunteering or interning will give you some sense of the day-to-day operations and whether it's something you think you'd enjoy.

Q: What resources might help someone interested in your field and job function?
A: Law schools that have an environmental law and policy concentration often have a corresponding center or institute, and they often have websites that are good sources of information.

Q: What do you look for when hiring a new employee?
A: Strong written and oral communication skills, an easygoing and cooperative personality, a good sense of humor, and a passion for the issues.

Spotlight on Health

As a subsector, health employs the most people and commands the largest share of revenue in the nonprofit sector. Almost every American interacts in some way with the health system—from general health (e.g., a visit to a clinic) to rehabilitative health (e.g., physical therapy). Overall, the country spends over $2 trillion on health care each year.

This figure is projected to hit $2.9 trillion by 2009 and $4 trillion by 2015, or 20 percent of GDP.[28] In 2006, the industry provided 13.6 million jobs for wage and salary workers, and 438,000 for the self-employed. Employment in this sector is expected to increase 22 percent through 2016 (as compared with 11 percent for all other industries combined), generating 3 million new jobs.[29]

Hospitals are probably the best-known institutions in the health subsector, employing 41 percent of health workers.[30] Many hospitals operate as charitable institutions and maintain a tax-exempt status. The nonprofit health subsector also extends beyond treating individuals. The field of public health (see "Public Health Careers," page 75) aims to improve community health, which might include providing education or helping disadvantaged populations to have more of a political voice in influencing health care policy.

Although this enormous sector comprises both for-profit and nonprofit institutions, areas in which nonprofits make up a significant percentage of the field are

- hospitals, especially acute care and rehabilitation facilities

- mental health services, including outpatient clinics and multiple service organizations

- residential treatment, including care for emotionally disturbed children, hospice, and home health

- centers and clinics, including community health, dialysis, organ and tissue banks, blood supply, family planning and reproduction, and groups addressing addiction

- health insurance, including health maintenance organizations (HMOs)

- research and organizations devoted to diseases or disciplines, including birth defects, cancer, bioengineering, geriatrics, neurology, and pediatrics

The work

Work in the nonprofit health subsector can be classified into three categories. The first is individual care: for instance, doctors, nurses, therapists, counselors, chiropractors, clinicians, laboratory technologists, pharmacists, and alternative medicine providers. The second is administrative support, including insurance officers, accountants, billing

public health careers

Public health is a major and growing health field, and one that taps into core values of the nonprofit sector: serving others and strengthening the health of a community. Public health focuses on the social context of disease. Strategies to promote health and prevent disease are applied to *populations* of individuals—in a village, a country, or across a continent. Public health professionals address issues such as access to health care, infectious diseases, environmental hazards, violence, and substance abuse. Specializations include epidemiology, biostatistics, and health services, as well as environmental, social, behavioral, and occupational health.

Nonprofit organizations play a critical role in public health initiatives, tackling complex issues using interdisciplinary approaches that depend on collaboration among nonprofits, government, and business (see, for example, "Government, Business, and Nonprofit Collaboration: The Case of the Female Condom in Zimbabwe," page 41). The work of public health involves research, public policy, education, advocacy, and service delivery. Organizations in this field look for scientists, researchers, lawyers, writers, and administrators, among others.

For more information on careers in public health, or to order the free publication *Advancing Healthy Populations: The Pfizer Guide to Careers in Public Health* (2002), visit www.whatispublichealth.org.

agents, and operations managers. The third involves work to improve health and health care on a large scale, serving as researchers, educators, or advocates on public health issues (see "Public Health Careers" at left), perhaps in partnership with major government agencies and programs. The organizations may focus on improving specific health issues of broad concern, such as clean water, immunizations, or HIV/AIDS prevention.

History and trends

Historically, hospitals in the United States were charities; their funding came from religious groups or a few wealthy individuals.

Although charitable hospitals continued to serve the poor and infirm, in the 1930s, many employers began paying for workers' health care. In 1965, the federal government created Medicare, providing health insurance for people over age 65; and Medicaid, providing health insurance for people with low incomes. As a result of these changes, either a business or the government subsidized the vast majority of Americans' health care. And due, in part, to these reliable sources of funding, in thirty years (1965–1995) the health care industry grew from 5 to 14 percent of the country's GNP. Yet for all the resources devoted to health care, not all Americans receive quality treatment, and, in the twenty-first century, the United States continues to lag internationally in infant mortality and life expectancy rates.

The combination of the necessity, scope, and money related to health care means the subsector is quite complicated—nonprofit health organizations often rely at once on government, foundation, and commercial funding, and they are subject to public policy decisions and numerous regulations. For nonprofits, having both financial and policy considerations can mean competing with for-profit institutions for clients and revenue, while at the same time maintaining their tax-exempt status as charities by donating some of their services for free.

To keep up with the pace of change, one trend for nonprofit health organizations is to operate more like for-profit enterprises, with an emphasis on cost efficiency and marketing. Another trend is to form coalitions to minimize expenses while maximizing resources.

A third, and perhaps more significant trend, is for nonprofits to alter their definition of health care from focusing on individual health to community health. Between 1995 and 2002, foundations tripled their support to health care nonprofits devoted to research, public education, and advocacy. They also increased their support for nonprofits working to improve overall health care policy.

Professionals new to this subsector will find a field that continues to be powerful both economically and politically. Insured Americans have greater access to a higher quality of health care than those without insurance; health care nonprofit organizations will find their role intensified as they seek to bridge this gap. They must also respond to widespread concerns such as obesity and epidemics. Finally, if health care nonprofit organizations can maintain their reputation for trustworthiness, stability, and quality, they will play an increasingly important role in sensitive areas such as mental health and substance abuse, reproductive and end-of-life issues, and HIV/AIDS prevention and treatment.

health jobs sites

In addition to the general nonprofit jobs websites listed in the Appendix, check out these sites for health-related (especially public health) jobs:

American Public Health Association
careers.apha.org/search.cfm

Public Health Employment Connection
cfusion.sph.emory.edu/PHEC/phec.cfm

Public Health Jobs Worldwide
www.jobspublichealth.com

Partners in Information Access for the Public Health Workforce
phpartners.org/jobs.html

PublicHealthJobs.net
www.publichealthjobs.net

facts and figures: health

- In 2005, health organizations accounted for more than 13 percent of all public charities. They reported $672 billion in total revenue.

- The health subsector is the subsector most dependent on fees for services and goods: more than 87 percent of its revenue comes from this source.

- Hospitals and primary treatment facilities account for nearly 75 percent of the subsector's assets, expenses, and revenue.

- In terms of number of organizations, the subsector is dominated by those classified as "other": family planning organizations, blood banks, public health organizations, and patient support organizations.

- The second largest group in the subsector is disease-specific organizations, such as the March of Dimes and American Cancer Society.

- In 2006, contributions to health organizations—more than $20 billion—represented a decline of more than 5 percent. In 2005, contributions had declined as well (by 0.6 percent).*

Sources: Unless noted, all data are from *Nonprofit Almanac 2008*.

* *Giving USA (2006)*, as reported in Hall, "Donations by Americans reached $295-billion in 2006."

CAROLYN PIZZUTO
Vice President, Revenue Management

Age: 49

Education: BS, education; MA, community health administration; AMA project management certification

Years at current organization: 20

Years in current position: 1

First job out of college: Customer service agent for an airline

First job in nonprofit sector: Teacher

March of Dimes

www.marchofdimes.com

Mission: The mission of the March of Dimes is to improve the health of babies by preventing birth defects, premature birth, and infant mortality. The March of Dimes carries out this mission through programs of research, community services, education, and advocacy.

Operating budget: $228 million

Number of employees: 1,450

Number of employees who report to you: 8, the directors of event marketing and communications, revenue and data analysis, national special events, and family team development; two managers of online fundraising; administrative assistant; and manager, revenue projects

Q & A

Q: Informally, describe your career track.
A: I started at the March of Dimes as a graduate intern while I was working as a health and physical education teacher in New York City. At March of Dimes, I moved from intern to community director to director of WalkAmerica to director of development, all at one chapter office. I then was promoted to executive director for another chapter office. I then came to the national office,

where I moved from national director of volunteer development to national director of online fundraising to my current position.

Q: What do you know now that you wish you had known when you were first job hunting?

A: With the Internet and other new technologies, access to information is so much better today. It is easier to prepare for interviews and learn about prospective employers. Looking back, I wish I had been better prepared for my interviews.

Q: Describe a representative work day.

A: I lead the March of Dimes National WalkAmerica Campaign. I also direct and support the expansion of our online fundraising capabilities and manage the National WalkAmerica training program. I travel frequently and get to work with our chapter staff and volunteers nationwide to help grow their WalkAmerica events. When not traveling, my day is spent working with other departments to ensure synergy in developing and executing materials, tools, and training. It is critical that the fundraising strategies effectively support the foundation's mission.

Q: What misconceptions do people have about your job? What's the reality?

A: A common misconception is that there is less accountability in the nonprofit world. Also, people often mistakenly think that there is less stress and that every day is easy. In truth, these are very real jobs in very professional settings. We are accountable and we work hard, even though we are working for a cause we believe in deeply.

Q: What do you love about your work?

A: I love that every day is different. Working with volunteers is truly an honor. In particular, it is an honor to work with those families who are affected by premature birth and birth defects.

Q: What advice would you give to someone interested in a career similar to yours?

A: Get out and volunteer. Explore opportunities that are a little bit outside of your comfort zone. Realize that the work that is done in the nonprofit sector is terribly important and that you can make a difference.

Q: What resources might help someone interested in your field and job function?

A: *The NonProfit Times* and the *Chronicle of Philanthropy* will keep you in touch with the nonprofit world. Also stay apprised of current business news outlets such as the *Wall Street Journal, Business Week,* and the *New York Times.* In my specific area I seek out resources to help me better understand Internet fundraising and the strategies that drive e-mail marketing. *Business 2.0* (published by www.CNNMoney.com) has been a great publication as well.

Q: What do you look for when hiring a new employee?

A: I look for passion and an outgoing and engaging personality. I also look for individuals who are well versed in the March of Dimes mission and people who have clearly done their homework before coming in for an interview.

Spotlight on Human Services

The human services subsector, also called *social services,* includes some of the giant organizations that many people think of first when they think of the nonprofit sector: American Red Cross, Urban League, Salvation Army, Volunteers of America, YMCA, and YWCA. Because of the enormity of its task—to restore, protect, maintain, and promote quality of life—this subsector is large, diverse, and overlaps with many other subsectors, especially health.

Human services organizations address

- family and children services, including counseling, adoption, foster care, and day care

- public safety and emergency assistance, including disaster preparedness and relief, travelers' aid, search and rescue, fire prevention and control, and first aid and safety training

- housing and shelter, including low-income and subsidized housing, retirement communities, housing search assistance, youth hostels, homeless shelters, assisted living, and services for the deaf and blind

- crime and legal organizations, including crime prevention, rehabilitation services for offenders, prison alternatives, court reform, dispute resolution and mediation, protection against abuse, correctional facilities, police departments, and public interest law organizations

- employment, including job training, vocational rehabilitation, Goodwill Industries, and labor unions

- food and nutrition, including food banks and pantries, farmland preservation, and farm bureaus

- recreation, sports, and leisure, including camps, physical fitness and community recreational facilities, parks and playgrounds, sports training facilities, social clubs, street fairs, amateur sports clubs and leagues, amateur sports competitions (including Olympic committees and Special Olympics), and professional athletic leagues

- youth development, including youth centers and clubs, scouting programs, and citizenship and religious leadership programs

- advocacy, including neighborhood change and development, welfare reform, immigration rights

The work

The vast range of human services organizations means that professionals with well-developed skills and passion for a specific issue are apt to be able to apply their experience and expertise to an agency in this subsector.

For instance, people with a background in law, immigration, child development, or geriatric care may find a niche in an organization focusing on a specific issue. Because the needs of individuals often are better addressed if the larger context is understood, professionals who know the contributing history, political, economic, and social factors can help an organization make strategic decisions and care appropriately for their constituents. Many of these agencies depend on a large team of frontline workers.

Another route for professionals may be to identify an organization with a mission that is particularly meaningful and apply their unique set of skills to advancing that mission. Most social service organizations depend on teaching or training, project management, operations and administrative support, fundraising, grants administration, counseling, therapy, research, and communications.

The U.S. government provides data on "social assistance, except child day care" establishments—both nonprofit and for-profit. The Bureau of Labor Statistics reports that this subsector provided 1.5 million nongovernmental jobs in 2006. Although half of all social assistance employers had fewer than five workers, in this subsector larger establishments account for most jobs (see Figure 1).

History and trends

Since the founding of the United States, families, friends, and neighbors have cared for the needy. Organized service providers became better established during the nineteenth century, with most focusing on children, widows, or mothers having trouble caring for the families—often called the "deserving poor." In the 1900s, a number of additional agencies were developed to respond to the needs of immigrants. Most organizations were funded by private donations and, to some degree, by businesses and state governments.

FIGURE 1

Half of all establishments in social assistance, except child day care, have fewer than five employees.

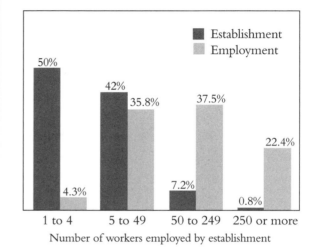

Source: Bureau of Labor Statistics, U.S. Department of Labor, *Career Guide to Industries, 2008–09 Edition*, Social Assistance, Except Child Day Care, available at www.bls.gov/oco/cg/cgs040.htm (accessed December 18, 2007).

To make the most of this funding, some organizations banded together to create Community Chests, which raised money jointly and then distributed donations among members.[31]

The human services subsector went through two significant changes in the mid-twentieth century. Many nonprofit organizations folded during the Great Depression, and the federal government stepped in to provide assistance. In the 1960s, the federal government declared a "War on Poverty," injecting the subsector with new funds and expanding it to include senior services, mental health, prevention of violence against women, foster care, and early childhood education and nutrition.

The federal government's involvement meant many organizations' funding streams changed from private donations to public money. The Community Chests gave way to a federation of organizations under the United Way, which in turn became less prominent as smaller, independent organizations cropped up throughout the second half of the twentieth century.

In the 1980s and 1990s, the subsector changed again when the Reagan administration introduced major budget cuts, and the Clinton administration reduced the number of people eligible for welfare and the amount of cash they could receive. With less federal money allocated to the human services sector, many human services organizations switched their emphasis from helping individuals directly to encouraging long-term development, including job training and child care. They also took advantage of other kinds of government support, including loans, tax credits, and tax-exempt bonds.

In addition to particular shifts in the landscape, this history also demonstrates an important reality for human services nonprofits: they are subject to changes both in the economy and in public policy. Fortunately, human services organizations don't lack for public awareness or opportunities to help. Especially after the terrorist attacks on September 11, 2001, and Hurricane Katrina, human services organizations gained added prominence. In addition, new factors—such as increased immigration, more single-parent households, households with both parents working, and longer life expectancy—mean the sector is likely to continue expanding and varying its services.

human services jobs sites

In addition to the general nonprofit jobs websites listed in the Appendix, as well as those listed in "So You Want to Be a Youth Worker?" page 121, check out these sites for human services jobs:

Coalition on Human Needs
www.chn.org/jobs/index.html

National Human Services Assembly
www.nassembly.org

SocialService.com
www.socialservice.com

SocialWorkJobBank
www.socialworkjobbank.com

facts and figures: human services

- With 100,436 reporting public charities, based on the of number of organizations, the human services subsector dominates. It accounts for more than 32 percent of reporting charities.

- In terms of missions, human services is the most diverse subsector. Its organizations include soup kitchens, farmland preservation alliances, and amateur sporting clubs.

- The greatest number of human services organizations focus on recreation and sports, which represent more than 24 percent of reporting groups. Second place goes to housing and shelter organizations, accounting for almost 16 percent of the sector.

- In 2005, human services organizations reported more than $148 billion in total revenue.

- Human services organizations receive slightly more than 53 percent of total revenue from fees for goods and services.

- Human services organizations receive almost 23 percent of their income from government grants, making this the subsector the most dependent on public funds.

- In 2006, social services organizations raised almost $30 billion, representing 10 percent of all charitable giving, and a decline of 12 percent from the previous year. However, when 2005 disaster gifts are deducted, contributions were just about flat.[*]

- In 2005, contributions to this subsector increased by almost 29 percent, due to contributions related to Hurricane Katrina.[†]

Sources: Unless noted, all data are from *Nonprofit Almanac 2008.*

[*] *Giving USA (2006),* as reported in Hall, "Donations by Americans reached $295-billion in 2006."

[†] Ibid.

Spotlight on International and Foreign Affairs

The international and foreign affairs subsector deals with issues that extend beyond national boundaries. It can address short-term, urgent needs such as emergency relief following a natural disaster or a refugee crisis. It also helps countries and populations create long-term, sustainable routes for improved peace and prosperity. Relief, recovery, or development is often part of the mission of organizations in this subsector.

Sometimes called nongovernmental organizations (NGOs) or international nongovernmental organizations (INGOs), many international and foreign affairs nonprofit organizations serve as intermediaries between a government and its population. Many NGOs have the benefit of working at the grassroots level, engaging with and responding immediately to the people whom they serve.

International NGOs frequently work on humanitarian, economic, or political issues. Specific areas of concentration include

- cultural and student exchange, including high school, university, teacher, and professional study

- development, including microfinancing and small business loans, health care, disease care and prevention, nutrition, water safety, agricultural assistance, reproductive health and family planning, transportation, and education

- disaster relief, including emergency food, shelter, medical, and sanitation services

- human rights, including civil society, freedom of the press, voting, legal issues, and safety

- refugees and migration, including camps, asylum, settlement, and negotiation

The work

NGO professionals can work in the United States or abroad; however, it's not as easy as one might imagine to work overseas, since many NGOs prefer to maintain a close connection with the people they serve by hiring local staff.

In the United States, professionals might find positions as program officers focusing on either a particular geographical area or an issue; as researchers, writers, or analysts in a think tank; as advisors on public policy or economic issues; or as marketers and communications specialists for advocacy organizations. Producing and disseminating information is often a key feature of NGOs. Professionals might also help organize conferences, hold competitions or seminars, or host gatherings.

Overseas, professionals might work as trainers or educators, as linguists or translators, as field staff providing practical and administrative support, or might provide technical ("how-to") support, especially for organizations seeking to build infrastructure.

It's important to note that, depending on their mission, NGOs can work in violent or unstable environments—conditions may be uncomfortable at best, dangerous at worst. In addition, because their work often has an impact on government and vice versa, NGOs may find themselves in politically sensitive situations. As is true for all nonprofit organizations but especially in this subsector, working in an international NGO often requires diplomacy, sturdiness, and stamina.

History and trends

International nonprofits began in the early nineteenth century, focusing on issues of broad concern such as ending slavery, providing hospitality, and studying ophthalmology. In 1864, the International Red Cross was founded to help injured and suffering soldiers. The subsector expanded after World War I to help all victims of war and to secure long-lasting peace.

In the 1960s, as many countries in Africa and Latin America achieved independence, international organizations began providing economic support as well as short-term relief. Often, these NGOs worked on a particular geographic area, being careful not to transgress political alliances. However, this code of behavior changed in the early 1970s, when Doctors without Borders insisted on going wherever medical help was needed, regardless of politics.

The four guiding principles of NGOs emerged as "humanity (preventing and relieving suffering); neutrality (not taking sides); impartiality; independence (from foreign governments or political or religious agenda)."[32] These values not only helped establish trust, but also protected the safety of NGO professionals. Although sometimes there was a lingering suspicion that an NGO worker was a spy or government agent, most NGO professionals could count on being seen as honest brokers for the cause they served. In return, NGO professionals were by and large not harmed in violent struggles.

The 1990s saw a rapid increase in the number of NGOs, as well as another change in the subsector. The end of the Cold War, civil wars, and food shortages prompted tremendous humanitarian crises, especially in Eastern Europe and Africa. Many NGOs sought to provide relief, but political and military realities often thwarted humanitarian efforts. Perhaps the best-known example is Rwanda in the early 1990s. Fighters infiltrated

---

international and foreign affairs jobs sites

In addition to the general nonprofit jobs websites listed in the Appendix, check out these sites for international and related jobs:

DEVJOBS
www.devjobsmail.com

Foreign Policy Association
www.fpa.org

InterAction (subscription required)
www.interaction.org

International Jobs Center (subscription required):
www.internationaljobs.org

the refugee camps and terrorized the very people NGOs tried to protect. In addition, international aid workers themselves became targets. Seeing that international political intervention was slow or not forthcoming, several NGOs concluded they were making the situation worse, not better, and withdrew. In addition to being horrific in itself, the episode in Rwanda prompted many in the subsector to reconsider the NGOs' commitment for total independence.

As NGOs play an increasingly prominent role in global affairs, they are challenged to demonstrate transparency and accountability. In some cases, NGOs are perceived as both threatening capitalism and as serving capitalist elites, as contributing to colonialism and interfering with local autonomy. New professionals may find the subsector responding to these criticisms in part by supporting entrepreneurial efforts to build locally owned infrastructure.

facts and figures: international and foreign affairs

- The total number of reporting international and foreign affairs organizations—5,075—accounted for less than 2 percent of the sector in 2005.

- This subsector reported almost $23 billion in revenue in 2005.

- Private contributions account for more than 67 percent of revenue, making this the subsector the most dependent on private contributions. Government grants account for almost 22 percent of revenue to international and foreign affairs organizations.

- Unlike other subsectors, international and foreign affairs organizations distribute almost 54 percent of their funds in grants and specific assistance to individuals.

- The wealthiest foundations in the United States increased support for "international affairs" by almost 41 percent in 2005, largely because of the Asian tsunamis. But their total giving to charitable projects abroad (such as education and health efforts) remained flat.[*]

- In 2006, giving to international affairs organizations fell by an estimated 12 percent when adjusted for inflation, to just more than $11 billion. Like the drop in human services giving, analysts attribute this to unprecedented levels of giving in 2005 for disaster relief.[†]

Sources: Unless noted, all data are from *Nonprofit Almanac 2008.*

[*] From a study by the Foundation Center of 1,154 charitable funds in the United States, as reported in Ian Wilhelm, "Giving by Big Foundations Rose 6% in 2005, Study Finds," *The Chronicle of Philanthropy* (March 8, 2007).

[†] *Giving USA (2006)*, as reported in Hall, "Donations by Americans reached $295-billion in 2006."

NOTES FROM THE ROAD
LIVING AND WORKING ABROAD

Q&A with **Victoria Ebin**
Consultant to international nonprofit organizations

Q: What's fun about working overseas?
A: I love the travel. I love getting on a plane, the adventure, meeting people on the other side of the world and learning about how they live. I feel lucky that I can look at a map and say to myself, "I know people there," and that I have some understanding of cultures very different from my own. There's a thrill that comes from being able to find my way in a new place, and also from landing in a spot I know well and slipping back into my past life and resuming a conversation with an old friend, as if I had never left.

Q: What are some of the challenges of the travel?
A: Spending short amounts of time in places you don't know well can be lonely. Dinners alone in hotels are really boring. But if you return to a place a few times and always make an effort to get out, you will meet people and develop friendships. But it's hard connecting with people and then leaving—I often wish I could get all my friends together in the same place because they are scattered around the world.

Q: Isn't international work also exhausting?
A: Yes, the travel can be very tiring. The most difficult trips are when you visit several countries in a short time period and are always in airports. On one of my earliest trips, a journalist from Burkina Faso and I went to six countries in three weeks. I learned things that I won't have to be taught again—for example, if you do wash in a humid country (such as Ghana), make sure you're sticking around long enough for the clothes to dry. I'll never forget lugging plastic bags of wet clothes through airports . . . it wasn't until I got to Mauritania that everything finally dried.

Q: Have you found that the pace of change is slower overseas?
A: It's true that it can sometimes be harder to get things done—and if you're working in developing countries you have to be patient, creative, and sensitive to the local culture and approach. You definitely can't march in with "your way" of doing things. You need to be open, and really interested in listening and learning. And if you are, you'll have interesting things happen to you, meet

(continued on page 88)

(continued from page 87)

more people, and enjoy unexpected adventures. Once while living in Senegal I wanted to take my dog to the vet. But I got the wrong number and ended up getting the private line of the cultural attaché to Burkina Faso. Not realizing who he was, I asked if he could give my dog a tick bath. We ended up meeting and became friends. I've learned to love the time one has in Senegal. People there spend a lot more time taking care of their friendships and are so much more tuned into other people.

Q: Are there health concerns with overseas work?

A: You have to be careful. Everyone knows to watch out for food, water, and mosquitoes. But another distressing and dangerous issue is the amount of toxic chemicals that are part of everyday life: household cleaners, paint, gasoline with lead, pesticides, industrial run-off. It's terrible to think of the people—and especially the children—who live in such toxic environments.

Q: Do you hang out with a lot of expats?

A: In many countries where I've worked, there are groups of foreigners who tend to live in closed communities and have very limited contact with the "locals." Many are perfectly nice people, but I have never understood why they choose to live like that, and I don't really consider that true international work. But absolutely, I have non-African friends throughout the continent. In Senegal, where I lived for five years, some very close friends are American and European. But they have lived in the country for years, speak Wolof, and are deeply connected to the local community.

Q: You keep the United States as your base, but do other people who work internationally live abroad permanently?

A: There are so many paths for an international nonprofit career. I chose consulting, and get to work with various organizations on different projects. The friends I mentioned before are good examples of another approach to international work. Lillian Baer and Gary Engelberg were Peace Corps volunteers in the 1960s. They liked living and working in West Africa so much that they decided to stay. They created a nongovernmental organization based in Dakar, called Africa Consultants International, www.acibaobab.org. It started as a center for cultural exchanges and health, and later expanded to become an internationally recognized NGO that works to raise awareness of AIDS. Lillian and Gary, along with the Senegalese staff they have recruited, are doing an enormous amount of good in the region, through the path they chose and their tireless commitment to Senegal and Africa.

Q: How important are language skills if you want to work internationally?

A: I think the happiest and most successful people working internationally are adept at languages and make a real commitment to trying to speak the local language. I speak French so can get around in the francophone African countries. But French only helps with the surface of life there. You have an enormous advantage if you can speak to people in their local dialect, and even learning the most basic greetings opens doors. It shows you're not just another foreigner who has no deep commitment—or respect—and expects everyone to speak English.

Q: Can someone new to the field get an international placement, or do those jobs go to people "higher up"?

A: It's competitive to land a good international job, especially at the entry level. You'll need to show some experience on the issue, and ideally you'll have devoted time to the organization that you would like to have place you overseas. International organizations are aware of the strains of living abroad and are reluctant to send out someone they don't know or with no overseas experience. It's best if you can demonstrate your capability first.

Q: How do you find an international job?

A: It's much more strategic to think about finding a job on the issue you want to work on, that is employing an approach that your skills are suitable for, and in a country or region you are familiar with. The world is just too big to say, "I want to work internationally." You need to focus in on a specific area and identify the organizations doing work you'd like to contribute to. And then be creative about how you get your foot in the door and demonstrate how capable you are. ■

Victoria Ebin specializes in training African journalists on AIDS and reproductive health. She worked in Haiti and throughout Africa, especially Senegal and Ghana (countries where she also lived for several years carrying out anthropological research and working as a consultant). Victoria's clients include Academy for Educational Development (AED), Groupe de Recherche et Echanges Technologiques (GRET), Institute de Recherche et Developpement (IRD), Guttmacher Institute, Population Council, and Population Reference Bureau (PRB), among other organizations.

Spotlight on Public or Societal Benefit

The broad subsector of public or societal benefit organizations relies on research, collective action, and strategic change to improve the quality of life for a group of people or for the public at large. Usually its goals are far reaching and long term. Missions of organizations in this subsector are likely to address aspects of a community's physical, intellectual, social, financial, or political well-being. For instance, nonprofit organizations in this sector might attempt to change public attitudes about smoking or wearing seatbelts, or to improve the living conditions in a neighborhood.

The public or societal benefit subsector addresses

- civil rights and social action, including efforts on behalf of the rights of minorities, people with disabilities, women, seniors, and lesbians and gays

- civic engagement, including voter education, registration, and political campaigns

- advocacy, including reproductive rights, anti-abortion initiatives, freedom of speech and freedom of the press issues, and euthanasia

- community improvement and capacity building, including neighborhood development, block associations, chambers of commerce, boards of trade, real estate organizations, community service clubs (such as Kiwanis, Lions, Jaycees), and nonprofit management support groups

- philanthropy, voluntarism, and grantmaking, including private foundations, community foundations, and fundraising federations such as United Way

Organizations concerned with scientific and social science research, the interests of veterans, public transportation, credit unions, consumer protection, and public utilities are also included in this sector.

The work

Regardless of the area on which they focus, professionals in the public or societal benefit subsector will probably find themselves engaged in some combination of the following four efforts: getting a message across to the public, influencing public policy, changing or enforcing laws, or investigating the root causes of social concerns.

There are ample opportunities in this broad subsector for people with skills in persuasive speaking, writing, and social marketing. Researchers, policy experts, lobbyists, and lawyers also have important roles, as do people with skills in planning, strategizing, and managing membership.

In addition, because having political clout often requires mobilizing as many people as possible, community organizing, communications, and media relations are also potential professions.

History and trends

Civic-minded organizations have been part of the American tradition of volunteerism and community engagement since the founding of the country. Many consider this subsector to be at the heart of American democracy: it expects that citizens will actively participate in furthering the public good, and encourages them to do so.

With the civil rights movement in the late 1950s and 1960s, advocacy and social change efforts increasingly took a direct-action approach—public sit-ins, protests, and marches became prevalent and powerful. Advocacy work adopted other strategies as well—fundraising, awareness-raising events (such as marathons and direct mail), and litigation were leveraged to advance the mission of organizations.

And, while television and print media historically have been essential tools to publicize a cause, the Internet suggests whole new ways to organize like-minded people, raise small donations from many individuals, and disseminate stories and information. (What's more, the Internet is a lot less expensive than traditional media.)

---

the 10 wealthiest foundations in the U.S. (2006 assets)

1. Bill & Melinda Gates Foundation (*Seattle*)	$33.0 billion
2. Ford Foundation (*New York*)	$12.3 billion
3. Robert Wood Johnson Foundation (*Princeton, NJ*)	$9.8 billion
4. William and Flora Hewlett Foundation (*Menlo Park, CA*)	$8.5 billion
5. W.K. Kellogg Foundation (*Battle Creek, MI*)	$7.8 billion
6. Lilly Endowment (*Indianapolis*)	$7.3 billion
7. David and Lucile Packard Foundation (*Los Altos, CA*)	$6.3 billion
8. John D. and Catherine T. MacArthur Foundation (*Chicago*)	$6.1 billion
9. Andrew W. Mellon Foundation (*New York*)	$5.8 billion
10. Gordon and Betty Moore Foundation (*San Francisco*)	$5.7 billion

Source: Noelle Barton and Ian Wilhelm, "Foundations Assets Grow Sharply," *Chronicle of Philanthropy* (April 5, 2007).

In terms of community improvement, volunteer and member organizations have long sought to make neighborhoods and towns safe, attractive, and prosperous. Since the 1970s, when federal funding made housing for people with low incomes more affordable, community development organizations have also provided financial guidance and investments to help nontraditional property owners buy homes.

Philanthropies are another significant element in this subsector. Many well-known foundations, such as Rockefeller and Carnegie, were established at the end of the nineteenth century, when oil, steel, coal, and other industries generated significant profits, and wealthy businessmen sought to give their money to worthy causes. Since they wanted their charitable impact to be as significant as their professional one, these leaders hired professional staff and advisors to invest their money in causes that would make strategic, long-term changes in line with the benefactor's preferences and goals. Public foundations and federations adopted a similar approach, with the view that private dollars would have the greatest impact if pooled with others.

Foundations typically receive their founding endowment from an individual, a family, or a corporation with investment assets. Foundations remain significant sources of both giving and public change; however, recent trends suggest foundation giving may be directed more by donors and less by top-down decision making by executives and board members. In addition, many corporations are developing philanthropic arms, and some charities seek to provide business as well as social benefits.

public or societal benefit jobs sites

In addition to the general nonprofit jobs websites listed in the Appendix, check out these sites for jobs in the public or societal benefit subsector:

Alliance for Justice
www.afj.org

Association of Fundraising Professionals
www.afpnet.org

The Chronicle of Philanthropy
www.philanthropy.com

Council on Foundations
www.cof.org

Dot.Org.Jobs
www.dotorgjobs.com

Foundation Center
www.fdncenter.org

Feminist Majority Foundation Online
www.feminist.org

National Organizers Alliance
www.noacentral.org

what is a community foundation?

Community foundations bring together the charitable donations of multiple donors. The foundation invests and administers targeted funds for its donors so that the grants have maximum impact on the top issues in a given geographic area. Community foundations work to understand and stay abreast of needs that are specific to a region, and they provide a structure making it easy for local philanthropists to give to their community. The first community foundation was established in 1914 in Cleveland; today there are more than 650 throughout the United States. Community foundations account for 1 percent of all grantmaking foundations, but almost 9 percent of all giving. They comprise one of the fastest growing sectors of philanthropy. In 2006, their giving increased by more than 13 percent, to $3.6 billion.

Source: Foundation Center, *Foundation Growth and Giving Estimates: Current Outlook* (2007), available at http://foundationcenter.org/gainknowledge/research/pdf/fgge07.pdf (accessed January 11, 2008).

facts about foundation jobs

Foundations represent only 7.4 percent of the nonprofit sector—or approximately 110,000 organizations in 2006. The majority operate with very few staff members who tend to have lower turnover than the nonprofit sector average; foundation staff tend to stick around. There is good news though: new foundations are popping up at a rate faster than for the rest of the nonprofit sector (foundations represented only 5.4 percent of the sector in 1996 so there was an 87 percent increase in ten years).[*] Vacancies, however, still are relatively rare in the foundation world.

The top five causes that foundations support (and the percentage of their contributions that go to them) are listed below. As such, foundations are more likely to be looking for program people with knowledge in these issue areas.

1. education (24 percent)
2. health (almost 21 percent)
3. human services (almost 15 percent)
4. arts and culture (12.5 percent)
5. public affairs, societal benefit (just over 11 percent)[†]

Sources:

[*] National Center for Charitable Statistics, "Number of Nonprofit Organizations in the United States, 1996–2006, available at http://nccsdataweb.urban.org/PubApps/profile1.php?state=US (accessed January 24, 2008).

[†] From a study by the Foundation Center of 1,154 charitable funds in the United States, as reported in Ian Wilhelm, "Giving by Big Foundations Rose 6% in 2005, Study Finds," *Chronicle of Philanthropy* (March 8, 2007).

facts and figures: public or societal benefit

- The 35,249 public or societal benefit organizations represented almost 12 percent of reporting public charities in 2004.

- This subsector reported more than $57 billion in revenue in 2004.

- Public or societal benefit organizations receive just more than 5 percent of charitable contributions.

- Total assets of U.S. foundations, one part of this subsector, totaled more than $510 billion in 2004.[*]

- Advocacy, grantmaking, and civic organizations employed 1.2 million wage and salary employees in 2006. The vast majority worked in establishments employing fewer than five people. Their earnings averaged $15.81 per hour.[†]

- In 2006, giving to public or societal benefit organizations increased by more than 2 percent, down a bit from the increase of 4 percent in 2005.[‡]

Sources: Unless noted, data here are from Pollack and Blackwood, *The Nonprofit Sector in Brief, 2007,* which is an earlier version of data presented in the *Nonprofit Almanac 2008.*

[*] Noelle Barton and Ian Wilhelm, "Foundation Assets Grow Sharply," *Chronicle of Philanthropy,* (April 5, 2007), available at www.philanthropy.com/premium/articles/v19/i12/12000701.htm#wealthiest.

[†] Bureau of Labor Statistics, U.S. Department of Labor, *Career Guide to Industries, 2008–09 Edition,* Advocacy, Grantmaking, and Civic Organizations, available at www.bls.gov/oco/cg/cgs054.htm (accessed December 18, 2007).

[‡] *Giving USA (2006),* as reported in Hall, "Donations by Americans reached $295-billion in 2006."

WORKING AT A FOUNDATION

Q&A with **Gregg Behr**

Executive Director • The Grable Foundation • www.grable.org

Q: Working at a foundation sounds like a dream job. Is it?

A: Yes, I think I have a dream job. Foundation work is tremendously interesting and rewarding. It offers the chance to have an impact on the world and help people and communities in need. The best foundation staff members are learning all the time about issues, organizations, and policies, and this makes for a very stimulating day. But awarding grants—at least doing it well and responsibly—is not easy work.

Q: How hard can it be to give away money?

A: Grant making involves real opportunity costs. A foundation has limited dollars to invest, and typically we must decline more organizations than we fund. It takes careful research and thought to identify the most appropriate recipients for the limited funds, and time and good administration to manage the grants effectively. Plus, it's sometimes uncomfortable to raise difficult matters or decline requests face-to-face.

Q: Is the structure and staffing of The Grable Foundation representative of a typical foundation?

A: I have a colleague who says, "If you have met one foundation, you have met one foundation." There are many types of foundations, including family, private, operating, and community foundations. These categories are all different, and the foundations in them are all distinct. The Grable Foundation makes grants totaling approximately $10 million per year and has a staff of ten. But the Richard King Mellon Foundation, also in Pittsburgh, awards close to $90 million in grants annually, and only has a staff of nine. There simply are no "typical" foundations.

Q: What type of person makes the best foundation program officer?

A: The two most important attributes I look for when hiring staff are curiosity and kindness. Foundation work is done best by people who are inquisitive, eager to learn about the world, and willing to go into communities to listen, without preconceived notions of the right solutions. Our work requires kindness because foundation staff

(continued on page 96)

(continued from page 95)

are in the customer service business. We work in service to our organization's mission, our trustees, and the vision of our founders. And we work in service to the communities we are charged with helping.

Q: What type of experience helps to land a job at a foundation?

A: Foundation work is a realistic, worthy career goal, but the truth is that it is hard to break into this world fresh out of college, or even right out of graduate school. Turnover is low, and the competition for the few vacancies is fierce. Foundation leaders look for candidates who have certain educational credentials but also significant experience in business, government, or the nonprofit sector—or some combination of the three. It's smart to gain good experience in the field, and then make yourself lucky enough to land your dream job.

Q: How can you "make yourself lucky"?

A: There's no magic formula for creating the career you dream of. But you make yourself lucky because you have excelled in the work you have done, been present and active in your community, and gained skills that match the skills a prospective employer seeks. There are times when I have been looking for a generalist. I just wanted an extraordinary person who would have succeeded in any position. And there have been other times

when I have needed specific knowledge around a certain issue area. In both cases, however, I've looked for passion and drive, intellect, experience, and, as I mentioned earlier, curiosity and kindness.

Q: When did you become passionate about public service and philanthropy?

A: I think it has always been part of who I am, but I began to understand my values and cultivate them through extensive volunteer work as both an undergraduate and graduate student. At Notre Dame, I spent all four years volunteering at the South Bend Center for the Homeless and the Center for Social Concerns. I then spent a year as a Jane Addams Fellow at the Center on Philanthropy at Indiana University. Throughout my education, I was passionate about public service, but I was only beginning to develop ideas on civil society. It wasn't until graduate school that I could really start articulating what I believed and why.

Q: Do you recommend graduate school to someone interested in a nonprofit sector career?

A: I recommend taking advantage of as many educational opportunities and service learning experiences as you can, so long as you do it thoughtfully and consciously. There is no single track that you must follow, and now more than ever there are a range of academic and extracurricular programs that someone interested in public service can pursue. Definitely explore all your options, talk to people, and be creative about the course of study and professional experiences you choose.

Q: What other resources would you recommend to someone interested in a foundation job?

A: It is great to attend as many conferences as you can. They aren't just networking opportunities; conferences allow you to immerse yourself in ideas and really think about the issues and the communities you care about. And read, read, read—journals, books, newspapers. ■

The Grable Foundation is a Pittsburgh-based foundation dedicated to improving the lives of children. Gregg Behr previously served as president of The Forbes Funds, another Pittsburgh-based foundation, and prior to that practiced as a litigator with a national law firm. While a graduate student in law and public policy at Duke University, Gregg founded The Content of Our Character Project, a nationally acclaimed ethics initiative (www.contentofourcharacter.org).

CATHLEEN I. PRICE
Senior Attorney

Age: 36

Education: BA, history-sociology; JD

Years at current organization: 10

Years in current position: 6

First job out of college: Paralegal in a law firm

First job in nonprofit sector: Intern at a nonprofit law firm

Equal Justice Initiative of Alabama

www.eji.org

Mission: The Equal Justice Initiative of Alabama provides legal representation to indigent defendants and prisoners who have been denied fair and just treatment in the legal system. We litigate on behalf of condemned prisoners, juvenile offenders, people wrongly convicted or charged with violent crimes, poor people denied effective representation, and others whose trials are marked by racial bias or prosecutorial misconduct.

Operating budget: Approximately $1 million

Number of employees: 15

Number of employees who report to you: We are not organized with direct lines of management, but I routinely supervise the work of 4 fellows, 2 junior attorneys, and legal interns

Q & A

Q: Informally, describe your career track.
A: I worked as a paralegal in a large corporate law firm, and then went to law school. While in law school, I worked in a number of nonprofit and for-profit firms, and ended up realizing that I wanted to devote my training and energy to fighting human rights abuses.

Q: What do you know now that you wish you had known when you were first job hunting?

A: I wish that I understood at the outset the value of focusing on developing strong organizational skills. Having good organizational skills ten years ago would have saved me countless hours in the middle of the night, I'm certain.

Q: Describe a representative work day.

A: I represent indigent prisoners on death row in Alabama. My job entails litigation of their appeals. This includes legal research and factual investigation as well as the preparation of litigation pleadings. A typical day entails responding to letters from clients, conducting legal research in my own cases, or consulting with other death penalty lawyers about what is happening in their cases.

Q: What misconceptions do people have about your job? What's the reality?

A: I think that most people envision lawyers' work as what happens in the courtroom, like the lawyers on television. The reality is that the bulk of the work of lawyers is accomplished long before the cases get into court, and entails many long days studying cases, and finding and developing witnesses.

Q: What do you love about your work?

A: I love knowing that I am part of a movement that is working for the world that I want. Less loftily, I love to write, and lawyering definitely entails a lot of writing.

Q: What advice would you give to someone interested in a career similar to yours?

A: I would encourage everyone to spend some time in internships in different nonprofit organizations. In addition to getting exposure to the substance of the work, I think it's a good idea to learn about how different organizations are run.

Q: What resources might help someone interested in your field and job function?

A: I would recommend the Death Penalty Information Center (www.deathpenaltyinfo.org) and the NAACP Legal Defense Fund (www.naacpldf.org) in addition to the Equal Justice Initiative of Alabama as good sources of information on the state of the death penalty and related legal challenges.

Q: What do you look for when hiring a new employee?

A: We look for interpersonal skills that will serve our clients and their families, as well as shrewd observational skills and good writing skills. We also look for high energy; if you don't really want to work hard, our agency is not a place where you are going to be happy.

Spotlight on Religion-Related

The religion-related subsector includes Christian, Jewish, Islamic, Buddhist, Hindu, interfaith, and other religious organizations, as well as religious media organizations. Most are part of the approximately 355,000 religious congregations in the United States, which account for more than 20 percent of all nonprofit organizations.[33]

This subsector—along with mutual/membership benefit organizations (see page 104)—is unusual among nonprofit organizations in that its mission is primarily to serve its members, and secondarily to serve the public. In addition, the vast majority of its funds come from individual donors (who are usually regular participants in the parish) rather than from foundations or public money. Finally, this subsector remains almost exclusively nonprofit, with little competition or partnerships with for-profit companies.

The religion-related subsector addresses

- care for members, including religious services, religious education, counseling, and administration
- social services, including soup kitchens, donations and drives, and shelters
- affordable housing, including redevelopment efforts, support for first-time home buyers, and Habitat for Humanity

- education and community support, including tutoring, job training, and substance abuse programs

The work

Clergy and religious leaders make up the bulk of the professionals in this subsector. Almost all have denomination-specific training programs, and their work varies with their religious affiliation. However, most church leaders devote the bulk of their time presiding over religious ceremonies and events, counseling and visiting members, studying and preparing presentations, and administrating organizational business.

Although few congregations have staff, non-clergy professionals in this subsector may find roles maintaining operations, serving as financial advisors, coordinating one of the organization's programs (such as youth, music, or college ministries), or managing volunteers. If this subsector continues in a recent trend to compete for government funding to provide social services, professionals may find their roles expanding considerably to include building more professional and institutionalized volunteer programs, grant writing and administration, and staffing social service initiatives.

Keep in mind that lines between all of the subsectors overlap and blur. In the case of religion, more than 20 percent of U.S. charities include religious practices and faith as a core part of their mission. As such, if you are looking for a job in the nonprofit sector with a religious underpinning, you might focus on the type of work you want to do in tandem with your religious interest.

History and trends

Religious organizations have historically provided many of the social supports the nonprofit sector offers. Since the founding of the United States, religious organizations have helped the poor and needy, established orphanages, and founded hospitals. In addition, they served as community halls, places to hold public meetings, centers for social change such as the abolitionist and temperance movements, and sources for volunteers and leadership to provide goods and services to soldiers.

In some ways, the role of this subsector has become less prominent as the nonprofit sector grew overall; many of the roles religious institutions played were taken over by specialized organizations. However, Americans continue to volunteer for and make charitable donations to religious organization more than to any other nonprofit subsector. In addition, religious organizations often intersect with other nonprofits, sharing space or resources, or providing the volunteers or motivation for new organizations. Even if new nonprofit professionals don't find work as staff for religious organizations, they might be mindful of the role this subsector plays in their own field of interest.

New professionals may also find that recent legislation inspires religious organizations to attend increasingly to a public calling. Introduced in 1996 and signed into law in 2000, "charitable choice" (sometimes called "faith-based initiatives") allows religious nonprofits to compete with other nonprofit organizations for government funding to provide social services. Caveats to the law spell out that religious organizations may not be discriminated against nor discriminate against others on the basis of religion. Furthermore, government funds are intended to go entirely toward social service goals rather than religious activities.

The law remains controversial. Some argue it threatens freedom of religion and separation of church and state; others claim religious organizations should not be restricted from providing appropriate social services.

For professionals in the subsector, the practical elements of charitable choice may be more significant than the philosophical debate. With the addition of public funds, religious organizations may need to add staff or change volunteers' roles; integrate more people into the community; make physical, time, and budgetary changes to the organization; develop mechanisms for public accountability; and reconceive their missions to consider the appropriate weight they should give to members' religious development and to the public's health and welfare.

religion-related jobs sites

In addition to the general nonprofit jobs websites listed in the Appendix, check out these sites for religion-related jobs:

ChurchJobs.net
www.churchjobs.net

Combined Jewish Philanthropies
www.cjp.org

JewishJobs.com
www.jewishjobs.com

Work Ministry
www.workministry.com

facts and figures: religion-related

- 80 percent of Americans state an affiliation with an organized church or other religious institution.[*]

- In 2005, nearly 36 percent of all private contributions were given to religious organizations, which is double the percentage received by any other subsector.

- In 2004, the 17,670 religion-related reporting public charities represented almost 6 percent of organizations. (However, this reflects only a fraction of religious organizations in the United States.)

- In 2006, giving to religious organizations increased by more than 1 percent; in 2005 it had increased by closer to 2 percent.[†]

- Religious organizations are the most popular site for volunteering: 35 percent of Americans devote the greatest amount of their volunteer time at religious organizations; 41 percent volunteer at a religious organization to at least some extent.[‡]

- More than 80 percent of congregations participate in social service, community development, or neighborhood organizing projects. The majority focus on emergency services.[§]

- More than 80 percent of congregations have food assistance programs. More than 66 percent have clothing assistance programs. More than 40 percent have programs for the elderly. Approximately 33 percent have tutoring or youth support programs.[**]

- 21 percent of U.S. charities include religious practices and faith as a core part of their missions.[††]

- Of the approximately $1 billion that foundations and companies contributed to relief efforts connected to Hurricanes Katrina and Rita, approximately 20 percent went to religious organizations.[‡‡]

Note: Churches, associations of churches, and other religion-related organizations are not required to file with the IRS. They also don't have to file Form 990 detailing their receipts and expenditures, as other nonprofits do. As such, only a small percentage of these groups are tracked through IRS records, and data on this subsector are incomplete.

Sources: Unless noted, data here are from Pollack and Blackwood, *The Nonprofit Sector in Brief, 2007.*

[*] Susan Raymond, "Faith in America: The Philanthropic Context," onPhilanthropy.com (March 3, 2006), available at www.onphilanthropy.com/site/News2?page=NewsArticle&id=5621 (accessed January 14, 2008).

[†] *Giving USA (2006)*, as reported in Hall, "Donations by Americans reached $295-billion in 2006."

[‡] According to the *2003 Volunteer Supplement to the Current Population Survey* conducted by the Bureau of Labor Statistics, as reported in Kimberly Spring and Robert Grimm, *Volunteer Management in America's Religious Organizations* (Washington, DC: Urban Institute, 2004); available at http://www.urban.org/publications/411143.html (accessed January 24, 2008).

[§] Ibid.

[**] Raymond, "Faith in America."

[††] *2003 Volunteer Supplement*, in Spring and Grimm, *Volunteer Management in America's Religious Organizations.*

[‡‡] From a study by the Foundation Center, as reported in Caroline Bermudez, "Companies and Foundations Give $1 Billion for Katrina Aid," *The Chronicle of Philanthropy* (September 6, 2007).

Spotlight on Mutual/Membership Benefit

Mutual/membership benefit organizations—including some unions, political groups, professional societies, business and trade associations, councils, communes, cooperatives, and neighborhood organizations—primarily serve their members' interests. Most work done by these organizations is conducted by the members themselves.

Many mutual/membership benefit organizations have their roots in eighteenth- and nineteenth-century mutual aid societies—usually single-gender, single-race organizations whose members helped each other financially and socially. Among other things, these societies provided members with property and business loans, moral and leadership education, opportunities for social networking, and charitable goods or services for members. When members died, the mutual aid society often provided cemetery and burial services. In addition, most mutual aid societies also had a public service component, supporting schools, hospitals, or the elderly.

Since the country's founding, mutual aid societies have played an important role in creating a civic fabric. They were particularly critical in establishing African American communities, especially for newly freed slaves after the Civil War, and for Mexican immigrants seeking at once to assimilate into American society and to preserve their own customs.

In the 1960s, when the federal government declared a "War on Poverty" and distributed funds to social service organizations, many mutual aid societies benefited; however, as other nonprofit organizations and for-profits have taken on similar roles, the number of mutual aid organizations, members, and social service projects have declined. Nevertheless, some vital membership organizations remain, and the nonprofit sector continues to recognize in this subsector organizations that provide insurance (other than health), pension and retirement funds, and cemeteries and burial services.

THINKING OF STARTING YOUR OWN NONPROFIT?
TEN QUESTIONS TO ASK YOURSELF BEFORE YOU "GO AT IT ALONE"

by **Ethan Hutt** and **Aaron Tang**

Codirectors • Our Education • www.oured.org

It takes more than a great idea and a healthy dose of passion to launch your own nonprofit organization. If you're considering this path, it is vital that you first confirm that building a *new* organization is the most effective way to implement your idea, and that you have the range of resources necessary to create and sustain it.

Here are some questions to ask yourself to determine whether founding an organization is right for you—and for advancing your idea.

1. Do you have a solid "lay of the land"?

If you're considering founding a new organization, you need to be an expert in your field. You also must carefully canvass existing organizations doing related work. After all, the burden of proof will be on you to convince potential partners, funders, board members, and other supporters that you understand the problem you want to address, and that a new organization will be a part of the solution. This due diligence has the added benefit of helping you network, identify new supporters, find a possible fiscal sponsor, and develop an even stronger plan. Don't short change the preliminary research you need to do.

2. Is your idea truly unique?

Your concept should be innovative on a variety of fronts. Does your idea target a population not currently being served in this way? Does your idea employ a strategy not currently being used to serve this population? Will your idea be implemented at a scale that is unique (e.g., it's a local initiative when all others are only national, or vice versa)? To justify starting a new organization, it's best if your idea is unique in all three areas—population served, strategy employed, and scale implemented. It definitely needs to be unique in at least one area.

3. Is your idea sustainable?

Ideally, you have leads to seed money to help you launch your organization. But are you confident that your idea will be attractive to the funding world (foundations, individual donors, government programs), and that you will be able to generate the financial resources necessary to survive—and thrive? Is your idea also sustainable from a human resource perspective? Will you be able to build a team of dedicated, talented professionals to advance your mission?

(continued on page 106)

(continued from page 105)

4. Could an existing organization launch your project?

Even if your idea is innovative, this does not mean it requires a new organization to implement it. Make sure that an existing organization isn't a more appropriate home for your project idea. Starting a new organization when it's not absolutely necessary may only dilute already limited dollars. If you can work within an existing structure, you'll streamline resources, secure immediate colleagues, and be able to tap into an existing infrastructure, not to mention save countless hours each week for programmatic work that might otherwise be needed for administrative operations. There are many benefits in hooking up with an established group—but if you plan to partner with an organization as a first step toward establishing an independent group, make sure that your host understands your desire and is willing to offer a supportive relationship.

5. Have you tested your idea?

Take your idea to your smartest—and most critical—colleagues. Brainstorm with those friends who love to disagree with you. Give them a chance to poke holes in your plan, and then assess how strong your "defense" is. Does your idea stand up to a strong challenge? Does an attack only serve to motivate you further, or do you lose confidence more quickly than you might have

expected? Make no mistake, if you're starting a new organization, you'll face innumerable challenges and setbacks. You must have the knowledge and stomach to face them.

6. Have you tested yourself?

Starting your own nonprofit organization is no small feat. It generally requires tireless energy, total commitment, and complete comfort with having to survive on limited resources. Are you at a stage in your life where such a focus is realistic and will make you happy? Moreover, building a lasting and effective organization is not just a quick and easy endeavor. Can you make the multiyear commitment required to get a new organization up and running? Do you have the experience necessary to make your project a success?

7. Do you have the trust of the population you want to serve?

Are you viewed as an insider or an outsider? Are you known and respected among your target audience? A good litmus test is to ask yourself, "If I were incorporated today as an independent nonprofit organization, would leading members of my target audience join my board with enthusiasm?"

8. Is starting a new organization what's best for your target population?

Mission must come first. In the research you've conducted and conversations you've had with experts in the field and members of your target audience, can you confirm that starting a new organization is what's best for the people you want to serve—as opposed to working with an already existing organization to improve one of their current programs? Your decision cannot be about personal ambition; it has to be about how best to serve your audience and accomplish the mission.

9. Can you stand up to the "But for . . ." challenge?

Can you say that a vital idea will not be advanced, a groundbreaking strategy will not be implemented, a population in critical need will not be served, and a pressing problem will not be addressed *but for* you starting a new nonprofit organization? Will a viable solution not be tested *but for* the creation of your organization?

10. If you are committed to starting a new organization, have you investigated the steps necessary to incorporate?

Make sure you really understand the process required to start your own nonprofit. One of the best handbooks is *How to Form a Nonprofit Corporation* by Anthony Mancuso.[34] Other excellent resources include the charities and nonprofits section of the IRS website (www.irs.gov/charities); your local state association of nonprofits, which

will likely have guidelines on starting a nonprofit; and the office of your state attorney general.

On paper, the challenges of starting your own nonprofit organization may seem to outweigh the benefits. But the scale should tip for other reasons. It is a fact that we can't solve all of our world's problems within existing structures. Today's most pressing issues require creative, innovative, radical strategies at times, and sometimes these strategies need their own organizations. If your idea stands up to the challenges of starting a new nonprofit organization—and if you can stand up to the challenge of making it happen—to you we wish good luck, courage, confidence, and humility. ∎

OUR EDUCATION

Ethan Hutt and Aaron Tang (both 2005 graduates) cofounded Our Education in 2003 with some fellow classmates. Their goal was to give students a voice in school reform efforts. Our Education's mission is to improve K–12 education by engaging and empowering America's youth in a national movement for better schools. Echoing Green named Ethan and Aaron two of the "World's Best Emerging Social Entrepreneurs."

In a Nutshell . . .

This chapter offered a sense of the fields of work within the nonprofit sector. When combined with the profiles found throughout the book, it offered direction on how to choose the issues you would like to work on and approach you would like to be part of. More than anything, the information should have reinforced the range of opportunity for impact that a career in the nonprofit sector offers. The nonprofit sector is working on all sorts of issues in every part of the world.

Be advised, however, that no single career guide can make you an expert in a given field. If you're hoping to launch a career in the nonprofit sector without a strong sense of the type of work you would like to do, this book provides some direction. But you will need to spend extra energy choosing an area to target and learning more about it. You should be reading constantly, attending workshops, taking extra classes, and networking aggressively to learn as much as you can about the issue. And for job seekers who believe they already are "up to speed" in their field, it cannot hurt to make sure you really are.

Now that you have a handle on what nonprofit organizations do, you're ready to move onto the next chapter to learn more about the nature of work at them. Chapter 3 describes specific job functions in the nonprofit sector.

three

JOBS IN THE
nonprofit SECTOR

The nonprofit sector offers as many types of positions as the for-profit sector—and then some. From accounting to writing, from telemarketing to research, from counseling to fundraising, your skills and interests can find a home with the right nonprofit organization.

Some job functions are virtually identical in the nonprofit and for-profit sectors; for example, an information technology specialist's job will vary more based on the size of the organization than what sector it is in. Other positions are unique to the nonprofit sector, such as volunteer manager or grants writer.

The types of jobs in a nonprofit organization can be grouped into five very broad categories of responsibility:

- senior management
- programs and service delivery
- administration, human resources, and finance
- development and fundraising
- communications

While the largest nonprofit organizations can have dozens of departments and hundreds of specific job functions and titles, this book describes the following subcategories of work for each of the five areas listed above.

- The *senior management* section focuses on the executive director and associate director positions.

- The *programs and service delivery* section covers advocacy, counseling and direct social services, education and training, and research and policy positions.

- The *administration, human resources, and finance* section covers the job functions of accounting and finance, operations, clerical and data entry, human resources (including volunteer coordinators), information technology, sales, telemarketing, and customer service.

- The *development and fundraising* section covers annual fund, grant writing and administration, major gifts, planned giving, and special events positions.

- The *communications* section covers the work of editing, writing, and publications; graphic design; marketing and advertising; media relations (or public relations); and web development and design.

Organizations and organizational structures vary dramatically. Not all organizations have dedicated staff for each of these five areas, let alone individuals handling the specific job functions that could fall within the departments. In the smallest nonprofit having only one paid staff member, a single person handles all of these responsibilities (with perhaps some assistance from volunteers and board members). In large nonprofit organizations, job functions may be organized in countless ways. For example, advocacy might be housed in a communications department in one organization, and under programs at another.

However, almost all organizations have a leader who serves as executive director. And most organizations perform at least some work in the areas of program, administration and finance, development, and communications, and therefore need staff members to handle these duties. Various nonprofit sector job functions (grouped under the remaining four broad areas of responsibility) are described on the next pages.

In addition, many organizations rely on consultants to help them advance their mission, and the job of consulting is covered as its own section.

Throughout this chapter, pay attention to the notes that fall within the different categories of work. These refer you to related profiles appearing in the book, as well as sample job descriptions found in the second part of this chapter.

words to the wise: job titles

As you embark on your career in the nonprofit sector, it's as important to think about the work you want to do as it is the type of organization you want to work for. However, the range of job functions an organization offers—and specifics on what a given job actually entails—depends on many organizational variables. For example, small and midsized organizations must fold more responsibilities into fewer positions. The largest organizations are more likely to have clearly defined departments and more specific job functions.

In addition, one job title can refer to wildly different job descriptions in the nonprofit sector. The reverse is also true: a variety of job titles can refer to substantively the same job. As you search for positions that suit you best, be sure to pay attention both to job titles and job descriptions. Consider the skills and experiences an organization is looking for more than the job title of a given vacancy. Learn how to read between the lines of job descriptions. Familiarize yourself with an organization's structure and the roles of the other employees so you can gain a better sense of the reality of the job beyond what you read in a posting.

Senior Management

Executive director

A nonprofit executive director (also called a president or chief executive officer [CEO]) is responsible for leading an organization. The executive director is hired by and reports to the organization's board of directors and has ultimate responsibility for carrying out the strategic plan of an organization and managing all of its activities. The position usually entails working with the organization's board of directors; overseeing the execution of programs and services, communications, and fundraising; managing human resources and making sure personnel policies comply with current laws; developing and managing the annual budget, and having responsibility for the fiscal health of an organization; and serving as the senior-most spokesperson on an issue.

In general, executive positions are rewarding but stressful, and require significant commitment. Many executives find they have limited time for other life activities, so they must truly love the work. Burnout can occur in some cases; research on executives in the nonprofit sector shows that many would not return to the position. Many, however, embrace the leadership responsibility and decision-making authority they hold in their field, on their issue, among their constituents, and with their staff.

so you want to be an executive director?

Many people embarking on a career in the non-profit sector dream of one day leading or founding an organization. The rewards can be rich—you have the opportunity to set an organization's course and ultimately be responsible for how well it achieves its mission. With the right team supporting you, an executive director can be a thought leader on an issue, affect policy, and have a major impact on a field. This leadership role can be the final and most rewarding chapter in a career dedicated to public service.

But being ultimately responsible for an organization brings with it certain challenges. Many executive directors are surprised by just how much time they spend managing people and dealing with personnel issues. Others become frustrated with the energy they have to put into fundraising and development; they would prefer to be in the field actually doing the work rather than finding a way to pay for it. Some people find that leading and managing an organization actually makes them feel uncomfortably disconnected from the work they are passionate about.

If your goal is to become an executive director, conduct due diligence on what it actually entails.

Study the profiles of executive directors found in this book. Meet with executive directors leading organizations similar to ones you'd like to run, and try to understand what their days are really like. Determine academic qualifications that are either helpful or required to be a leader in your field, and find model career paths that might suit your goals. Identify and develop the skills you will need to be successful in the role of executive director—make sure you are working to become an expert on your issue as well as on how to raise money, communicate ideas, and manage people.

And, perhaps most importantly, work to realize your leadership potential. Be as thoughtful about the work you do as how you do it. Cultivate a mentor and solicit advice on your management skills and leadership abilities. Test your penchant for making tough decisions, asking for advice, and building consensus. Find as many opportunities to lead as early in your career as possible—at your place of work, through volunteer activities, and with professional development programs that focus on leadership development.

Typically, an executive is the institution's lead spokesperson and spends much time dealing with its constituents, volunteers, staff, and board. The executive serves as the face of fundraising efforts and as lead advocate for legislative and regulatory policies and practices that affect the organization's mission. Most executives spend a significant amount of time (and emotional energy) managing their board of directors, ensuring a smooth relationship with it and among its members.

Executives who work their way up the ranks may miss the direct contact with mission work that first called them to the field, but may find great (if less immediately rewarding) compensation in their ability to influence important decisions that ultimately benefit the people their organization serves. People who are comfortable exercising judgment, making decisions, working in and managing complex social and political situations, communicating to groups, and raising money—and who know how and when to seek advice—will feel more natural with the leadership demands an executive faces.

For More Insight on
Being an Executive Director . . .

See Brian Gallagher's interview ("Great Leadership in the Nonprofit Sector," pages 116–119); the sample executive director job description (pages 156–157), the boxed text "So You Want to Be an Executive Director?" (page 112); and the profiles of Yvonne Forman (pages 66–67), Marc Morial (pages 14–15), and Esteban Ramos (pages 114–115).

Associate director

Associate directors (also known as associate executive directors, among other titles) typically function as the "right hand" or second-in-command to the executive director. They work closely with the top leader on strategy, programs, fundraising, administration, and all of the other key departments in an organization. The associate director may be more responsible for smooth day-to-day operations than the executive director, often handling prickly personnel issues or unexpected crises. Depending on the organization and its size and structure, an associate director may be assigned areas of particular focus; for example, the associate director may provide extra leadership on research if the organization is a "think tank," on member services if it is a membership organization, or on fundraising if it is a start-up organization concentrating on resource development. Many of the skills and experiences required to be a successful executive director apply to the associate director position as well.

ESTEBAN RAMOS
Associate Executive Director

Age: 29

Education: BA, social work; MSW; Youth Studies Certificate Program

Years at current organization: 8

Years in current position: 2

First job out of college: Youth aide for a youth services program

First job in nonprofit sector: As above

Fresh Youth Initiatives

www.freshyouth.org

Mission: To support and encourage the efforts of young people in Washington Heights to design and carry out community service projects, develop leadership skills, fulfill their potential, and realize their dreams.

Operating budget: $850,000

Number of employees: 12

Number of employees who report to you: 8, three senior program directors, one senior group leader, and four group leaders

Q & A

Q: Informally, describe your career track.
A: I started as an intern at Fresh Youth Initiatives (FYI), organized through Public Allies (www.publicallies.org). As an intern, I helped establish a new satellite program. When the director of that satellite site resigned, responsibility for it practically fell on my lap and I took the reigns. After my ten-month internship was complete, FYI asked me to stay on as a full-time staff member. I kept acquiring new and expanded responsibilities—moving from program director, to senior program director, to associate executive director when the codirector of the organization resigned. I didn't apply for the position of associate executive director; it was offered and I accepted.

Q: What do you know now that you wish you had known when you were first job hunting?

A: I learned that the higher degree you have, the higher the pay you can command, and the greater impact you can make in an agency and in your field.

Q: Describe a representative work day.

A: I am responsible for creating and implementing the new vision for the organization and, at the moment, I am also responsible for transferring our organization to our new four-story building. I manage all programming at our sites along with recruiting, training, and cultivating our new generation of leaders. I also supervise eight staff members. I regularly tell new employees that you could have 100 percent of your day planned, but leave open 20 percent for the unexpected. I have days where a young person needs my immediate and full attention. When something comes up, we must make time to address it quickly and professionally.

Q: What misconceptions do people have about your job? What's the reality?

A: Many people believe that dedicating energy to young people is a waste of time—you can't make a difference. The reality is that children need nurturing and proper guidance; their heads and hearts are changing and growing as they figure out what type of person they want to become. Quality programs can positively affect our next generation's development—we can have an impact!

Q: What do you love about your work?

A: I love working with young people. The gratification I receive when I know that I have made a difference in their lives cannot compare to any monetary compensation. I call it a payment for the soul. And I love helping other people find that same satisfaction through their work or volunteer activities.

Q: What advice would you give to someone interested in a career similar to yours?

A: You can only go as far as your education. With solid education, training, and experience you can advance in the nonprofit sector and make a decent living.

Q: What resources might help someone interested in your field and job function?

A: Explore the Partnership for After School Education (www.pasesetter.org) and their publication *After School Matters.* I've also learned from certain experts and their books: Rosalind Wiseman's *Queen Bees & Wannabes: Helping Your Daughter Survive Cliques, Gossip, Boyfriends, and Other Realities of Adolescence;* Larry Brendtro, Martin Brokenleg, and Steve Van Bockern's *Reclaiming Youth at Risk: Our Hope for the Future;* author Erik Erikson's work on identity development in adolescence; Aristotle's *The Doctrine of the Mean;* Plato's *The Allegory of the Cave;* and Jonathan Kozol's *Savage Inequalities: Children in America's Schools.*[35]

Q: What do you look for when hiring a new employee?

A: I look for innovation, an awareness of the significance of young people's needs as they reach adolescence, and a genuine desire to help the community. Also, being bilingual is an asset.

GREAT LEADERSHIP IN THE NONPROFIT SECTOR

Q&A with **Brian Gallagher**

President and CEO • United Way of America • www.unitedway.org

Q: What makes a great leader?
A: In my mind, great leaders are purpose driven, and their sense of purpose extends beyond their individual organization. Great leaders can articulate a vision that is so compelling it motivates people to change. They are able to inspire people to work together toward a goal that they all understand and that they all want to achieve.

Q: Do you have to be a great public speaker to inspire people?
A: Some very quiet people are great leaders. But even if quiet, you still must be a good communicator. It's communication that allows you to motivate people from the inside out; that is, to motivate your own team, and then go on to motivate external audiences.

Q: How else do leaders motivate people?
A: Good leaders focus on outcomes and are willing and able to align their work and their organization's programs toward clear goals and specific results. Good leaders are also team oriented. They believe in building successful teams and know how to get people to participate effectively in them. And, more often than not, good leaders are kind.

Q: Why is kindness so important in leading?
A: You probably can be unkind and succeed for a while, but in the end you're apt to fail. People have choices. Your staff members, your partners in the field, your supporters—everyone has choices. People want to be part of organizations that are successful as well as fundamentally good. A leader who is purpose driven, team oriented, and kind is likely to attract people who share these attributes. This makes for a good leader and a good organization.

Q: Once you've attracted talent, what keeps people committed?
A: People are motivated by being part of something that is bigger than they are. I mentioned that great leaders articulate a shared vision and generate passion around it. But the best leaders are also clear about defining specific roles. Team members understand their roles and how they can contribute. A good leader listens to staff and makes appropriate assignments, and positions people—and the organization—to succeed.

Q: How is leadership different from management?

A: Management is a more definitive discipline. It has proven practices that have been developed and tested over decades; understanding and applying these practices is vital. Leadership, however, is more elusive. It comes from inside a person, not a book. To develop your leadership potential, you must be self-aware and build on who you are. Tap your strengths and manage your weaknesses so that the leadership approach you develop feels natural.

Q: How is leadership different in the nonprofit sector versus in business?

A: I don't see a great difference. The more critical distinction is how centralized or decentralized your organization is. A leader running a highly decentralized nonprofit shares more with a business leader managing a decentralized firm than she does with a leader of a highly centralized nonprofit.

Q: What academic training do you have, and how did it prepare you for your work?

A: I have an undergraduate degree in social work and a graduate degree in business. I believe this type of background—one that joins expertise in a chosen field and concrete skills in how to manage a business—is increasingly vital for careers in the nonprofit sector. Absolutely, you must have knowledge and passion for your organization's mission. But you also need to know about operations, finance, governance, creating strategic plans, and even brand development.

Q: What experiences shaped you as a leader?

A: Almost everyone in life is faced with challenges growing up, but most people have a choice in how they respond to them. Can you learn from adversity, and even failure? Can you develop competencies that allow you to excel in the face of challenges? Are you self-confident enough to ask for help? Have your experiences helped you develop deeper empathy for others? People who

(continued on page 118)

(continued from page 117)

are empathetic—a characteristic that I believe is developed very early in life—are more likely to take on leadership positions because they can put themselves in other people's shoes.

Q: How do you make tough decisions?
A: My belief is that you make the best decisions when you put the community (the "greater good") first, your institution second, and your individual interests third. If you put self-interest first, you will fail pretty quickly. If you put your institutional interests first, you might succeed for a while, but over the long haul your organization will not thrive. If you put the community or the sector first, you not only will serve your interests but your decisions will be sustainable.

Q: Do you have a mentor who has helped your career?
A: I have a community of mentors who are important to me. These people include both professional contacts as well as personal friends. The common thread is that they are wise and thoughtful, I trust them, and they are willing to sometimes offer tough advice. I think the best mentors come naturally and the relationships develop organically. I didn't seek out these advisors. Potential mentors are all around you. You can cultivate them and guide them so that they help

you professionally and personally, but you can't force their creation.

Q: What opportunities can a young professional pursue to build leadership skills?
A: You need to take risks. That might mean taking the job that no one else will take if it offers learning potential. It might mean moving to a new community or giving up a pay raise one year to take advantage of an interesting challenge. Mostly, it means saying "Yes!" when asked to step outside your comfort zone, try something new, make a sacrifice, and take a risk.

Q: How important is it for leaders to hire and cultivate great talent?
A: It's everything. Great leaders are confident and not afraid to surround themselves with strength. They recognize that it is people who develop strategy, create vision, and do the work to fulfill missions. If your leadership team has mediocre talent, then you will develop mediocre strategies and deliver mediocre programs. This is true for the sector as a whole too. Here at United Way of America we spend an extraordinary amount of time thinking about how to fill our pipeline of talent, how to make sure that talent reflects the faces of the people we serve, and how to retain our staff members.

Q: Why is a representative workforce so important?

A: Diversity is critical both for my organization and the nonprofit sector overall. It's vital, in part, simply because it is morally right. Diversity and inclusion also are important for business reasons—we need the best talent, and this means looking for it in all people. Finally, a diverse staff allows you to innovate. Multiple perspectives and experiences enable us to develop new strategies and programs that will reach new audiences. And it's worth noting that diversity isn't just about race and ethnicity. We need to include the next generation of talent in order to innovate as well. ∎

Brian Gallagher began his career as a management trainee with a United Way affiliate in 1981 and has served the organization since then. He served at several regional United Ways (including Winston-Salem, NC; Reading, PA; Providence, RI; Atlanta, GA; and Columbus, OH) before assuming the leadership of United Way of America in 2002.

Programs and Service Delivery

"Programs" refers to the actual work an organization does to meet its mission—the programs it runs, the services it delivers, the products it distributes. The wide variety of work nonprofit organizations perform means that there's an almost limitless range of types of jobs within this broad category of work. A program director might be responsible for a national women's rights campaign at one organization, or an after-school pottery class at another. A program director might need a law degree at one organization and research experience at another.

Because program work is often the "meat" of an organization, program staff—especially program directors—are usually expected to collaborate with other departments. For example, they might work with administration and finance on staff recruitment and program budgets, with communications staff on media campaigns, with development staff on developing grant proposals, and with their executive director on designing the overall strategy of the organization.

Some of the more common program-related job functions involve

- advocacy
- counseling and direct social services
- education and training
- research and policy

Positions exist at many levels for all nonprofit sector areas of work. For example, there are advocacy directors, advocacy associates, and advocacy assistants. We describe the general categories here, without trying to make distinctions among different levels of positions.

Advocacy

Advocacy work in the nonprofit sector typically refers to an organization's activism around a specific issue. It is often framed as campaign work (similar to lobbying) and involves developing and implementing the external strategies an organization employs to advance its mission, engage target audiences, educate, and enact change. Advocacy staff reach out to governments, organizations, private companies, policymakers, the media, and private citizens. Advocacy sometimes falls under an organization's communications department because it is so connected to motivating people and influencing decision makers.

Advocacy jobs attract strong leaders, organizers, coalition builders, networkers, educators, public speakers, and writers who know their issues inside and out.

For More Insight on Advocacy Jobs . . .

See Marcia Avner's sidebar (pages 16–17), the sample advocacy associate job description (page 150), and the profiles of Lisa Dardy McGee (pages 72–73) and Cathleen I. Price (pages 98–99). Refer also to the Public or Societal Benefit subsector discussion (page 90).

Counseling and direct social services

Counseling and direct social services jobs cover a wide range of work for a tremendous diversity of organizations and the even greater diversity of people those organizations serve. Most generally, this is frontline work involving direct interaction with children, adults, or families to make their lives better and their communities stronger. It includes social services jobs from social work, case management, and substance abuse treatment to domestic violence counseling and mentoring. It covers jobs at schools, in health care facilities, and at nonprofit organizations that run camps, after-school programs, or programs for senior citizens, for example.

Frontline workers who provide direct services to clients often have administrative responsibilities as well. Their work may include training staff and volunteers, keeping records and managing files, verifying information and responding to inquiries, or fundraising to support programs.

Counseling and direct social services jobs attract individuals with great "people skills," who enjoy hands-on work and are patient, attentive, and giving. They often have a lot of energy and know how to take care of themselves in their personal lives so that they don't burn out. The educational requirements vary greatly; some positions will require an MSW (master's of social work), others only a high school diploma. The skills required

so you want to be a youth worker?

Youth work is one large category of counseling and direct social services jobs. Youth workers support the personal, educational, and social development of young people. They might run a recreational program, community or environmental project, or an arts class; or provide mentoring or counseling services. A youth worker's role can vary greatly, but often the programs are aimed at disadvantaged youth to redress inequalities they face and empower them to lead healthy, happy, functional lives. Youth workers are expected to assess the needs of their young clients, provide support, and often connect them to other services that might benefit them. Sometimes youth workers connect with their clients' family members as well. Youth workers work in a range of settings, including youth centers, clubs, schools, and places of worship.

Some of the largest organizations providing youth programs in the United States include

- Boys & Girls Clubs of America (www.bgca.org)
- Boy Scouts of America (www.scouting.org)
- Camp Fire USA (www.campfire.org)
- Girls Incorporated (www.girlsinc.org)
- Girl Scouts of the USA (www.girlscouts.org)
- National 4-H Council (www.fourhcouncil.edu)
- YMCA of the USA (www.ymca.net)
- YWCA (www.ywca.org)

Most of the national organizations have local chapters, and hire frontline youth workers through those branches (whereas the national offices seek administrative professionals). In addition, thousands of community-based youth services organizations are spread across the country.

The National Collaboration for Youth (NCY) is a coalition of fifty nonprofit organizations that focus on youth development (they are all members of the broader National Human Services Assembly). Collectively, these organizations serve more than 40 million young people, employ more than 100,000 paid staff, and depend on more than 6 million volunteers. They are present in virtually every community in the United States.

For more information on the field of youth development, visit NCY's main website (www.collab4youth.org), as well as its dedicated site for youth workers, the National Youth Development Information Center (www.nydic.org). Two other good resources are the Medical Foundation's Youth Work Central (www.youthworkcentral.org) and the Alliance for Children and Families (www.alliance1.org).

will also depend on the specific position and types of clients served. Knowledge of a second language is often required.

For More Insight on Counseling and Direct Social Services Jobs . . .

See the sample after-school counselor job description (page 151), and the profiles of Wendy Terra (pages 186–187) and Christopher Murray (pages 234–235).

Education and training

Education and training jobs may be similar to counseling and direct social services positions. Educators and trainers develop and implement curricula, design assessment tools to evaluate the success of the educational programs, and manage support staff (including other educators). They may create training manuals, multimedia visual aids, and other collateral materials to support the programs. If electronic learning activities are involved, the work will require familiarity with computers and the Internet. For some organizations, these positions involve fieldwork and traveling to other communities and countries; for other groups, a training position exclusively involves internal programs designed for the staff of that organization.

Education and training jobs attract individuals who have a particular commitment to a target population, and usually some experience (even if just volunteer) working with that population.

The work relies on strong communication and organization skills, sensitivity to cultural diversity, enthusiasm, and motivation. These jobs may require advanced degrees in education or related fields and a willingness to work irregular hours, when the trainings take place.

For More Insight on Education and Training Jobs . . .

See the profiles of Brigette Rouson (pages 174–175), Sharon Williams (pages 208–209), and Shash Yázhí (pages 224–225).

Research and policy

Research and policy staff direct projects, evaluate programs, design surveys and other data-collection instruments, and serve as spokespeople to the media and other target audiences on their areas of expertise. They may manage and maintain data files and track new research developments and media coverage of key issues. They often prepare reports, fact sheets, policy briefs, charts, and other educational materials for web and print distribution. They may make public presentations on the organization's research and policy work. They are as likely to spend all of their time in the field as they are sitting behind a computer writing a report. Research and policy positions sometimes fall within a communications department.

Research and policy staff often work closely with other staff members of their organization to provide data and information and evaluate legislation or policies. They contribute to an organization's policy agenda and general strategic plan. They also collaborate with other organizations and may be the individuals assigned to participate in coalitions of organizations working collaboratively toward a specific advocacy or policy goal.

Research and policy jobs attract individuals with a scholarly background and experience with quantitative work. They often require familiarity with statistical software, excellent project management and writing skills, and possibly an advanced degree.

For More Insight on Research and Policy Jobs . . .

See the sample job descriptions for research associate (page 160) and youth services program director (page 164), as well as the profiles of Andrea Browne-Phillips (pages 42–43) and Lisa Dardy McGee (pages 72–73).

Administration, Human Resources, and Finance

Administrative and finance jobs handle the operational systems and practices of a nonprofit organization. If an organization is large enough to have a director of administration and finance, the position will report to the chief executive officer and be responsible for the financial management, operations, and human resources of the agency.

Specific areas of work within administration and finance include

- accounting and finance
- operations
- clerical and data entry
- human resources, including volunteer coordinators
- information technology
- sales, telemarketing, customer service

If an organization is large enough to have separate departments for these functions, they are likely to work closely with one another. Otherwise, many of the functions may be collapsed within a single position, such as director of operations. Work in this field often involves very specific responsibilities that require very measurable experience. Read job descriptions carefully to make sure you are qualified for the posting.

Administration and finance positions often require specific skill sets and certain educational credentials, as well as experience in nonprofit sector financial procedures. For finance positions, organizations may look for a degree in accounting or require applicants to be Certified Public Accountants. They may seek candidates with extensive experience with bookkeeping and certain software applications their organizations use. In general, administrative and finance positions attract people who love systems and have strong, advanced administrative skills.

NONPROFIT ACCOUNTING 101

by **Jeanne Bell** and **Elizabeth Schaffer**

Coauthors, *Financial Leadership for Nonprofit Executives* [36]

In our book *Financial Leadership for Nonprofit Executives,* we explain that effective nonprofit businesses—those that strike the balance between mission and money—are the result of financial leadership. In today's climate of increased scrutiny of the nonprofit sector, every nonprofit organization needs skilled leaders to manage its financial systems and processes.

In small and midsized organizations, the accounting function may be shared by a consulting bookkeeper, administrative staff, and the executive director. Larger organizations are likely to have dedicated staff members responsible for financial systems and oversight. If you're an accountant with an interest in public service, there's a job for you in the nonprofit sector. If you hope to run programs or events, a basic knowledge of accounting practices will help you develop sound plans. And if you have aspirations to be a senior manager or executive director of a nonprofit organization, understanding nonprofit financial practices is a must.

Core accounting principles and practices apply equally to nonprofit organizations and for-profit enterprises. As such, any basic accounting and financial management training will serve you well in the nonprofit sector. However, there are some key areas where nonprofit sector finances differ with those in the for-profit sector.

- Nonprofit organizations classified as 501(c)(3) with the IRS are tax exempt and allowed to receive contributions that are tax deductible to the donor. (See "What Is a Nonprofit Organization?" pages 10-12, for more information on this classification.) Nonprofit accountants need to know how to track and report these contributions, and many contributions require special handling.

- In addition, the accounting profession has established guidelines for responsibly tracking monies that the donor restricted for a specific use (e.g., buying a new building, starting a new program, or adding to the endowment). How these monies are tracked and reported depends on such issues as the nature of the donor's restriction; what conditions, if any, the donor has imposed on the organization before it can actually receive or use the money; and when any restrictions are met.

- In the area of capitalizing and depreciating assets—which occurs with nonprofit and for-profit enterprises alike—nonprofit organizations can give special treatment to some assets, for example, museum collections.

- Nonprofit organizations must report expenses by their "functional expenses classifications," basically either program services or supporting activities such as management, fundraising, and membership development. Specific knowledge is required to report expenses appropriately in the nonprofit sector.

Accountants interested in working at a nonprofit organization can gain the sector-specific training they need through internships or on-the-job training, so long as they come with solid financial management training. In addition, some colleges and nonprofit resource centers offer courses in accounting, budgeting, and financial reporting for nonprofit organizations. ∎

Jeanne Bell is the executive director of CompassPoint Nonprofit Services (www. compasspoint.org), a consulting, research, and training organization. She has served as the organization's associate director since 2000. Elizabeth (Liz) Schaffer is chief financial officer for the Women's Funding Network (www.wfnet.org), an international organization of 125 member funds that make grants to improve the status of women and girls. Liz also works as a consultant to nonprofits, specializing in financial management.

Accounting and finance

Accounting and finance staff handle the daily management of financial systems and procedures, including annual organization budgets, department budgets, monthly financial statements, accounts receivable and payable, payroll, audits, and tax filings. They prepare financial management policies, procedures, and controls, often working very closely with the executive director and instructing staff on these policies. Accounting and finance staff may be responsible for the financial aspects of fundraising events, and they will work with department staff to prepare financial reports as requested by foundations, government, and other funding sources. They often negotiate and manage contracts with outside vendors and consultants.

For More Insight on
Accounting and Finance Jobs . . .

See Jeanne Bell and Elizabeth Schaffer's sidebar ("Nonprofit Accounting 101" at left) and the sample bookkeeper job description (page 152).

Operations

Operations staff oversee the administrative work of an organization. They handle purchasing, contracting, and maintenance of office equipment, including computers and supplies. They are responsible for ensuring smooth daily operations of the organization's facility and will handle relationships with service vendors. As an organization grows or becomes more sophisticated, operations staff will be responsible for any necessary move to expanded space and implementing new information technology systems. They may supervise administrative and accounting staff, oversee staff meetings and retreats, handle the logistics of other special events, and manage issues surrounding the legal compliance of an organization. Operations staff may be responsible for insurance for the organization and board members, training and other issues surrounding transportation for groups that transport clients, or real estate (in cases where an organization manages multiple sites). A senior director of operations may be responsible for managing other administrative and finance job functions, such as accounting, human resources, and information technology.

Clerical and data entry

Clerical staff provide administrative support and are needed in all departments of an organization, not just the administration and finance division. The work can cover a range of responsibilities from filing to sophisticated systems development work. Clerical staff answer phones, maintain files and calendars, arrange meetings, make travel arrangements, and prepare correspondence and other communications. They may be expected to offer copyediting assistance, as well as perform more advanced editing and writing. They often must be adept at a range of software applications, including word processing, spreadsheets, and slide show presentations.

Data entry staff also perform administrative functions but are apt to be assigned specifically to database management work. They are often responsible for inputting, updating, and maintaining files for current and prospective donors; generating mailing lists; performing mail merges and assisting with print and electronic mailings; tracking direct mail and other solicitation responses; and producing reports. Depending on an organization's mission and the data it tracks, data entry staff may contribute to work that covers much more than development, fundraising, and donor or member management.

For More Insight on
Clerical and Data Entry Jobs . . .

See the sample job descriptions for administrative assistant (page 149) and database manager (page 155).

Human resources

Human resources (HR) staff handle all personnel-related responsibilities. They develop job descriptions and post openings, recruit applicants, review applications, check references, make recommendations on candidates, and oversee the interviewing and hiring processes, often in collaboration with program and executive staff. They are expected to develop creative strategies for finding diverse applicants with the skills, experiences, and commitment to mission that their organization needs. HR professionals design and manage training and new employee orientation programs. They help identify professional development opportunities for staff members and coordinate participation in them. They ensure an organization's compliance with federal, state, and local laws and mandates in areas of employment, benefits, compensation, harassment, nondiscrimination practices, and affirmative action. They develop personnel policies, establish salary structures, manage benefits programs (and make sure that participants understand them), and oversee performance evaluations. HR staff make recommendations to senior staff on compensation packages that will enable the organization to compete for exceptional staff. They serve as the primary liaison between employees and insurance carriers. HR staff are expected to understand employment law and regulations and stay apprised of changes in policies.

For More Insight on Human Resources Work . . .

See David Eisner's sidebar ("The Volunteering Imperative," pages 24–25), the sample job descriptions for human resources assistant (page 159) and volunteer coordinator (page 162), and the profiles of Melissa Schulz (pages 196–197) and Michael Watson (pages 128–129).

volunteer coordinator

Organizations are becoming much more professional in managing volunteers. For groups that rely extensively on volunteers to perform the day-to-day work of their organization, volunteer coordinator is a critical human resources specialization. Volunteer coordinators recruit, screen, train, schedule, monitor, evaluate, and support volunteers. Depending on the mission of the organization and the work it performs, a volunteer coordinator might work with specific populations of volunteers, such as business and corporate professionals, students, young people, elderly people, or people with disabilities.

Volunteer coordinators are often the first point of contact for individuals wishing to contribute to an organization. They identify and hold networking opportunities in the community to promote the work of their organization and educate new audiences about the organization's volunteer needs. Volunteer coordinators develop special events and other programs to recognize volunteers.

Volunteer coordinators often have similar qualifications as educators and trainers, since they, too, must develop training programs and the support materials to accompany them. Volunteer coordinator positions attract team players with strong organizational and communication skills. They need to be good at managing people and often come to the job with prior experience in coordinating special events.

MICHAEL WATSON
Senior Vice President, Human Resources

Age: 48

Education: BA, economics; MS, organizational management and human resource development

Years at current organization: 8

Years in current position: 8

First job out of college: IBM marketing representative

First job in nonprofit sector: Current position

Girl Scouts of the USA

www.girlscouts.org

Mission: Girl Scouting builds girls of courage, confidence, and character, who make the world a better place.

Operating budget: Approximately $60 million

Number of employees: 435 employees at headquarters and more than 9,500 employees in affiliate organizations across the country

Number of employees who report to you: 5, vice president, human resources; director, compensation, benefits and human resources information system (HRIS); chief learning officer; human resources project manager; and administrative assistant

Q&A

Q: Informally, describe your career track.
A: I began my career as a marketing representative for IBM and later joined GE's Human Resource Management Program. After several years of human resources positions of increased responsibility at GE Capital and Time Warner, I returned to IBM, where one phone call from an executive search firm changed my life. I became the quintessential "sector switcher" when I joined Girls Scouts of the USA, and launched a new chapter where I can apply the skills and experiences I developed in the for-profit sector to a nonprofit organization.

Q: What do you know now that you wish you had known when you were first job hunting?

A: Start early. The job hunting process begins freshman year in college. The classes, subject major, volunteer activities, and summer internships that you choose all play a role in your ability to find the job you want.

Q: Describe a representative work day.

A: I lead a team that provides all aspects of human resources—hiring, benefits, compensation, employee development, and retention. Our department works with management to hire and retain high-caliber employees and create a work environment where employees can best contribute to the organization's mission. Each day is different, but a representative day could include working with teams on projects, attending budget meetings, interviewing candidates, answering questions for new employees, or working with members of the human resources team to create a new program that will help develop or retain employees.

Q: What misconceptions do people have about your job? What's the reality?

A: One misconception is that nonprofit sector human resources work is easier than work in corporations. The importance of attracting, retaining, and developing the best talent to accomplish the organization's work is the same in both sectors.

Q: What do you love about your work?

A: I like our mission and where we are going as an organization. I have a great deal of respect for our CEO, and am excited about the opportunity to make a difference in the lives of girls across the country.

Q: What advice would you give to someone interested in a career similar to yours?

A: Research potential employers and talk with as many people as you can at those organizations, in your field, and in similar job functions. Network in a professional and systematic manner. Select an organization that is a good fit—whose mission you believe in and that needs and appreciates the experience and skills you offer. If you choose well, you will have a meaningful and exciting career.

Q: What resources might help someone interested in your field and job function?

A: Our website is a good source of information on our mission (www.girlscouts.org). For people interested in human resources, I recommend several books: Ed Michaels, Helen Handfield-Jones, and Beth Axelrod's *The War for Talent;* Michael Watkins's *The First 90 Days: Critical Success Strategies for New Leaders at All Levels;* and Jim Collins' *Good to Great: Why Some Companies Make the Leap—and Others Don't.*[37] The Society for Human Resources Management (www.shrm.org) is the largest professional association for human resources professionals and has student chapters.

Q: What do you look for when hiring a new employee?

A: I look for individuals who have a passion for the work we do and who are smart, talented, and possess superior communication and interpersonal skills.

Information technology

Information technology (IT) staff manage an organization's information and telecommunications systems, applications, and services. They are responsible for e-mail, phone, voice mail, and desktop computer support for an organization's staff, and provide training on both hardware and software. IT professionals often are responsible for website development and maintenance and collaborate with an organization's communications and development staff to use the Internet to advance the organization's mission. IT staff develop strategic plans for information technology systems, and implement and evaluate those plans.

For More Insight on IT Work . . .

See the sample web designer job description (page 163).

Sales, telemarketing, and customer service

Nonprofit sector sales, telemarketing, and customer service jobs might fall under a development department (covered later), as they are often connected to fundraising, membership services, or donor support.

Sales jobs are found in nonprofit organizations that have earned income programs. These organizations sell goods or services either because the goods themselves are part of the mission or to generate income to advance their mission. For example, a nonprofit theater sells tickets as part of its mission of providing performances in a

---

membership services

As a career category, membership services is an excellent example of the wide range of departments a given position can be housed in. An organization might place a membership services professional in marketing or communications, in development (also called fundraising), or in database management and customer service. For insight on one membership services career path, see Byron Hatch's profile (pages 254–255).

---

community, whereas Girl Scouts sell cookies to fund their programs serving young girls.

Sales staff develop and implement business plans and direct marketing and promotional efforts. They may be expected to use a range of media in their work, including postcards, posters, press kits, e-mail, the web, radio, television, and direct mail. They often are responsible for identifying and reaching out to prospective customers, and may be involved with customer service. Some development positions, such as those involving membership solicitation, are billed as sales jobs, since these staff are "selling" the organization as they try to recruit new members.

Telemarketers are more junior-level sales positions. The majority of their work is conducted via the telephone, calling existing and potential donors and members to solicit support.

Large social services organizations that deliver goods or services to an extensive client base often have a customer (or client) service function. This work involves answering communications from clients, tracking and resolving complaints, and providing recommendations on how the organization can administer the highest quality services.

Development and Fundraising

Development covers the work that an organization performs to cultivate donors and volunteers and secure funds. Development staff conduct prospect research; write grants; manage direct mail, online, telephone, and major gift solicitations; and plan special events. The best development professionals think long term and perform work that is deliberate and involves relationship building. They identify individuals, foundations, and corporations with shared passion and values, and deeply engage them in advancing the mission of an organization. Supporters are cultivated over time, and become emotionally (and eventually financially) invested in the work of the organization.

In the healthiest nonprofit organizations, the development function intersects with all other departments. Development staff are apt to work particularly closely with the executive director (who often spends a significant portion of time on fundraising), senior program staff, and the communications department. Depending on the size, structure, and funding sources of an

organization, a development director or associate may be responsible for an annual fund, major gifts, endowment and capital campaigns, and foundation and corporate partnerships. In the largest organizations, these areas of responsibilities will have dedicated staff, with titles that match (e.g., major gifts officer).

Five of the most common specializations within a development department are

- annual fund
- grant writing and administration
- major gifts
- planned giving
- special events

While not all organizations have an endowment or annual fund, the development staff at even very small organizations are apt to write and administer grants and assist with some form of special events.

Annual fund

Annual fund professionals cultivate donors who make yearly gifts to an organization, often to cover core operating support. These gifts are usually unrestricted—that is, not earmarked for specific programs—and frequently considered the bread and butter of support for a nonprofit organization. Unlike major gifts, organizations can realistically hope that donations to an annual fund will be renewed every year (although they might represent larger gifts that are pledged over time). An annual fund director may recruit and train volunteers who make phone solicitations, plan and implement direct mail solicitations, and, at a university, develop reunion and leadership gifts, for example.

Grant writing and administration

Grant writers and administrators manage and execute activities connected to raising funds through government, foundation, and major donor grants. They conduct research on prospective foundations and understand application guidelines, build relationships with foundation staff, and prepare letters of inquiry to request the invitation to submit a full proposal. Grant writers and administrators arrange meetings for their organization's senior staff member with foundation program officers and other key personnel.

Grant writers work closely with their own program staff to understand funding priorities and educate their colleagues about funding opportunities, and then to develop specific ideas for grant proposals. They write proposals and compile all required collateral materials for submission, including budgets, timelines, staff biographies, IRS documentation, and relevant research documents. Grant writers and administrators prepare interim and final reports to funders, update and maintain donor databases, create grant calendars identifying deadlines for interim and final reports, and handle other related communications and administrative tasks.

Organizations receiving support from government agencies often seek grant writers and administrators with specific experience navigating the more complicated application and reporting procedures required for federal funds.

Major gifts

Major gift officers cultivate and secure "once-in-a-lifetime" gifts from major donors. These donors are frequently individuals who have had a long relationship with the organization and who are motivated to make a sizeable gift—either restricted or not—to it. And they may expect some sort of recognition. Staff members in this department manage prospect research, build long-term relationships with donors (and understand their philanthropic goals), solicit gifts, and identify and coordinate appropriate recognition (e.g., naming opportunities). Major gift officers spend a great deal of time out of the office, at events, and holding one-on-one meetings to cultivate their prospects.

Planned giving

Major nonprofit organizations such as educational institutions and hospitals often have planned giving staff who manage charitable gifts of estate assets. Some departments are so large that planned giving officers are responsible for a specific geographic region of prospects. Planned gifts may be deferred gifts that are arranged by an individual and fulfilled upon his or her death. Planned giving professionals are knowledgeable in the legal aspects of estate planning and the many different

WHO WANTS TO FUNDRAISE? I DO!
OR WHY THE DEVELOPMENT DIRECTOR HAS THE BEST SEAT IN THE HOUSE

by **Richard Potter**

Vice President of Development and Communications • American Humanics • www.humanics.org

Fundraising can get a bad rap in the nonprofit sector. Fundraisers are sometimes referred to as "professional beggars" seen shaking a tin cup and pleading for money. They must constantly manage the stress of making "the ask"—and endure regular rejections.

Development is hard work and dealing with rejection is part of the job. But development work can be tremendously engaging, and really does offer one of the best seats in the house. In 2008, *U.S. News & World Report* rated fundraising as one of the Top 31 Best Careers—not just nonprofit sector careers, but the top 31 best careers *overall*.[38]

The development professional works closely with many of the top thinkers and program implementers in an organization. A development professional must know the issues inside and out, so part of the job description includes staying apprised of developments in the field. You get paid to read, attend conferences, and learn. Development involves both concentrated periods of working independently while writing a grant proposal, as well as the opportunity to make site visits, network, and meet with leading philanthropists in your field.

In addition, experienced fundraising and development professionals are a hot commodity in the nonprofit sector and often command some of the highest salaries in an organization. A strong development function is vital to an organization's success and this career path is one of the most viable in the nonprofit sector. If you do your job well and demonstrate quantifiable accomplishments, serving as a development director offers tremendous job security. Even in an era of downsizing, an organization would be hard-pressed to let go of a competent development professional. ∎

Richard Potter has served as American Humanics vice president for development and communications since 1996. Previously, he served six years as development director at the University of Dubuque (Iowa) and four years as a project administrator in telecommunications. He holds an MBA and a BBA in marketing.

planned giving vehicles available. They frequently work with a potential donor's lawyers and other estate planners. In smaller organizations, planned giving officers may also be responsible for major gifts and other fundraising programs.

Special events

Special events staff design and manage programs raising awareness about an organization and its issues, cultivate volunteers, and generate funds. Special events include walks, runs, and other programs where participants solicit sponsorship; awards ceremonies and benefit concerts; annual luncheons or dinners; and rallies and demonstrations to name just a few. Often, these events take place outside of business hours, so special events planners should be prepared to work unconventional hours.

Special events work involves strategizing with an organization's other staff members to set a calendar of events for the year, and establish revenue and marketing goals for them. For each program, a special events professional will form an event committee, solicit sponsors, recruit participants and volunteers, manage a budget, and be responsible for all logistics. The work often involves overseeing designers and other consultants to create invitations, posters, programs, and related materials, and collaborating with the organization's communications department to market the event. (If the organization does not have a communications staff, development staff would be responsible for all marketing as well.)

Development jobs attract professionals with excellent people skills and real business acumen. They know how to interact in the corporate, government, and philanthropic worlds. They have passion for an organization's mission and the ability to communicate that passion to engage diverse audiences. Development professionals must juggle many different relationships and tasks concurrently, be highly organized, excel at creating systems, embrace deadlines, and work well under pressure. The best development directors are superb and creative writers and communicators. They can distill complicated issues down to compelling calls to action that appeal to lay audiences.

Because this area of nonprofit sector work is specific to the sector, leaders often look to hire development professionals with concrete and directly transferable experience. Employers are likely to ask for samples of a candidate's work on a grant proposal, letter of inquiry, or special events program, as well as proof of the results you have secured.

For More Insight on
Development and Fundraising Work . . .

See the sidebars by Richard Potter ("Who Wants to Fundraise?" page 133) and Stacy Palmer ("The Development Field," pages 135–137), the sample job descriptions for grants manager (page 158) and special events coordinator (page 161), and the profiles of Carolyn Pizzuto (pages 78–79) and Jamie Roach (pages 26–27).

The Development Field

Q&A with **Stacy Palmer**

Editor • *The Chronicle of Philanthropy* • www.philanthropy.com

Q: What kind of degree does a fundraiser need?

A: Fundraisers come from a variety of academic backgrounds, but a growing number seek accreditation by the organization Certified Fund Raising Executive International (http://cfre.org). CFRE offers continuing education programs to master fundraising skills.

Planned giving—helping people prepare bequests, charitable trusts, or other deals—attracts people with law degrees or advanced financial training. This has been a growth area in fundraising because of the expected intergenerational transfer of wealth where trillions of dollars are likely to flow to nonprofit organizations over the next few decades. And some nonprofit groups recruit people with marketing, banking, and sales experience in the hope those skills can be transferred into a fundraising position.

While fundraising has become far more professional in the past decade, many fundraisers get their earliest experience working as volunteers for causes they care about, or as undergraduates helping their colleges or universities seek money from alumni. Experience, whether paid or volunteer, helps develop critical skills and demonstrates to potential employers that you understand development.

Q: Are fundraisers who start out working for one type of organization—say environmental or educational—permanently locked into that field?

A: Many fundraisers are so dedicated to a particular mission that they never want to change fields. But others find that a number of causes inspire their passion and that working for different types of organizations allows them to learn about new issues and apply their skills in different ways. Still, some recruiters are wary of fundraisers who want to switch causes—as are some donors—so it's best to commit to one or two areas, rather than switching from cause to cause to cause.

Q: What is the average tenure in the job?

A: Fundraisers are in such high demand that they are offered many opportunities for advancement. As a result, the average fundraiser keeps a job for two years and then moves into a new role, often at a larger, wealthier, or more prestigious institution.

(continued on page 136)

(continued from page 135)

Q: What are the prospects for advancement within development?

A: Fundraisers often stay in positions where their main responsibility is obtaining money and other resources for a nonprofit group. But because fundraising is such an important skill for nonprofit chief executives, some fundraisers have advanced into top leadership positions. As baby boomers start to retire, and as nonprofit organizations continue to be created, demand will become even more intense for leaders who understand how to raise money and work closely with wealthy donors, government officials, and others involved in the development process.

Many fundraisers with experience working for individual institutions also go on to jobs where they serve as consultants to organizations needing assistance. Those jobs often give fundraisers more flexibility and higher pay than they might otherwise receive.

Q: Does fundraising involve much travel?

A: Yes, often. Raising money from wealthy people requires in-person meetings to get them excited about giving. And a capital campaign may involve soliciting donors who are outside the community where the nonprofit organization is based.

College fundraisers often travel to events at alumni clubs, including travel overseas. Many charities send fundraisers to areas where large numbers of wealthy, retired people live part of the year—for example, a hospital in the Northeast might raise money at galas in Florida or send its top doctors there for an educational session with potential donors.

Q: Does everyone in the development office go out and meet donors? Are there other opportunities?

A: Fundraising offices work to identify potential donors, and many hire people who specialize in such prospect research. Bigger fundraising offices often have specialists who maintain electronic databases and track information so that earmarked money is directed appropriately. In addition, some fundraising offices hire their own personnel specialists because recruiting top-notch fundraisers is so challenging.

Q: Do fundraisers ever get to move into jobs where they give away money?

A: Yes, though there are far fewer jobs in grant making than in the grant-seeking field. Still, some fundraisers make the transition—especially those who work closely with wealthy families who create family foundations and need an expert to help them figure how to give money away.

Q: What are some of the newer specializations in the development field?

A: A growing amount of money is raised online, and charities increasingly need to communicate with donors via the Internet. Charities seek people skilled in cultivating online communities and using video, audio, text messaging, and other tools that are popular with donors, especially younger donors. ■

Stacy Palmer is editor of *The Chronicle of Philanthropy*. Published bi-weekly, it is a leading news source for charity leaders, fundraisers, grantmakers, and other people involved in the philanthropic enterprise. *The Chronicle* features an extensive listing of development job postings. (A subscription includes access to the paper's website and news updates by e-mail.)

Communications

Communications covers the work involved in communicating with an organization's various audiences, through all mediums. Most broadly, the work involves coordinating and implementing a comprehensive communications program that supports the organization's mission. Staff create and disseminate materials and messages to influence and engage members, donors, volunteers, policymakers, and other decision makers in the field, and the media.

Nonprofit sector leaders look for staff members who have strong communication skills, no matter what their position. This is because virtually every job is better performed if the person who fills it is a skilled writer and speaker. Communications professionals will work with other staff on communications strategies, and work particularly closely with the development department. (Frequently, a small or midsized organization employs a single director of communications and development.) However, a communications director has final responsibility for the efforts, and ensures that outreach is done strategically.

Typical specializations within a larger communications department include

- editing, writing, and publications
- graphic design
- marketing and advertising
- media relations (or public relations)
- web development and design

Editing, writing, and publications

Nonprofit editing and writing jobs—sometimes billed as publications positions—involve developing plans for, researching, and writing newsletters, annual and other reports, speeches, opinion pieces, web content, and other print and electronic materials that are the vehicles for an organization's messages. Editors, writers, and publications directors will copyedit content prepared by program and other staff, and they may be responsible for assisting with the preparation of foundation grant proposals and presentations. They will oversee the production of materials, working with graphic designers, printers, and mail houses. They will manage schedules and set deadlines for the dissemination of materials.

Depending on the nature of the nonprofit organization's work, a publications professional may be responsible for more elaborate materials, such as the production of a program book for a symphony, a monograph for a research institute, or a complete book to accompany an exhibition for a museum. Oversight of these materials may involve assigning content to outside authors, researchers, and board members and other supporters with issue-specific expertise. These staff may also be responsible for directing sales efforts to secure advertisements to include in the material.

Graphic design

Only the largest nonprofit organizations—and only those with significant publications and Internet programs—will have graphic designers on staff. (More often, an organization will contract with a graphic design consultant or firm to handle this work.) Graphic designers design and provide art direction and production management for print and electronic communications materials. They will design anything from the organization's logo, business cards, invitations, and programs to its website. Graphic design staff may manage freelance photographers and illustrators and be responsible for the use of the organization's logo by outside parties.

Marketing and advertising

Marketing and advertising staff work to brand an organization to build its reputation, raise awareness of its issues, and cultivate support by using various free and purchased media. They work closely with development and other communications professionals on staff to create marketing strategies and implement media or advertising campaigns, and they may work with corporate partners on cause-related marketing initiatives. They may create messages; design direct mail campaigns; create marketing materials such as logos, brochures, newsletters, stickers, and posters; and develop advertisements or public service announcements for print, radio, television, and the Internet.

For large organizations with affiliate offices nationwide or worldwide, marketing staff work to ensure that use of the agency's brand style is maintained and standardized. They will design and oversee the production of merchandise to support special events and thank donors, including tote bags, mugs, or T-shirts. They understand their organization's target markets and develop opportunities for reaching them to cultivate support. Advertising and marketing staff create budgets and set schedules for campaigns.

Media relations (or public relations)

Media relations staff develop and implement communications strategies using radio, television, newspapers, magazines, and the Internet to advance the organization's mission. They cultivate relationships with journalists who may cover issues relevant to the organization, and they work to develop and place news and feature stories in targeted media outlets. Media relations staff are responsible for writing press releases and press advisories, opinion pieces, letters to the editor, and materials necessary for a press kit (such as "pitch" letters suggesting news coverage, staff biographies, timelines, background papers and other fact sheets, and past news coverage). They will build and maintain target media lists, track news coverage of the organization and its issues, and maintain files of press clippings.

Media relations professionals—especially associates or more junior-level staff—may spend a significant portion of their time on the telephone calling journalists with a potential news story. They call to pitch the release of a report, a major policy development, or an upcoming special event or demonstration, and, if they generate interest, they work with the reporter to develop the story. They provide background information, present their organization's experts as key spokespeople on the issue, and arrange interviews. For major news events, they may organize formal press conferences. For other press worthy events, media relations staff register and manage press who attend.

Media relations professionals at most organizations tend to spend significantly more time reaching out to the press than responding to inquiries. However, most communications departments field at least some calls from journalists, and some—especially those with high-profile spokespeople or working on particularly "hot" issues—may need a full-time associate assigned exclusively to managing calls. These staff members provide the reporter with appropriate background information, oversee requests for interviews, and help shepherd the inquiry into coverage that serves the interests of the organization and the clients or issues it works for.

WHAT IS CAUSE-RELATED MARKETING, AND WHO DOES IT?

by Timothy J. McClimon

Vice President of Philanthropy • American Express Company

American Express helped coin the term "cause-related marketing" in 1983 when it launched a campaign to raise money for the restoration of the Statue of Liberty. The company donated one cent to the Statue of Liberty effort every time someone used one of its charge cards. The Statue of Liberty benefited with close to $19 million raised in additional support. American Express benefited as well: it is widely reported that the number of new cardholders increased by 45 percent and card usage went up by 28 percent.

Cause-related marketing involves a for-profit company partnering with a nonprofit organization in a campaign that raises brand awareness of the company and financial support for the organization. The collaboration may involve the joint sponsorship of events, public service announcements, or display advertisements. It may also involve the production of merchandise targeted to a specific client base that features both the company's and nonprofit organization's logo.

Cause-related marketing is usually separate from corporate philanthropy, which is the direct donation of funds by a corporation to a nonprofit. Cause-related marketing programs tap into existing marketing budgets and are designed to increase consumer spending. The funds a company spends on cause-related marketing campaigns are typically not tax deductible as charitable contributions, but they may be tax deductible as business expenses. Nonprofit organizations and corporations have embraced cause-related marketing campaigns because of their "win-win" nature (everybody benefits) and the fact that they may offer access to previously untapped sources of funds. Partnerships have been formed to address everything from breast cancer to literacy to historic preservation.

At a nonprofit organization, communications and development staff usually oversee a cause-related marketing program. Or, if the agency is large enough, a director of marketing may have responsibility for the initiative. At a for-profit company, the work is most often handled by a marketing executive although there may be involvement with the philanthropy staff as well. ∎

Timothy J. McClimon is responsible for the American Express philanthropic program, which incorporates employee volunteer activities and grants in the areas of economic independence, cultural heritage, and community service. Previously, Tim directed New York's Second Stage Theatre company and, prior to that, AT&T's philanthropic program. Tim began his career by specializing in nonprofit law in private practice.

Finally, media relations experts train senior staff, board members, and the executive director on how to serve as effective spokespeople. They hold mock interviews and press conferences and teach staff how to speak in "soundbytes," field (or deflect) confrontational questions, and generally are comfortable and skilled enough to leverage the press effectively. Media relations staff are also responsible for "crisis communications"—handling the press and minimizing the damage when the organization, one of its staff members, or a client it serves generates negative attention.

Web development and design

Web development and design work may be handled by an organization's information technology department or its graphic designer. If it is a dedicated function, the web developer is apt to work with colleagues in communications and IT to design, develop, and maintain the organization's website. This involves keeping content and graphics current, monitoring the site to ensure that all elements function as planned, and developing innovative ways to use the web to reach all of the organization's target audiences and advance its mission. A web developer is also responsible for harvesting information collected via the web.

Communications positions attract strong writers and speakers and also individuals having an understanding of public relations, marketing, message development, and the business of news. Like grant writers, nonprofit sector writers, editors, and publications professionals need to be able to translate often complicated and esoteric issues into compelling and accessible prose. Organizations hiring communications staff will look for candidates who have solid knowledge—if not expertise—in the work of the organization. They may look for candidates with a "Rolodex" of contacts to journalists, as well as those with professional journalism experience themselves. For positions that involve marketing and advertising, organizations will look for candidates with creativity and may often be attracted to past experience with a for-profit advertising agency.

For More Insight on Communications Work . . .

See Timothy J. McClimon's sidebar ("What Is Cause-related Marketing, and Who Does It?" page 140), the sample communications officer job description (page 153), and the profiles of Christopher Herrera (pages 142–143) and Erika Lindsay (pages 60–61).

CHRISTOPHER HERRERA
Director of Communications

Age: 43

Education: BA, English

Years at current organization: 7

Years in current position: 7

First job out of college: Editor of a small independent trade publication

First job in nonprofit sector: Publications coordinator at a civil rights organization

Tides Foundation

www.tidesfoundation.org

Mission: Tides Foundation works with individuals, families, and institutions, providing philanthropic services to support positive social change.

Operating budget: $5 million

Number of employees: 35

Number of employees who report to you: 2, a communications manager and a communications associate

Q&A

Q: Informally, describe your career track.
A: After working for several years at a painfully boring trade publication for the legal community, I took the graphic and editorial skills I had acquired—along with my English degree—and luckily found a communications job for an organization in which I strongly believed. I have worked in the nonprofit sector developing communications materials and strategies ever since.

Q: What do you know now that you wish you had known when you were first job hunting?
A: That nonprofit organizations desperately need good writers.

Q: Describe a representative work day.

A: I am responsible for all institutional communications and marketing efforts, including websites, publications, media relations, and developing key messages about our mission and services. A typical day involves writing, rewriting, telling consultants to rewrite what they've written, then rewriting that in between rewriting content provided by staff. Then editing that down to half the length. Then lunch. Then a meeting, perhaps with senior managers to discuss and develop the foundation's five-year plan. Then maybe some more meetings about new foundation initiatives. Perhaps a conference call with partner organizations on a joint project. Then a meeting—you guessed it—to go over some rewrites.

Q: What misconceptions do people have about your job? What's the reality?

A: There are fewer misconceptions than there is open ignorance. I don't mean that in a pejorative sense, but people often ask, "What exactly do you do?" The reality is that I write a great deal, generating content for various communications vehicles, and edit and review even more content from staff and consultants. I also manage quite a few consultants, directing and reviewing projects.

Q: What do you love about your work?

A: Tides Foundation funds great organizations doing great work. From economic justice to Get Out the Vote efforts, we move significant money to support work on important issues. I am proud to be a part of that.

Q: What advice would you give to someone interested in a career similar to yours?

A: This career is very achievable. Take the low-paying (but perhaps necessary) entry-level positions as early as possible, when your living overhead is low and your physical and emotional resiliency is high. Gain expertise in specific issues as well as hard skills that can be applied to those issues—be they policy analysis, organizing, fundraising, or communication.

Q: What resources might help someone interested in your field and job function?

A: For those interested in a communications position, hone your writing skills via workshops, classes, and especially hands-on experience while working or volunteering in the field. And stay abreast of visual design trends and communication technologies as much as possible. There are many good organizations connected to social change: The Opportunity Agenda, The Spin Project, Center for Community Change, Open Society Institute.

Q: What do you look for when hiring a new employee?

A: A good writer. Being able to take a relatively abstract concept and turn it into compelling copy for publication is often the goal. That requires someone who can quickly grasp issues and organize ideas into clear language. I also look for a general technological facility, meaning either experience with layout or web-based software or indications that there would be a quick and welcome learning curve to gain those skills. And a finely tuned sense of humor also doesn't hurt.

Consulting in the Nonprofit Sector

Many nonprofit organizations depend on consultants for their work. Consultants may be hired to do just about anything—from preparing strategic plans, helping with board development, researching and writing reports, or designing and implementing a media strategy, to creating communications materials, assisting with fundraising and development, developing a website, or serving as an interim staff member.

For the nonprofit organization, a good consultant offers focused expertise, new contacts, fresh perspective, and an "outsider's" eyes. Also, a consultant may be hired for project-specific work, so costs (and overhead expenses) can be lower than if the work were assigned to a full-time staff member. For the successful consultant, the career path offers independence and the chance to pick and choose projects, develop an area of expertise, work with a range of organizations while being your own boss, and freedom from sometimes frustrating office politics. The busiest and most business-savvy consultants may earn more than a comparable full-time staff member of an organization.

Independent and entrepreneurial workers make the best consultants. You have to be a go-getter who is able to sell your strengths. And you have to be comfortable with risk, since you have less job security working for yourself on a contract-to-contract basis. You also should be happy to go at it alone. You may partner with others, but you are not officially part of a team, and the day-to-day work is often quite solitary. You don't gain a lot of management experience as a consultant, and while some have transitioned to full-time staff positions at organizations, consulting is not a typical career path toward becoming a nonprofit executive.

Solo practitioner versus consulting associate

A nonprofit organization may hire a consultant who is a solo practitioner (or independent contractor). Also known as freelancers, these consultants work for themselves, but may partner with staff members and other consultants on larger projects. Nonprofit sector consultants are not usually incorporated as nonprofit organizations, but they work on behalf of the nonprofit sector and their careers are dedicated to public service. Often, consultants have both a functional and issue area of expertise (e.g., grant writing around international public health issues).

A nonprofit organization also may hire a consultant, or team of consultants, through a firm. Firms that specialize in consulting work to nonprofit organizations may or may not be incorporated as nonprofit organizations themselves. But like specialized solo practitioners, their work is dedicated to the nonprofit sector. Local, regional, and national nonprofit sector consulting firms exist around functional needs (e.g., executive recruitment and board development), and with subsector expertise (e.g., health). Working at a consulting firm offers the employee the opportunity to work for a range of organizations and on diverse projects, but brings with it less independence and perhaps slightly more job security than operating as a solo practitioner.

Launching a nonprofit sector consulting career

Selling yourself as a consultant requires experience and an extensive network of contacts who trust you and respect the work you do. Client organizations are hiring an expert and have little interest in training or mentoring a consultant who is under contract with them. As such, most consultants have not started out as consultants. Rather, they began as staff members at organizations, developed experience and skills, built a strong network in a given field, and then transitioned into launching their own businesses. Others have entered the consulting field immediately, but at a consulting firm for the job security and experience it offers.

The financial uncertainty in being a solo practitioner usually is greatest in the start-up period. Unless you have a strong financial safety net, it's smart to have some savings and at least one substantial consulting gig in place before you head out on your own. Knowing you have a four- or six-month contract confirmed—even if it is not full-time work—will give you the freedom you'll need to build your business.

As with any career you might pursue, if you are interested in consulting work, conduct research and talk to professionals in the field. Ask nonprofit organization leaders about the consultants they work with, and meet with those individuals for informational interviews and specific career advice. Plus, if you impress the consultants you meet, they may pass contracts they can't handle to you.

It is critical for a consultant to have a professional portfolio of sample work—even more so than if you were applying for a staff position. Remember, you're pitching yourself to potential clients. You want to show them the work you have produced, and you need to be able to articulate the results it delivered. If you're thinking of moving from a staff to consulting position, use your current work to create the portfolio you'll need.

For More Insight on Consulting Work . . .

See the interview with Victoria Ebin ("Notes from the Road," pages 87–89), the sample consultant job description (page 154), and the profile of Diane J. Johnson (pages 146–147).

DIANE J. JOHNSON, PHD
Founder and President

Age: 45

Education: BA, communications;
MS, nonprofit management; PhD,
interdisciplinary studies; certified in
conflict mediation

Years at current organization: 14

Years in current position: 14

First job out of college: Press representative
for a national television and radio network

First job in nonprofit sector: Program
assistant for a grantmaking foundation

Mmapeu Consulting

www.mmapeu.com

Mission: Mmapeu Consulting works to support and develop vibrant and relevant community change organizations. We provide consulting, training, facilitation, research, and program evaluation in the areas of organizational development, nonprofit management, board leadership, cultural assessment and diversity, coalition building, and project management.

Operating budget: Approximately $200,000

Number of employees: 1 with numerous affiliate consultants

Number of employees who report to you: Solo practitioner

Q & A

Q: Informally, describe your career track.
A: My first career out of college was in corporate communications and media sales. I was totally unaware of the nonprofit sector as a career option. After four years of corporate work, it finally dawned on me that maybe I could get a "real job" in the nonprofit sector. While volunteering at a symposium, I met an expert in nonprofit organizational development who became my mentor. That professional relationship led to an internship,

then a part-time job for a foundation, and, eventually, a full-time development position. Soon after starting my first nonprofit job, I pursued a master's degree in nonprofit management. After six years in the sector at various organizations, with increasing responsibility, I created Mmapeu Consulting. For fourteen years, I served as principal working on myriad regional and national projects and initiatives.

Q: What do you know now that you wish you had known when you were first job hunting?
A: That it would take four jobs until I found one that I felt matched my talents, skills, passion, and drive.

Q: Describe a representative work day.
A: As a consultant there is really no typical work day. Each day can be a combination of client development, relationship building, responding to client crisis, conducting a training, facilitating a national meeting, collecting qualitative data, or presenting at a regional conference. I work with client organizations to help them achieve specific organizational goals. And there is always the back-office work to contend with.

Q: What misconceptions do people have about your job? What's the reality?
A: People often feel they can be a nonprofit sector consultant without having substantive and extensive experience in the field. Effective, responsive, and dynamic nonprofit sector consulting requires deep and broad knowledge in targeted issue areas—either as a generalist or a content expert.

Q: What do you love about your work?
A: My talents, skills, expertise, values, and perspectives are of use to clients; and my work culminates in facilitating community and social change.

Q: What advice would you give to someone interested in a career similar to yours?
A: Identify your skills, competencies, and your passions. Secure opportunities (both paid and volunteer) to broaden your knowledge and talents. Actively build networks—develop relationships and mentoring opportunities with individuals you respect. Participate in industry-wide associations and go to conferences (even if you have to pay for them yourself). Read poetry and literature, develop a spiritual practice, and remember to integrate community, fun, and laughter into your life.

Q: What resources might help someone interested in your field and job function?
A: I'd recommend publications and organizations such as the Association for Research and Nonprofit Voluntary Action (ARNOVA) (www.arnova.org), Independent Sector (www.independentsector.org), *Nonprofit Management & Leadership Journal,* The Alliance for Nonprofit Management (www.allianceonline.org), and *Stanford Social Innovation Review* (www.ssireview.org).

Q: What do you look for when hiring a new employee?
A: I look for a range of experience and expertise, enthusiasm, an entrepreneurial spirit, a balance between confidence and humility, patience, and a sense of knowing what one doesn't know and a corresponding desire to learn.

147

Sample Job Descriptions

The following section provides fifteen sample job descriptions representing a range of job functions housed at diverse fictional organizations. They include

The job listings are fictional, as are the recruiting organizations, but they were drawn from real-life, recent, and particularly descriptive postings. They accurately reflect how a vacant position might be described and the skills and experiences an organization might seek. Use these descriptions to identify the type of work that sounds appealing to you and that you are qualified to perform. Ignore the information about the organization if you just want to concentrate on the work, or use the mission of the organization to help you also think about what field inspires you (and then return to the appropriate subsector description in Chapter 2).

As you read, think about how you would draft a cover letter to apply for a particular job. Consider what credentials you offer, as well as any additional experience you might want to gain as you think about advancing your career.

ADMINISTRATIVE ASSISTANT, DOMESTIC VIOLENCE SHELTER

Organization: House of Hope (*fictional*)
Location: Detroit, MI

Organization:

House of Hope is a domestic violence shelter serving women in need in the Detroit area. We work to empower survivors of domestic violence and their families. We provide shelter and direct services to women and children who have experienced domestic violence. We run educational programs to inform the community about the impact of domestic violence and ways to fight the epidemic. House of Hope employs five full-time staff members but depends on the generosity of our network of more than fifty volunteers. We receive support from civic and religious groups, local corporations, private citizens, and the government. We also raise funds through our bookstore in downtown Detroit.

Job Description:

House of Hope seeks an administrative assistant to handle the full and heavy administrative workload of our organization. The administrative assistant supports the work of our full-time staff members and their communications and calendars. She or he answers phones, files, makes photocopies, schedules meetings, and maintains our databases. She or he manages relationships with key vendors, helps us produce our quarterly newsletter, and executes all mailings. The administrative assistant also assists in the planning, preparation, and execution of various fundraising activities and special events for House of Hope. She or he reports to all five of our full-time staff members.

Main Responsibilities:

The administrative assistant will

- answer phones
- update and maintain databases
- assist with the word processing needs of full-time staff
- schedule meetings for full-time staff and manage their calendars
- sort and deliver incoming mail; oversee production and execution of all outgoing mailings
- assist with special events logistics
- perform other administrative tasks as needed

Qualifications:

Computer literacy in Microsoft Office programs including Excel, Access, Outlook, Word, and Powerpoint. Fluency in other programs such as Adobe Photoshop a plus. Excellent interpersonal and communication skills. Pleasant phone manner. Excellent organization skills, multitasking abilities, and attention to detail. The ability to prioritize a multitude of tasks amid frequent deadlines. Flexibility, self-motivation, and patience. Fluency in Spanish a plus, but not required. Deep commitment to House of Hope's mission and sensitivity to issues surrounding our work.

ADVOCACY ASSOCIATE, AFFORDABLE HOUSING

Organization: Affordable Housing Now *(fictional)*
Location: Chicago, IL

Organization:

Affordable Housing Now is an unprecedented grassroots alliance of civic, business, religious, and labor leaders committed to tackling Chicago's affordable housing crisis. Affordable Housing Now is dedicated to raising the issue of affordable housing to the top of the civic agenda—through forums, public events, reports, media outreach, and other organizing efforts. The coalition also is advancing a plan for public and private investment to develop and preserve affordable housing for Chicagoans.

Job Description:

Affordable Housing Now seeks a positive and self-motivated person to develop and coordinate our advocacy program. The advocacy associate will help us build our coalition, educate and mobilize diverse constituencies, act as a spokesperson to the media, and find additional ways to develop political and grassroots support to advance our affordable housing agenda. The advocacy associate will report to the convenor of our coalition and will be in charge of several student intern field organizers.

Main Responsibilities:

The advocacy associate will

- assist the convenor in guiding the coalition in all of its organizing, advocacy, and relationship building with the media, politicians, public officials, and other decision makers
- help plan the organization's advocacy agenda

- develop and maintain relationships with grassroots constituencies, other coalitions and campaigns, government officials, and other community leaders
- organize rallies for affordable housing and other special events such as letter writing campaigns
- track, monitor, and analyze local government decisions related to affordable housing
- track, monitor, and analyze media coverage related to affordable housing
- interact with and advocate before government officials
- recruit and supervise student interns
- attend all coalition meetings and report on advocacy events

Qualifications:

High school degree; bachelor's degree in public policy, government relations, or related area preferred. Significant knowledge of affordable housing policy, and willingness to build knowledge. Knowledge of state and local legislatures, state agencies, and nonprofit organizations. Experience in grassroots organizing and education, with proven track record working in and building local coalitions. Experience lobbying. Excellent written and verbal communication skills, including public speaking skills. Creativity in developing messages. Experience working with the media and at public forums. Ability to work independently in designing and implementing activities but also as part of a team effort. Bilingual skills desirable.

AFTER-SCHOOL COUNSELOR, AT-RISK PRE-TEENS

Organization: The Atlanta Family Center (*fictional*)
Location: Atlanta, GA

Organization:

For more than fifteen years, the Atlanta Family Center has provided a full range of human service programs to help children, adults, families, and communities realize their potential. As part of its mission, the Atlanta Family Center offers an after-school program for at-risk elementary school children that provides homework help, mentoring, arts and crafts programs, and counseling services.

Job Description:

The Family Center is looking for an after-school counselor who will develop, facilitate, and manage after-school activities for approximately twenty-five at-risk elementary school-aged children. The activities will include homework and tutoring, recreational activities, mentoring programs, and counseling services. The counselor will develop partnerships with community organizations—bringing in guest speakers and arranging for special projects or initiatives—to augment on-site services and activities. The counselor will be responsible for securing and managing volunteers. Most importantly, she or he will be the lead counselor for the children and provide direct supervision to youth involved in various programming during after-school hours.

Main Responsibilities:

The after-school counselor will

- recruit, screen, and admit participants
- develop, facilitate, implement, coordinate, and supervise daily programming for all youth enrolled in the program; serve as lead counselor for the children
- recruit and manage volunteer counselors
- organize biannual parent-teacher-student day
- routinely communicate with social work staff to improve service delivery to students; connect students with additional services as required
- develop a wide network of community-based resources and establish partnerships to augment on-site programming
- regularly communicate with parents or guardians of children; communicate with children's teachers as necessary
- participate in all staff meetings and staff development activities
- represent the program at public events

Qualifications:

Bachelor's degree. A premium is placed on candidates with experience working with adolescents, particularly from traditionally underserved communities. Experience in tutoring, mentoring, managing volunteers, and developing programs. Excellent written and verbal communication skills. Strong capabilities in math, reading, and other general academic studies, as well as creativity and organizational skills. Common sense and good judgment. Candidates must be passionate about engaging youth and acting as a positive role model and be flexible, patient, and supportive. Fluency in Spanish is highly desirable.

BOOKKEEPER, FAMILY FOUNDATION

Organization: The Longaker Foundation (*fictional*)
Location: Little Rock, AR

Organization:

The Longaker Foundation is a family foundation founded in 1995 and based in Little Rock, Arkansas. Its grants, totaling $15 million annually, are directed to nonprofit organizations and their programs that work on three core issue areas: family planning and reproductive health, the fight against global warming, and early childhood education. The foundation supports approximately forty organizations working in the United States and internationally.

Job Description:

The Longaker Foundation seeks a bookkeeper who will report to the chief financial officer. The bookkeeper will be responsible for the day-to-day fiscal reporting needs of the foundation. She or he will handle general bookkeeping and management of the general ledger, including cash receipts, accounts payable, and accounts receivable, and other work related to financial systems. The bookkeeper will oversee check and wire issuance, daily deposits, and voucher and expense processing. This person will assist in monitoring all financial transactions for the foundation. She or he will support our monthly closing process.

Main Responsibilities:

The bookkeeper will
- maintain the general ledger and chart of accounts
- perform monthly reconciliations of bank accounts, accounts receivable, accounts payable, and revenue
- ensure internal controls exist and are functioning effectively
- prepare checks for signature and mailing
- assist with financial reporting
- prepare 1099 forms
- provide accounting assistance to foundation staff
- work to improve current bookkeeping and other accounting systems and procedures
- assist with other administrative responsibilities as required

Qualifications:

Associate's or bachelor's degree in accounting and finance, or equivalent training required. At least two years bookkeeper and accounting experience with a nonprofit organization. Knowledge of MIP accounting software package preferred, or knowledge of other accounting software package required. Heavy data entry experience, highly organized, and strong oral and written communication skills. Commitment to the foundation's mission.

COMMUNICATIONS OFFICER, PUBLIC HEALTH

Organization: Malaria Research International *(fictional)*
Location: Geneva, Switzerland

Organization:

Malaria, one of the most common infectious diseases in the world, kills more than one million people and afflicts as many as 500 million people annually. Every thirty seconds, a child dies from malaria. The disease is both a result and cause of poverty and a major obstacle toward economic development. No vaccine currently exists. Malaria Research International is an international research center dedicated to research around the prevention and treatment of this deadly and widespread disease, with a particular emphasis on developing an effective malaria vaccine.

Job Description:

The communications officer will be based in Malaria Research International's Geneva, Switzerland, headquarters. She or he will report to the director of communications and assist with the full range of press-related responsibilities to help communicate information about malaria research and the work of Malaria Research International to the organization's target audiences worldwide. The communications officer will help use the media to educate policymakers, community leaders, funders, and the general public about malaria. Our offices are bilingual English and French.

Main Responsibilities:

The communications officer will

- develop and maintain target media lists of journalists worldwide

- help draft, edit, and disseminate press releases and advisories via fax, e-mail, and mail
- help draft and produce press kits
- make follow-up "pitch calls" to journalists on appropriate news stories related to malaria and the work of Malaria Research International
- track news coverage of malaria and maintain binders of press clippings; prepare media reports for office staff on press coverage
- help organize press conferences and press briefings; manage press registration
- handle inquiries from the media, maintain logs of incoming media calls and forward requests to appropriate staff members, and arrange interviews for organization's spokespeople
- ensure that press section of website is up to date
- conduct administrative work as necessary (photocopying, filing, etc.)
- recruit and manage communications intern

Qualifications:

Bachelor's degree and some experience in a nonprofit organization's communications department required, preferably in a health or research organization. Understanding of the business of news. Some knowledge of public health issues generally, or malaria in particular. Superior writing and editing skills. Excellent administrative skills and stickler for detail. Experience managing lists. Pleasant phone manner and willingness to make "cold calls" to journalists. Fluency in English and French.

CONSULTANT (BOARD DEVELOPMENT), CHILDREN'S HOSPITAL

Organization: Saguaro Children's Hospital *(fictional)*
Location: Phoenix, AZ

Organization:

Saguaro Children's Hospital is one of the leading pediatric medical centers in the United States. The private, nonprofit health facility is dedicated to enhancing, sustaining, and restoring children's health and development. The hospital provides treatment for children from birth to age twenty-one, conducts research, and functions as the training site for medical students. The hospital is governed by a diverse, fifteen-person board of directors who are leaders in the community and volunteer their time to advance the hospital's mission.

Job Description:

By the end of the year, five of Saguaro Children's Hospital's board members will retire. In light of this, the hospital recently underwent a rigorous evaluation of its board composition and effectiveness. The evaluation produced a five-year strategic plan for board development. The hospital seeks a board development consultant to engage in a one-year contract with the hospital to apply the strategic plan and to support board development.

Main Responsibilities:

The board development consultant will

- review the hospital's current strategic plan; assess all existing board materials and evaluate the functioning of the current board of directors, including its fundraising goals and accomplishments
- prepare a yearlong work plan with goals, timeline, and budget for the board

- identify expertise and skills missing from current board members, identify potential board members to recruit, and develop a board recruitment package
- revise the existing board orientation manual
- develop job descriptions for board members and assist with definition and understanding of roles and responsibilities
- train executive director on board management and effective board communications; engage executive director and existing board members in recruiting new board members; and organize one board retreat, an orientation for new board members, and trainings for existing board members
- prepare final report on consulting contract and recommendations for future actions

Qualifications:

The consultant must have substantial experience in board development and knowledge of the health care arena and governance of hospitals. Past non-profit organization references are required, preferably from hospital clients. He or she should be an adept facilitator, trainer, writer, and strategist. The consultant should have a portfolio of sample board development materials (e.g., evaluations, recruitment packages, orientation manuals, retreat programs, and training modules).

DATABASE MANAGER, CONSERVATION ADVOCACY

Organization: Marine Mammals Movement (*fictional*)
Location: Boston, MA

Organization:

The Marine Mammals Movement is an international grassroots environmental organization working to protect the world's ocean mammals. We are a membership organization with five offices internationally and more than 200,000 members worldwide who are committed to helping preserve marine mammal species. Our members receive our quarterly newsletter and periodic e-mail and mail communications, attend meetings, and organize their own grassroots fundraising and public education efforts. Our Boston office handles U.S. operations and serves and cultivates our 25,000 members in the United States.

Job Description:

The database manager will maintain and enhance the organization's membership database, record individual gift revenue, and perform a variety of related tasks in support of the development department's data and development needs. She or he will use Raiser's Edge software. She or he will be responsible for overseeing direct mail and e-mail appeals, including membership upgrade letters, membership acquisition mailings, annual appeals, acknowledgement letters, and the production of membership materials such as membership cards. The database manager will assist in procurement of and outreach to new prospect lists. This full-time position reports to the vice president of development.

Main Responsibilities:

The database manager will

- enter and update membership information; maintain accuracy and consistency in coding and data entry; conduct regular database maintenance and clean-up
- oversee gift acknowledgements and ensure that acknowledgements are mailed promptly
- work closely with the organization's advocacy and programming staffs to create opportunities to identify and solicit new members
- create and run Raiser's Edge reports as needed and run queries as requested by other staff members
- manage special projects, such as importing data from large events, supporting special mailings, and procuring new prospect lists
- provide customer service to new and current members and manage all membership inquiries; send information packets
- stay current on updates to Raiser's Edge software

Qualifications:

Bachelor's degree or equivalent professional experience in membership and customer service. Experience with database management and Raiser's Edge software. Ability to manage efficiently a significant workload and pay close attention to detail. Appreciation and enjoyment of achieving a high degree of accuracy. Pleasant phone manner. Strong writing and organizational skills. Willingness to work with and report to numerous staff members.

EXECUTIVE DIRECTOR, ORCHESTRA

Organization: Rocky Mountain Orchestra *(fictional)*
Location: Salt Lake City, UT

Organization:

Founded in 2000, the Rocky Mountain Orchestra (RMO) is a new American orchestra based in Salt Lake City dedicated to programming a wide range of music, including that by new American composers. It has an annual operating budget of $5 million and an administrative staff of twelve full-time employees who are responsible for concert production, marketing, public relations, education, community engagement, fundraising, customer service, accounting, and financial reporting. The RMO employs more than seventy-five professional musicians each year and dozens of guest conductors. The orchestra performs thirty classic, pops, and holiday concerts annually at venues throughout Colorado, Utah, Idaho, and Montana. In addition to its concerts, RMO is committed to delivering high-caliber educational programming for young people and families.

Job Description:

RMO seeks an executive director to lead the organization and manage all human and financial resources to advance the orchestra's mission. The executive director reports to the board of directors and works closely with the organization's music director. The executive director works with the board to develop and implement the organization's long-term plans; directs fundraising activities; collaborates with the music director to set artistic direction, select guest artists and conductors, and develop programs; produces concerts and educational programs; manages marketing and promotion; and oversees all financial and administrative functions. The executive director manages six direct reports, including an assistant; a general manager; and the directors of development, business operations, educational programs, and communications and marketing.

Main Responsibilities:

The executive director will

- advise the board of directors on matters concerning the orchestra, serve as ex-officio member on all board committees, and manage board meetings and activities
- implement the orchestra's current five-year strategic plan and assist with the creation of the next plan
- prepare and monitor operating budgets, manage sound financial practices, and oversee monthly financial statements
- play an active role in key development and fundraising efforts; serve as lead representative of the orchestra at special events, with major donors, and at foundation meetings; oversee grant applications, corporate foundation solicitations, and individual donor fund drives

- work with the music director to develop and implement artistic programs, hire musicians, and select guest artists and conductors; oversee the negotiation of orchestra member and guest artist contracts; serve as the spokesperson to the musicians for policy and administrative issues
- work with the general manager to schedule concerts, rehearsals, and other programming; secure appropriate venues; and manage other operational issues
- manage marketing campaigns for the orchestra and serve as lead spokesperson for the organization in interviews
- hire and manage consultants as appropriate
- recruit and supervise operations and administrative staff; manage communications, insurance, compensation and benefits packages, job descriptions, and payroll functions; ensure that the orchestra operates in accordance with all local, state, and federal laws

Qualifications:
Bachelor's degree or higher. Strong leader with solid knowledge of classical music and with senior management experience, preferably in an orchestra setting. Passion for the mission of the Rocky Mountain Orchestra. Adept at working with a board of directors, managing and motivating staff, and creating and implementing programs. Experienced fundraiser with demonstrable success raising significant funds from a variety of funding sources, preferably in the Rocky Mountain region.

GRANTS MANAGER, MUSEUM

Organization: Museum of Glass (*fictional*)
Location: Denver, CO

Organization:

The Museum of Glass is Denver's newest museum. It offers a diverse collection of glass pieces, ranging from drinking glasses to contemporary art installations. The museum's permanent collection includes works by European, Asian, African, and American glass makers. The museum is dedicated to promoting the work of the next generation of glass artists and craftspeople, providing high-quality educational programs and workshops, and serving as a center for research.

Job Description:

The Museum of Glass is seeking a writer to serve as grants manager. The grants manager will develop and implement a comprehensive plan to generate income for the Museum through government and private foundation grants. The grants manager will identify prospects, develop and track grant proposals, and maintain relationships with funders. She or he will support other development activities of the museum and will report to the director of development in the museum's small development department.

Main Responsibilities:

The grants manager will

- conduct prospect research on potential government and private foundation funding sources; build and maintain orderly files on prospects and share information on grant opportunities with program staff

- schedule brainstorming meetings with program staff on new funding opportunities and specific grant proposals
- draft grant proposals and project budgets and revise documents as necessary based on input from program staff and director of development; prepare all necessary collateral materials for grant applications; submit and track grants
- arrange in-person meetings for museum staff with foundation program officers
- prepare update memos for museum staff on prospects, grants applied for, and grants secured; prepare interim and final reports for foundations on grants secured
- remain up to date on arts-related funding trends
- participate in and support other development activities as appropriate

Qualifications:

Bachelor's degree. Experience in writing government and foundation grants and preparing budgets. Experience in prospect research. Willingness and ability to cultivate relationships with funding sources. Strong and comfortable telephone skills. Highly organized, self-motivated, and goal oriented. Ability to create and manage efficient systems and handle multiple projects. Candidates must have exceptional and versatile writing skills and the ability to translate program ideas into compelling narrative. Candidates must have a portfolio of professional writing samples, preferably including successful grant proposals.

HUMAN RESOURCES ASSISTANT, CULTURAL ADVOCACY

SAMPLE JOB
POSTING
10

Organization: Association for American Jewish People (*fictional*)
Location: St. Louis, MO

Organization:

The Association for American Jewish People is a national Jewish organization working to combat anti-Semitism, strengthen the Jewish community, provide services to Jewish people in the United States, and advance an advocacy agenda on behalf of Jewish people worldwide. We are an advocacy and education organization. We organize educational symposia, publish manuscripts and books on issues relevant to Jewish life, and collaborate with partner organizations to advance our mission.

Job Description:

The Association for American Jewish People is looking for a human resources assistant to join the human resources department of our national office, based in St. Louis. The assistant will help manage personnel policies and procedures. She or he will maintain personnel files and ensure they are in compliance with regulations and industry standards. She or he will assist with payroll administration and all aspects of recruitment, new employee orientation, benefits administration, and coordinating the annual performance review process.

Main Responsibilities:

The human resources assistant will

- review job descriptions and job announcements for consistency and appropriateness
- post jobs using various media, and manage the job posting budget
- coordinate the recruitment process in collaboration with hiring manager
- assist in developing and coordinating employee orientation and staff trainings
- act as primary contact for the payroll processing organization
- collect, review, and input timesheets
- prepare and maintain employee personnel files, records, and information
- communicate information on benefits, policies, and programs to employees; update employee handbook periodically
- oversee the maintenance of benefits records and direct the documentation necessary for implementing benefit coverage

Qualifications:

Bachelor's degree and at least one year's experience in a human resources department, either as an intern or as an associate. Knowledge of fundamental human resources laws and principles. Certification as a professional in human resources (PHR) by the Society for Human Resource Management (SHRM), or expectation to be certified within one year. Strong communication and problem-solving skills. Understanding of the media and experience placing advertisements. Exceptionally well organized, detail oriented, and self-motivated. Must set rigorous standards for accuracy and efficiency. Proficiency with Microsoft Office applications. Must be reliable with confidential, sensitive information.

RESEARCH ASSOCIATE, VOTER ADVOCACY

Organization: Your Vote Counts (*fictional*)
Location: flexible

Organization:

Your Vote Counts (YVC) believes that having every vote count is the fundamental tenet of American democracy. YVC is a DC-based coalition of academics, attorneys, and educators. We work to protect the integrity of U.S. elections through litigation and advocacy in support of legislative reforms to ensure reliable elections and to protect the exercise of fundamental voting rights. We educate policymakers, the public, and the courts on issues surrounding electronic voting machines and advance legislative solutions to problems posed by existing voting systems. YVC associates conduct research, pursue advocacy, and implement litigation in state capitols throughout the country. The research associate need not be based in Washington, DC, but must be willing to travel.

Job Description:

Your Vote Counts seeks a research associate. Our researchers conduct original research on a range of electronic voting issues, but concentrate on procedures and policies adopted by local jurisdictions for the use of new voting technologies. The research associate will help plan research studies, develop survey instruments, conduct research interviews, and create and maintain data sets. She or he will assist in the analysis of findings and writing and dissemination of research reports and policy briefs. She or he will report to the national research director.

Main Responsibilities:

The research associate will

- support the management and execution of research projects related to electronic voting; conduct research into the actual practices surrounding the use of electronic voting technology by elections officials, maintain subject databases, create and maintain data sets, recruit and track research participants
- assist in preparing research findings for public presentations by senior staff
- participate in developing and maintaining a knowledge base of current literature regarding electronic voting technology, certification protocols, and state regulatory practices nationwide
- respond to external requests for information about YVC's work and electronic voting issues
- assist in identifying funding opportunities for new research projects

Qualifications:

Bachelor's degree. Graduate degree in public policy or statistics preferred. Familiarity with and commitment to YVC's mission. Experience conducting quantitative and qualitative research and statistical analysis. Proficiency in SPSS software. Excellent written and oral presentation skills. Ability to make academic research accessible and compelling to lay audiences. Organizational skills and ability to work as part of a team with team members working in satellite offices.

SPECIAL EVENTS COORDINATOR, EDUCATION ASSOCIATION

Organization: Charter Schools America *(fictional)*
Location: Los Angeles, CA

Organization:

Charter Schools America is an educational organization whose mission is the preparation of traditionally underserved students for higher education, regardless of the students' race, gender, or socioeconomic group. To accomplish this goal, the organization starts and manages groups of charter high schools in specific geographic regions.

Job Description:

Charter Schools America is looking for an experienced special events coordinator who will lead the planning, management, and implementation of special events and related development projects. The special events coordinator will direct day-to-day operations to ensure an effective and efficient specials events program for the organization. The special events coordinator reports to the development director, but will work closely with program directors, the executive director, and other members of the staff.

Main Responsibilities:

The special events coordinator will

- create an annual special events strategy, events calendar, and events budget for the organization
- manage all aspects of organization's annual fundraising lunch: identify speakers and honorees, secure corporate sponsors, manage graphic designers and other vendors, develop marketing materials and invitations, secure media coverage, and achieve fundraising goal for lunch

- prepare follow-up report on lunch for staff and board members
- create and run other fundraising and special events to generate new resources and support for the mission and goals of the organization
- organize organization's board meetings and corresponding social activities
- develop written materials to support special events and development activities
- recruit and manage volunteers to assist with special events
- collaborate with members of the development department to ensure that special events complement other development activities
- travel to support regional events and activities as required

Qualifications:

Bachelor's degree and at least three years of special events experience in a nonprofit setting. Ability to develop creative and well-executed programs, handle multiple tasks and details simultaneously, and function well under pressure. Proven track record in donor prospect research and volunteer management. Strong oral and written communication skills, and knowledge of database management. Successful candidate is goal oriented and results oriented, and can engage others in planning and execution of special event fundraisers.

VOLUNTEER COORDINATOR, DISASTER RELIEF

Organization: Hurricane Katrina Relief Network *(fictional)*
Location: New Orleans, LA

Organization:

The Hurricane Katrina Relief Network is a faith-based organization that recruits, trains, and places volunteers with partner organizations providing assistance to those affected by Hurricane Katrina. Our volunteers are recruited through our network of Louisiana churches. We match them with our partners (local and national nonprofit organizations) depending on the type of volunteer service they are interested in. They might work on home debris removal, tree removal, tree planting, light construction, family and children outreach and care, or animal care.

Job Description:

The volunteer coordinator plans, coordinates, and manages all volunteer program activities for the Hurricane Katrina Relief Network. The volunteer coordinator recruits, trains, assigns, supports, and tracks approximately 200 volunteers. She or he travels extensively to churches throughout the state to make presentations on the Hurricane Katrina Relief Network to prospective volunteers. She or he oversees the volunteer application process and matches volunteers with partner organizations. The volunteer coordinator provides oversight to the partner organizations' programs, ensuring that they are effectively utilizing volunteers. The position reports directly to the executive director.

Main Responsibilities:

The volunteer coordinator will

- recruit, train, assign, support, and track a network of approximately 200 volunteers
- develop and maintain relationships with partner churches to recruit volunteers
- arrange and deliver presentations on the program to prospective volunteers at churches
- review volunteer application forms
- develop and maintain relationships with the organization's network of partner nonprofit organizations to identify volunteer programs
- make site visits to assess volunteer programs and volunteers' satisfaction with activities
- handle all inquiries from prospective volunteers
- manage evaluation of volunteer programs
- participate in strategic planning discussions with the organization's program staff to improve programs and build the organization

Qualifications:

Bachelor's degree. Experience in volunteer management or other supervisory work. Ability to motivate others. Excellent administrative, organizational, communication, presentation, and time management skills. Exceptional interpersonal skills. Ability to engage effectively with a wide range of people. Experience with coordination and event planning. Willingness to travel. Willingness to convene night and weekend informational sessions. Commitment to Hurricane Katrina Relief Network's mission.

WEB DESIGNER, LGBT SERVICES

Organization: Gay Services Center *(fictional)*
Location: Dallas, TX

Organization:

The Gay Services Center serves the lesbian, gay, bisexual, and transgender communities of the Dallas region. Every week, more than five hundred people visit our multiservice organization for social service, public policy, educational, cultural, and recreational programs. In addition, dozens of organizations use our meeting spaces for their own events. Gay Services Center staff work on public policy and advocacy issues to support the gay community locally and nationally.

Job Description:

Gay Services Center's constituencies depend on the center's website for information on programs, advocacy efforts, and health and human services. We seek a web designer and developer who will manage, update, and improve all web-related materials. This is both a design and web development position, and candidates must be well-versed in HTML software and have graphic design experience. The web designer and developer reports directly to the communications director. The Gay Services Center offers a relaxed, energetic, dog-friendly, and highly productive office.

Main Responsibilities:

The web designer will

- maintain, update, and improve website content and design; work with program staff to gather appropriate content to keep the website accurate and up to date

- coordinate electronic communications, including e-newsletters and fundraising appeals
- develop and implement web-based marketing
- analyze website traffic and modify the site as appropriate for the mission of the center
- provide technical and administrative assistance to the center's staff

Qualifications:

Four-year college degree in computer-related field or equivalent experience. Two years' experience in website and electronic communications work, preferably in the nonprofit sector. Mastery of HTML and CSS. Ability to produce clean code and smooth-functioning websites. Experience preparing web graphics and managing site content. Perfectionist—willingness to test and troubleshoot web pages across multiple browsers, platforms, operating systems. Ability to work independently, but with strong people skills and eagerness to work with many different staff members. Ability to handle routine maintenance of website content and design, as well as develop creative ideas to use web-based vehicles to more fully inform and engage audiences.

We encourage applications from women, people with disabilities, and people of diverse ethnic, racial, religious, and socioeconomic backgrounds, educational and work experiences, geographic and national origins, sexual orientations, and ages.

YOUTH SERVICES PROGRAM DIRECTOR, COMMUNITY FOUNDATION

Organization: Fulton County Community Foundation (*fictional*)
Location: Gloversville, NY

Organization:

The Fulton County Community Foundation is dedicated to supporting philanthropy and strengthening communities in our upstate New York region. We serve as a vehicle by which donors can identify and realize their philanthropic goals. We create and manage charitable funds and implement initiatives, partnerships, and strategic grantmaking. We were founded in 1990 and since that time, we have made grants of more than $15 million and now have assets of more than $20 million in more than sixty different funds.

Job Description:

The Fulton County Community Foundation seeks a program director in youth services to manage the foundation's youth services-related grantmaking processes. She or he will link opportunities in the nonprofit community with the resources and vision of donors to our foundation. She or he will develop appropriate funds to support youth-serving programs and work with grant applicants and the foundation's decision-making committees to oversee the allocation of resources in the community.

Main Responsibilities:

The program director will

• maintain expertise in the field of youth services

• prepare and deliver presentations to grantors and foundation staff on developments in the field and the work of local nonprofit organizations

• identify and develop relationships with prospective donors

• oversee the grantmaking process; meet with prospective grant applicants, conduct proposal review and research, and present recommendations to the appropriate decision-making bodies at the foundation

• make site visits to nonprofit organizations receiving support

• monitor grants; prepare progress reports, manage payment schedules, maintain regular communications with grantees and grantors

• manage program associates and interns working on youth services grant programs

• serve as a spokesperson for the foundation in the philanthropic field

Qualifications:

Master's degree and five years' related experience in the nonprofit sector. Expertise in the field of youth services. Familiarity with the Fulton County region and its opportunities and challenges. Excellent analytical, verbal, and written communication skills. Ability to interact with grant seekers, board members, donors, and foundation staff from diverse backgrounds. Strong team player. Passion for the work of the Fulton County Community Foundation.

In a Nutshell . . .

The discussion of the range of job functions that exist in nonprofit organizations, along with the review of the sample job descriptions, demonstrates just how many different skills, experiences, and educational backgrounds nonprofit sector employers need. Virtually any skill set and area of functional expertise can be applied to a nonprofit organization setting (although you may have to target larger organizations if you want to pursue a more specialized position). The information should have helped you identify the type of positions that you are interested in and qualified for. This knowledge, when combined with that around the issues (or subsector work) discussed in Chapter 2 that resonates most strongly with you, can help direct you to the nature of the career you hope to pursue. Chapter 4 offers advice on how to prepare for that career.

four

PREPARING FOR A CAREER IN THE *nonprofit* SECTOR

Regardless of whether you're a high school or college student, recent graduate, or midcareer professional, it's never too early—or too late—to think about your career goals.

By picking up this book you've indicated an interest in the nonprofit sector as a possible professional path. But the sector is large and varied, and it's not enough to say that you "want to make a difference" in the work you do. If you haven't done so already, you'll want to hone in on some issue areas of particular interest to you. Better yet, you'll identify a passion for one field, and focus exclusively on it. Then you'll mesh your intellectual interests with your skills to identify the types of organizations and positions you should pursue.

Determining what you want to do is a lifelong quest for many people and one often fraught with turmoil and ambiguity. But at a certain point, you need to make decisions, concentrate on a specific career objective, and act. The bottom line in this quest is that knowledge is power. The more you know about issues, organizations, and jobs—through classes, volunteering and interning, part-time work, and talking with experts in the field—the better equipped you will be to focus on a field and develop a course of action for finding a job.

In this chapter you will explore two facets that will help you prepare for a career in the sector. The first is to understand who you are and how your interests can shape the kind of nonprofit career you choose. Next is to look at the educational and experiential options that will help you prepare for a nonprofit career and land a great job.

Understanding Yourself

It may seem obvious, but it's often overlooked: The most important preparation you can make is to know yourself. The following questions will help you clarify who you are so you can set your professional goals and career objectives.

- What are the issues you care about?
- What type of work have you enjoyed?
- What are you good at?
- Where and how do you want to live?
- What do you want to do?

Each of these questions will be explored in depth in the following pages.

What are the issues you care about?

The nonprofit sector offers plenty of opportunities for employment if you just want or need "a job," and, as in every sector, nonprofit organizations have their share of 9-to-5ers. But the sector succeeds because the people in it are motivated by something much deeper than a paycheck. And it is these leaders with passion whom nonprofit sector employers want to recruit.

Building an interesting and meaningful career (and landing a truly rewarding position) requires drive, determination, and enthusiasm around a certain issue. It's likely that you already know the subject matters that interest you. Depending on where you are in your academic training, you may have begun thinking about a major, or you may have already completed all of the coursework required for your concentration. But as you contemplate your professional career, especially one in the nonprofit sector, you'll want to explore what drives your heart and mind beyond just your coursework.

This type of introspection is often challenging, but not impossible. And the time you devote to asking yourself key questions about what you care about will pay off during your job search. Having ideas about what you want to do and the type of organization you'd like to work for will help you target your outreach efforts and increase your chances of securing a good fit with your first full-time job in the sector.

To identify the field you'd like to work in, you might begin by asking yourself some questions about who and what has motivated you in your personal, academic, volunteer, and professional life so far. For example:

- Who are the people you admire and why? What do they do with their lives and why is this inspirational to you?

- To what causes and organizations do you volunteer your time?

- What issues influence the way you vote?

- What challenges in your family life or within your community affected you or those around you? What type of leaders or organizations presented solutions that made sense to you?

- What websites, television programs, newspaper sections, radio broadcasts, books, documentaries, or similar issues-oriented media are you first drawn to? What articles or coverage do you follow from start to finish?

- What social problems make you angry enough to write a letter, attend a protest, or donate your time or money?

- At dinner with family or friends, what conversations engage you the most deeply? What policy issues make your ears perk up and keep you up at night debating?

- What C-SPAN policy coverage captivates you to such an extent that you forget dinner?

- What classes inspired you to go the extra mile with a paper or project? What was it about the subject matter, the professor, the readings, or the fieldwork that stimulated you?

- What did you dream of doing as a child? What is your "dream job" today?

Use the answers to these and similar questions to identify core issues you care about—that is, the type of organizational mission you are attracted to. And then think about the types of approaches or solutions to the problems that make sense to you, and that you would like to be part of.

What type of work have you enjoyed?

As important as it is to think about what you care about, it's equally vital to see where your passion intersects with your actions, or where "the rubber hits the road." You might find yourself saying, "I am deeply opposed to the death penalty," but, in fact, you spend every weekend working tirelessly at your local animal shelter. Or you might have taken a half dozen classes on the environment and written a winning thesis on global warming, but every evening you are at the senior center doing art projects with its residents. Is there a disconnect between what you believe in and what you do? Do your actions offer more insight than your words?

Forget for a moment about the assumptions you have regarding your political, ethical, and spiritual beliefs and look instead at how you actually spend your time.

- What clubs did you join in high school and college and how did you spend summer vacations?

- Where have you volunteered?

- Where have you traveled, and what did you do while on the road?

- What have been your favorite internships and jobs?

- What public events, meetings, workshops, and other extracurricular programs do you attend?

Use the answers to these and similar questions to conduct a realistic appraisal of how you spent your time. Try to find common themes in your experiences (themes that, if they match your career objectives, you will want to communicate in your résumé). Acknowledge what you did and what you enjoyed, and use this knowledge to help figure out what you might like to do. And

specialist or generalist?

Many people interested in a career in the nonprofit sector are driven by a well-defined passion for a specific cause or issue—they seem to have been born knowing that one day they will work to protect the environment, end racial discrimination, support international public health initiatives, or bring arts education to young people.

Other people committed to public service careers just want to fall asleep at night knowing that they have contributed their time and skills to an organization doing good work. As long as they are helping people or the planet, they may not think it matters whether they are working to assist migrant farm workers or to battle malaria. Or they may have a range of interests, and no specific issue generates more "fire in their belly" than another.

Whether you have a specific calling or a more general commitment to public service, it's important to hone in on an issue area (or two) and develop substantive knowledge and practical experience in that field. The variety of work in the nonprofit sector is endless—and often overwhelming—as

shown in the discussion of subsectors in Chapter 2. Without some direction during your college days, you'll miss out on an opportunity to focus on classes, faculty members, clubs, service learning programs, and the wide range of other campus-based resources and opportunities that can help prepare and connect you to a certain field of work and land your first job.

A thoughtful, intentional course of study combined with appropriate extracurricular activities will help you build the skills and experiences that will be attractive to a nonprofit sector employer. And it will help you build a passion for a mission, grounded in demonstrable knowledge, that all nonprofit sector leaders say they seek in new staff members. Of course, no one expects a recent college graduate to be an expert in a particular field. The key, however, is to be able to show personal and professional direction in your life, and then to be able to communicate your knowledge, skills, and commitment to a potential employer.

remember, if where you have been complements where you are headed, the individuals connected to your past experiences will be vital additions to your network.

What are you good at?

Ideally, we all do what we enjoy, and enjoy what we are good at. The most satisfying work and successful careers tap into our passions and allow us to leverage our strengths. In the nonprofit sector, this is especially important. You can't serve others well unless you are happy and feel fulfilled. You need to pursue work that you are good at and that allows you to accomplish goals that make you proud. This doesn't mean it has to be easy work; embracing new challenges and developing skills will always stimulate you and keep you engaged. But, equally, the work shouldn't feel relentlessly hard; you don't want to feel stuck in a position that isn't a good fit for your expertise or where you struggle with tasks.

Ask yourself some questions about the type of work that seems to come naturally to you.

- Are you a hands-on person? Do you want to provide services directly to the clients an organization serves? Do you want to be working in the field?

- Do you like to be a part of a team, do you prefer to work independently, or are you comfortable with a combination of solo and team work?

- Are you more comfortable focusing on one large task, or juggling many smaller tasks, or some mix of both?

- What are your core skills—person-to-person contact, writing, speaking, technology, number crunching, invention, compassion, analysis, people management, and so forth—and in what combination?

- Are you happy to ask people to invest their time and money in a cause that you care very deeply for?

- Are you good at dealing with office politics and managing people?

- Can you organize complex projects and develop systems?

Is there a functional area that appeals to you in particular—human resources, accounting, programs, research, development and fundraising, technology, media and communications, or volunteer management?

Also consider how other people describe you and your work. What strengths have past managers recognized in you? Did they point out areas needing improvement? How would colleagues or friends describe your personality and what do they see as your leading assets?

Knowing what you are good at will help you identify career paths that fit. It will also allow you to sell yourself honestly and persuasively during interviews and informational meetings.

And while an area of expertise is tremendously helpful, remember that strong communication skills are vital in almost all aspects of life, and certainly for most jobs. Your résumé and interviews should demonstrate that you are a competent communicator and care enough to proofread your materials, and that you have experience working on a range of professional documents. Writing samples sometimes are required in an application process, and it's a bonus to list them as "available on request" at the bottom of your résumé. You'll also want to show that you have strong verbal communication skills.

In addition, most organizations (especially small and midsized ones) value staff members who understand the role fundraising and development plays in fulfilling their mission. Even if you are not hired to write grants or plan special events, prospective employers find experience in these areas very attractive, and it's likely that any job you land will be expected to support fundraising efforts in some capacity. And it's true more generally that managers often expect their staff to multitask—you may be assigned one job, but you are expected to jump in and help in other areas as well and often.

As such, having a range of skills and experiences can be attractive. However, just as prospective nonprofit sector employers look for a clear commitment to their organizational mission, so too do they look for clearly defined skills and experiences. And, once again, it's important for you to be able to communicate in an interview and on a résumé what you bring to the table. You want to be able to say (and prove), "Here's what I am good at. Here's what I have done. Here's what I would bring to your organization."

Where and how do you want to live?

In addition to the mission of the organization and the nature of the work or job function, you'll also want to ask yourself questions about where and how you want to live. Questions about the type of community you want to call home, the part of the country where you would like to be based, and the size and culture of the organization you envision working for will help you narrow your job search. For example:

- Do you want to live in a small town or a large city, or someplace in between?

- Where in the country do you want to be based? What type of climate do you like?

- Is the type of work you're interested in specific to a certain region, population, or type of community?

- Do job opportunities exist in the region where you attended school? Do they exist in your hometown?

- Where do you have the strongest network of friends, family members, and colleagues whom you can tap to be part of your networking and job search effort?

- Do you have the financial resources to set yourself up for job hunting in a large city where living costs are significantly higher (but where more opportunities usually exist)?

- Would you prefer to work in a large organization that is likely to be based in a major metropolitan area or in a smaller organization that could be based anywhere?

- Do you prefer a more structured work environment or a more relaxed and intimate setting?

The questions listed above and others similar to them will help you determine some of the geographic parameters you can put on your job search. They also may help you choose between large versus small organizations.

It is much easier to find a job in the region where you are based during your job search. Being physically present in the town or city where you want to work literally helps you get your foot in the door with networking, informational meetings, and for interviews when vacancies pop up—all of which tend to be more successful if you conduct them in-person.

Furthermore, many organizations don't have recruitment budgets and are unwilling or unable to pay travel costs associated with interviewing out-of-town applicants. Many organizations also are suspicious of applicants applying from afar, believing that they have no guarantee that the applicant will relocate if offered the position, so they are reluctant to invest the time and resources in interviewing out-of-towners. Plus, organizations feeling strapped for resources often shudder at the thought of paying relocation costs.

All of this is to say that if you can decide where you would like to live—which, hopefully, is a place that has job opportunities in your field—your best bet is to get yourself there for your job search. However, this is not always possible. You may need to line up your first job while you are still completing coursework or you may have other financial or personal constraints on your ability to relocate before you have a job in hand. If this is the case, don't despair. It is absolutely possible to land a good job from afar; you'll just need to be even more diligent about the networking and outreach efforts that Chapter 5 discusses.

BRIGETTE ROUSON
Leader, Education Initiatives

Age: 50

Education: BA, communications; JD;
MA, communications and culture

Years at current organization: 5

Years in current position: 3

First job out of college: Journalist for a
political journal

First job in nonprofit sector: Writer for a
newspaper trade association

Alliance for Nonprofit Management

www.allianceonline.org

Mission: The Alliance for Nonprofit Management is the professional association of individuals and organizations devoted to improving nonprofit management and governance capacity to assist them in fulfilling their mission.

Operating budget: $1 million

Number of employees: 7.5

Number of employees who report to you: None

Q&A

Q: Informally, describe your career track.
A: I started out in journalism, completed law school, and became a lawyer. I then worked in public policy for a newspaper association and later as a grantmaker in the women's funding community. Finally, I moved into nonprofit management consulting—first with a nonprofit organization, then in independent practice, and now with the Alliance for Nonprofit Management. This last opportunity arose because of my volunteer leadership of a People of Color group and publications experience. Looking back, my path has been

informed by paying attention to cultural identity and social justice, primarily through forming and supporting collective activity.

Q: What do you know now that you wish you had known when you were first job hunting?
A: I wish I had known that there is much more to life than the structures, types of authority, and ways of operating that embody mainstream concepts of achievement or service. I now recognize that my own moral compass is more important—and empowering—than conformity.

Q: Describe a representative work day.
A: My work falls into four categories of activities: (1) develop and implement program activities; (2) write and edit publications; (3) draft funding proposals and reports; and (4) recruit members and respond to inquiries from the public. I start each day by drafting a work list. I then check and immediately respond to as many messages as possible. I will work on project items such as contracting agreements, planning events, and convening meetings. I review relevant publications to stay informed of our key issue areas. And I schedule phone appointments to talk with capacity builders in the nonprofit sector.

Q: What misconceptions do people have about your job? What's the reality?
A: The misconceptions are at two ends of a continuum—either that my role is focused on one piece of work, or that it includes nearly everything. The reality lies somewhere in between. I have a range of work responsibilities, which makes for real cross-fertilization.

Q: What do you love about your work?
A: I love connecting with people who care about the common good and are willing to take risks in investing their energies in social change. I love finding ways to uncover and influence power relations to strengthen the hand of people who have been excluded.

Q: What advice would you give to someone interested in a career similar to yours?
A: Develop a diverse wisdom circle (including mentors and colleagues), make regular contact (not necessarily frequent) to gain a deeper sense of their experiences, shared aspirations, lessons learned, and suggested approaches and connections.

Q: What resources might help someone interested in your field and job function?
A: I'd recommend Fieldstone Alliance books, Alliance for Nonprofit Management reports, African American news media such as *Diversity* and *YES!;* and books such as Ron Takaki's *A Different Mirror,* Samuel Yette's *The Choice,* and Howard Zinn's *Voices of a People's History.*[39] Explore the organizations CompassPoint (www.compasspoint.org), National Community Development Institute (www.ncdinet.org), National Network of Grantmakers (www.nng.org), Interaction Institute for Social Change (www.interactioninstitute.org), and Joint Center for Political and Economic Studies (www.jointcenter.org).

Q: What do you look for when hiring a new employee?
A: I look for warmth, resourcefulness, a team spirit, intellectual as well as practical skills, and commitment to social change.

estimated nonprofit salaries by experience and job level

The following data represent average salary ranges and are based on aggregated available studies and general experience. Individual opportunities may vary widely (possibly by $30,000 or more in either direction) and be influenced by organizational size, type of position, geography, and other factors. Readers should adjust for inflation and various other factors.

Years of experience after school	Entry-level jobs (coordinator, assistant, associate)	Mid-level jobs (manager, associate director, officer)	Senior-level jobs (director, VP, chief officer)
0–5 years	$25,000–40,000	$40,000–55,000	$55,000–70,000
5–10 years	$35,000–50,000	$50,000–75,000	$75,000–100,000
10+ years	$45,000–60,000	$60,000–85,000	$85,000–125,000

Note: These data are based on the assumption of an undergraduate college degree and on 2007 salary data for a midsized non-profit organization in a metropolitan region. Without a college degree, average salaries may be decreased. With a master's-level degree, numbers may increase by $10,000 to $20,000 or more. Doctoral-level degrees may increase averages by $20,000 to $40,000. Data provided by Commongood Careers.

the IRS Form 990

When the federal government grants an organization nonprofit status, the organization is required to file an IRS Form 990 annually. Churches, organizations with annual revenue below $25,000, and some other organizations have been exempt from this requirement. However, as of 2008, small tax-exempt organizations are required to file electronically Form 990-N (also known as the e-Postcard) with the IRS annually; but churches are still exempt.

Completed Form 990s are available online through GuideStar, at Foundation Center libraries, and on request from the organization itself. Properly completed forms can tell a reader a great deal about an organization, including its financial condition, how it raises and spends its money, and compensation of staff members. The Form 990 is a good resource for learning more about an organization, especially as you try to determine your earning potential.

COMPENSATION IN THE NONPROFIT SECTOR

Q&A with **James Weinberg**
Founder and CEO • Commongood Careers • www.cgcareers.org

Q: The nonprofit sector has a reputation for low salaries. What's the reality?

A: Nonprofit salaries may be more competitive than you realize, and they're getting more so all the time. Successful organizations understand that they compete with for-profit companies for talent, and pay close attention to market rates. You probably won't get rich by working in the sector, but with education, experience, and wise management of your personal finances, most nonprofit sector jobs will allow you to live comfortably.

Q: But how much money can I really expect to make?

A: Earning potential depends on many factors, such as your own level of education and experience, as well the type of job, organization budget, and geography. Always try to know two specific numbers: your minimum salary requirement and your estimated "market value."

Q: How can I determine my minimum salary requirement?

A: Remember, nonprofit jobs should be about service, not sacrifice. While you aren't pursuing a nonprofit sector career for the money, you need to cover your living costs. Itemize your monthly expenses for housing, food, transportation, child care, entertainment, incidentals, and student loans or other debt payments. A regular "set-aside" for savings should also be part of your financial plan, regardless of your age or the amount you can save each month. Tally up the numbers to determine your personal bottom line, be honest about that number, and never accept a salary that would leave you struggling to make ends meet.

Q: How can I figure out my market worth?

A: Completely separate from your minimum salary requirement—and possibly higher or lower—is an average salary value that a person can expect based on education, experience, geography, and desired type of work. Employers may offer much more or less than this number, but understanding the average is important data in evaluating a specific job offer. While it's hard to find information about nonprofit salaries, following are some resources to start with:

• **GuideStar** offers a searchable database of more than 1.5 million nonprofit organizations, including Form 990 tax return data that documents salary information for the highest-paid positions at specific organizations. GuideStar also offers a fee-based nonprofit compensation report and salary search tool. (www.guidestar.org)

(continued on page 178) 177

(continued from page 177)

- *The NonProfit Times* publishes an annual special report on salaries, with benchmarks primarily for senior-to-executive management positions across budget size and geographic location. (www.nptimes.com)

- *The Chronicle of Philanthropy* conducts regular surveys and publishes data on various aspects of salaries, especially at the executive level. (www.philanthropy.com/stats)

- **Professionals for NonProfits** publishes annual surveys of nonprofit sector salaries in New York City and Washington, DC. (www.pnp-inc.com/1.asp)

Q: How should I handle interview questions about my salary requirements?

A: Discussing salary can be frustratingly delicate. Both the prospective employer and employee hope the other party will disclose salary range first. Both hope that they are within negotiating range of the other. And neither one wants to be deceived at any stage in the process. In many cases, employers will say that compensation depends on experience and then require job seekers to first share their salary histories and expectations. Be honest. It is never advisable to stretch the truth about your salary requirements just to get yourself to a further round of interviewing. Before the first conversation occurs, learn as much as you can about average compensation for that type of role in the area. Informational interviews and Form 990s can provide valuable information.

Q: How much flexibility might a nonprofit organization have with its compensation?

A: In general, there is not a lot of room for salary negotiations with nonprofits because they operate on such tight budgets. Except at the most senior levels, a nonprofit making an offer might expect you to request 10 percent to 15 percent more than their initial offer, and they may or may not be able to meet you halfway. It's unlikely they can go much higher. Pushing a negotiation too hard can backfire. Instead, stress areas where you can be flexible and explore creative solutions. Remember to always consider the reasons behind the numbers. To the extent it is appropriate, share why you believe you deserve a certain salary. Try to understand the reasoning behind the organization's offer. Nonprofits often struggle with equity issues, meaning how much one job pays in comparison to what other employees currently earn. Finally, keep in mind that you may be able to negotiate more aspects of compensation than just your base salary.

Q: How is salary different from compensation?

A: Your salary is the base amount of money you are paid annually before taxes, and is just one piece of how employees are compensated. Financial compensation may also include bonuses and health care benefits. Although limited resources may constrain nonprofit salaries, many organizations try to compensate with other tangible benefits such as vacation and flexible scheduling. Nonprofits are also famous for their intangible benefits such as personal fulfillment from work, casual workplace cultures, and rewarding camaraderie with colleagues. Remember to consider these often-overlooked forms of compensation when evaluating a position.

Q: How common are bonuses at nonprofits?
A: Performance-based bonus systems are still relatively uncommon in the nonprofit world, although their use is gaining in popularity, especially in organizations with managers who have private sector experience. Bonuses are most commonly seen with fundraising and development positions. You can suggest using a bonus system for any type of position, however, as a way to bridge a salary gap and to lower the risk of an employer spending a lot of money and not seeing the returns they want.

Q: In addition to salary, what specific benefits might be negotiated?
A: Some benefits are often standardized for all employees at an organization. These might include medical, dental, and life insurance; retirement investments like 401(k)s, 403(b)s, or IRAs; and vacation and personal days. Be careful, because it is not always appropriate to negotiate these with an employer—but you may wish to inquire about flexibility in the percentage of your health care insurance that you are required to cover or the

rate of an employer's matching of your retirement savings. Flexible hours and additional vacation days are generally the easiest things for an employer to provide.

Q: Would it really hurt to settle for less money than I need, just for a year or two?
A: If the job is a great opportunity for you, you might consider settling for less than you want, but never settle for less than you need. Agreeing to a salary that will make you unhappy in the short term or long term can have real repercussions for your career. Remember that in the end, many aspects of compensation really come down to feeling respected and valued. If an organization cannot offer you what you need, it is better to walk away from the opportunity. However, if you consider other aspects of compensation and come to an agreement that works for both parties, you may end up in a rewarding and personally fulfilling position. ∎

Commongood Careers is one of the nation's leading nonprofit search firms. Previously, James Weinberg served as national development director at BELL (Building Educated Leaders for Life), and executive director of the Homeless Children's Education Fund. James has a master's degree in management and public policy, a bachelor's degree in psychology, and is a past Coro Fellow.

big versus small organizations

The differences between small and large organizations can be dramatic. On the small end of the spectrum, a nonprofit organization may have just a couple of paid (or just part-time) staff members, an annual budget in the mere thousands of dollars, and may depend on volunteers to execute the bulk of its work. On the large end of the size spectrum, an organization may have thousands of employees and hundreds of affiliates, a formal hierarchy, and a budget in the hundreds of millions of dollars. Working at an organization at one end of the spectrum or the other can be a very different experience. While generalizations are not true for all organizations, job seekers will want to consider a range of basic issues when deciding where to hunt for work.

Larger organizations tend to have

- larger budgets and higher salaries

- more clearly defined (and rigid) job descriptions

- a greater range of positions available

- more formal work environments and more traditional work cultures

- better and more comprehensive benefits

- more opportunities for advancement and a more clearly defined career ladder, but a greater likelihood that staff are "tracked" in a certain job function

- less access to senior leaders (both executives and board members) for entry-level and junior staff members

- a slower response to developments in the field

Larger organizations are more likely to be based in major metropolitan areas, so even if salaries are slightly higher, staff members' living costs may be higher as well.

Smaller organizations tend to have

- more opportunities for employees to develop a range of skills and experiences

- a greater emphasis on multitasking

- more contact among board members and senior and junior staff

- a greater "family" culture and team spirit among all staff members

- less financial security

- fewer benefits and lower salaries

- greater freedom in responding quickly to the news of the day

Smaller organizations can be based in any size community.

A number of issues that relate to organizational strength and culture do not depend on the size of an organization. **Other organizational issues** that you may want to consider include

- What funding sources does the organization utilize?

- How diverse is the organization? What is the climate for people of color, gay staff members, people of faith, and people from other diverse backgrounds?

- How collaborative is the organization? Does it partner with other groups and is it a member of any coalition efforts in its field?

- How connected is the organization within its community, to local colleges and universities, and to policy leaders?

- Does the organization (and its funders) depend on a single "star" executive director? Is she or he a founding executive director and, if so, what is the impact of this? Does the leader work collaboratively with the entire staff?

- Do senior staff members serve as mentors to younger staff? How does the organization demonstrate a commitment to cultivating new leaders and providing opportunities to junior staff?

- Who sits on the organization's board of directors? How diverse are they—vis-à-vis age, race, sexual orientation, and ethnic identity?

- What type of media coverage does the organization generate?

- What is the organization's policy regarding flexible work schedules, benefits, and leaves of absence?

- How high is the turnover rate?

When job hunting, job seekers—especially very junior-level ones—often feel that "beggars can't be choosers" and they must take whatever they are offered. But just as recruiting organizations are assessing your qualifications and whether you will fit within their organizational culture, so, too, should you be active and engaged in your assessment of your potential employer. Learn as much as you can about all aspects of the organizations where you interview. This will make you a much stronger interviewee and enable you to ask smart questions and thereby increase the likelihood that you will be offered a position. And it will also provide you with the information necessary to be able to choose an organization where you will be happy to work.

What do you want to do?

You've focused on the issues you care about, reflected on the type of work you have done and enjoyed, identified what you are good at, and considered the type of organization you might like to work for. Now it's time to try to establish how your beliefs, experiences, personal style, and goals come together to create sign posts that might direct you toward what you want to do professionally.

This personal reflection may be sufficient and the signs may be clear. You may know precisely the type of organization you want to work for and the specific position you will try to secure. If so, great. You can flip to the next chapter of the book to read about strategies for landing the job you know you want.

However, it is possible that you know you're committed to a career of public service, but you need more information to decide exactly what you want to do. If you're still in school, now is the time to tap every available campus and community resource to build your knowledge and secure new experiences, and, in doing so, explore a range of career possibilities. By the time you're job hunting in your final year, you will want to have a clear idea of the work you want to do.

Even if you're out of school, it's not too late to find new experiences that will help you test different career possibilities. The newest and the most seasoned professionals alike can benefit from volunteering, networking, professional development opportunities, continuing education coursework, and countless other opportunities providing insight into various fields and knowledge about various professional opportunities.

Exploring Different Career Possibilities

You now have a sense of who you are. But career preparation requires that you build knowledge about and gain experiences in the nonprofit sector in pursuits that range from the academic to the experiential. The opportunities for how you can spend your time are endless; what's vital is that you are intentional about your choices. What you learn and experience will inform your understanding of the different career possibilities in the nonprofit sector. Some knowledge- and experience-building opportunities that you can target to your nonprofit sector interests include

- educational tracks
- certificate programs
- advanced degrees
- volunteering
- interning
- other extracurricular activities
- mentoring
- professional development opportunities
- year-of-service programs

There are a limited number of hours in the day, so you can't pursue all of these. But career development and personal growth is an ongoing process. Some opportunities may be appropriate for you now, others might make sense to try down the road. Be strategic: identify the holes in your knowledge and the best avenues for filling them. Pack your days and structure your time so that when you look back on your year, you can say it was a rich and rewarding one, you spent your time wisely, and you know more about where you want to head than you did twelve months prior.

Educational tracks

A savvy student can parlay virtually any major into a nonprofit sector career. If you want to be an environmentalist, you can make a degree in English just about as useful as one in biology. In part, this is because your academic pursuits are only one piece of the puzzle, and you will sell yourself by all that you have studied and done. It's also because you will graduate from college with many more courses than just those in your major, and your electives might tell as important a story as your concentration. Your studies should help you gain expertise in a field but also develop solid critical-thinking skills; employers are apt to be more interested in how your brain works than in what your major was.

With that caveat in mind, it's still important to create a course of study appropriate to your professional goals, to use classes to become an expert in certain issues, and to learn more about various career opportunities. But how do you decide what educational track is right for you?

A few majors are explicitly career focused. Business, law, education, nursing, and social work are examples of degrees that lead to very specific professional paths. Some fields (e.g., nursing) may actually require a degree or appropriate certification for you to get the job. For others, the degree is helpful but not required. If you are absolutely certain of your career goals, these educational tracks will make sense for you.

However, the majority of majors do not prescribe a career. Most liberal arts degrees (anything from history to political science) can help form the intellectual foundation for a vibrant nonprofit sector career. If your course of study is rigorous, you will learn reasoning and communication skills that you can apply to almost any job. But some majors might be more suitable for either your functional interests (the type of job you might do) or your issue-area focus (the type of organization you want to work for). For example, an English or journalism major might suit someone interested in being a communications director one day. A public policy degree might appeal to someone seeking a researcher or program director position.

Nonprofit management is offered as a formal program at many colleges, either as a master's degree or a concentration. A nonprofit sector-focused education track may also be called leadership studies or philanthropy. This type of educational track may be of interest to students with a clear commitment to the nonprofit sector. Your electives or a second major might focus on the issue you are most interested in, for example, public health, ecology, or education.

How do you choose among the different educational options? Research. Spend careful, quiet time with your college bulletin and highlight the classes that sound appealing to you. Talk to your academic advisor, junior and senior students, faculty members, career counselors, deans, and anyone else you can think of for advice. If you know you want to attend graduate school shortly after graduating, talk with administrators, students, and faculty members at the graduate schools of interest to you, and ask those individuals what they look for in applicants. Schedule informational meetings with professionals sooner rather than later. (See "What Is an Informational Meeting?" page 232 for details.) Ask them what they studied and what they might have done differently

academically if they had the chance. Read syllabi that are posted online and sit in on classes. Follow your heart and create a course of study that feels right to you. And remind yourself that while your coursework is important, everything you do outside the classroom is vital as well.

Certificate programs

Nonprofit sector-focused certificate programs cover a range of subjects and offer an opportunity to build your knowledge, develop your leadership potential, and fine-tune specific skills relevant to public service careers. Some take a weekend to complete, others require a multiyear commitment. These tangible credentials help communicate to a potential employer your commitment to and preparation for a nonprofit sector career.

Some certificate programs are delivered through a college or university and available to students currently enrolled in school. Others are sponsored by a local nonprofit organization and are targeted to professionals currently working in the sector. Online certificate programs are also available. Some programs focus broadly on management and leadership development, others concentrate on specific skills such as fundraising.

American Humanics (AH) offers the only national undergraduate certificate program that prepares students for nonprofit management and leadership responsibilities. (See page 281 for more information on AH.) Available on nearly seventy-five campuses, the AH program is founded in experiential education. Students are required to participate in internships of at least three hundred hours, be active in leadership and service-learning opportunities, complete rigorous coursework related to core competencies, and attend the three-day AH Management/Leadership Institute learning symposium. In addition, students complete a major field of study as required by the university or college to obtain a baccalaureate degree. The student's major provides a concentrated area of study.

A campus that doesn't offer the American Humanics program may have its own certificate program or nonprofit sector concentration. If not, you certainly can create your own. Talk to your advisors, faculty members, and internship coordinators to develop your own certificate tailored to your specific interests.

Advanced degrees

More than one hundred universities offer a graduate degree in nonprofit management, public policy, or public administration. Relevant doctoral programs tend to be housed in schools of public administration or public policy (or public affairs), social work, or business administration. In addition, law degrees, master's in business administration (MBA), and master's in social work (MSW) degrees are valued and sometimes required by certain nonprofit organizations, depending on the job you want.

Students tend to find they make better selection and use of graduate programs if they have had some professional experience before attending. Consider taking a year or two off between your undergraduate and graduate studies. (See "Why Wait?" pages 188–189.) The skills and experiences you acquire may help you better leverage and apply more fully the opportunities a graduate program offers.

WENDY TERRA
Clinical Social Worker III

Age: 39

Education: BS, business economics; MSW; postgraduate certificate in treatment of interpersonal violence and trauma

Years at current organization: 10

Years in current position: 10, I transferred programs within the agency, but primarily my job function remains the same

First job out of college: Custody and securities operations clerk for a trust company

First job in nonprofit sector: Social worker I, The Children's Village

The Children's Village

www.childrensvillage.org

Mission: The Children's Village works in partnership with families to help society's most vulnerable children so that they become educationally proficient, economically productive, and socially responsible members of their communities.

Operating budget: $52 million

Number of employees: 805

Number of employees who report to you: None

Q & A

Q: Informally, describe your career track.
A: I worked as a custody and securities operations clerk in the financial field for approximately two years before deciding I needed a career change. I moved abroad to work as an au pair for eighteen months, and decided I wanted to work with children. I chose social work because I felt it would provide more opportunities. When I returned to the United States, I pursued my MSW degree. When I graduated, I began my first position at The Children's Village.

Q: What do you know now that you wish you had known when you were first job hunting?

A: Prior to graduate school, I was not aware that facilities such as residential treatment centers existed; I was completely unfamiliar with the child welfare system. Had I been aware of such facilities, I would have volunteered at one to become familiar with the field and gain some relevant experience.

Q: Describe a representative work day.

A: I am a primary therapist for boys ages 10 to 15 in a residential treatment facility. I provide individual, family, and group therapy as well as crisis intervention. I perform fieldwork, including home visits and court appearances. My calendar often doesn't begin to describe what my day will actually look like. I usually begin my day with paperwork and phone calls, and getting briefed from the staff about residents. Then off to meetings—treatment conferences, team meetings, discharge planning meetings, school meetings. I reserve late afternoons for family sessions or individual therapy sessions. In between all of these scheduled appointments, there is often a child in crisis, who becomes the priority.

Q: What misconceptions do people have about your job? What's the reality?

A: A common misconception I confront is that the kids and families we serve are "bad," "criminal," or "crazy," and that the work is very dangerous. The reality is that I am often working with kids who have great potential. I often am amazed when I first meet a resident; the referral material might describe him in predominately negative terms, and then I meet him and the positive aspects just jump out—he's likeable, articulate, or has a great sense of humor, for example.

Q: What do you love about your work?

A: I love the direct contact I have with the kids and families, and making a connection with them. It's a privilege to bear witness to their strength, resiliency, and accomplishments. I love the possibility (and hope) of an opportunity to make a positive impact—even a small one—in their lives.

Q: What advice would you give to someone interested in a career similar to yours?

You need real passion for any nonprofit sector work. But you also need to understand the reality and challenges of the situations you'll face and the limited resources you'll struggle with at times. Social workers are merely transient in the lives of the people we help, and we cannot control the outcome of our interventions. However, with every encounter we are granted an opportunity to make a difference. You may never bear witness to the impact you made in someone's life, but when these rewards present themselves, you will experience a profound sense of achievement.

Q: What resources might help someone interested in your field and job function?

A: Some helpful organizations and websites include: Council of Family and Child Caring Agencies (www.cofcca.org), Child Welfare League of America (www.cwla.org), and, for the field of social work, National Association of Social Workers (www.naswdc.org).

Q: What do you look for when hiring a new employee?

A: Someone who is grounded, able to think on their feet and handle stress, flexible, proactive, and able to separate professional from personal issues.

WHY WAIT?
SOME OF THE BENEFITS OF TAKING TIME OFF BEFORE GRADUATE SCHOOL

by **Dr. Robert F. Ashcraft**

Director • Lodestar Center for Philanthropy and Nonprofit Innovation • Arizona State University
and Executive Director of ASU's American Humanics program • http://nonprofit.asu.edu

Are you running, not walking, to graduate school? Some undergraduate students feel they have such clarity on their education and career goals that they're convinced it makes sense to head straight on to their advanced degree upon graduation. Others don't know what they want and think graduate school will buy time before they have to make a decision. If you're in either camp—superconfident or utterly flummoxed about your career goals—at least consider taking a break from academia. In the end, such a postponement may not cost you time, but actually help you make better, and more efficient, use of the next few years of your life.

Here are some of the benefits you might receive from taking a year or two off before graduate school to work, volunteer, or travel.

- *You can roll up your sleeves and apply your learning to the real world.* You may have volunteered or worked in the past, but this may be your first chance to live and work in the world—and test out your ideas—without the backdrop of school.

- *You can learn more about the field you want to study.* The practical experience you gain by working a couple of years before graduate school will help you make smart decisions about what to study later on. It will also provide a rich background to help you apply and test the ideas you learn in the classroom. This is especially important because many graduate degree programs employ the case study method and assume students will engage in discussions and analysis informed by considerable real-world experiences.

- *You can rest and recharge in a new setting.* If you're a go-getter, your time off is likely to be anything but that. However, you've spent a long time in school, which presents a unique set of stress and pressure. Wouldn't your heart and mind say thank you to a change of pace for a period of time? In ten or twenty years, won't you cherish a year of memories where you did good work and just had fun?

- *You can make and save money.* You may be graduating with student debt, and looking ahead to incurring more debt to finance graduate school. Working for a few years can help you make a dent in your outstanding loans and save so that you don't have to work as much in school.

(AmeriCorps opportunities may include education awards that can be applied to future education or student loans. See "Year-of-service programs," page 212 for details.)

- *You can gain maturity and wisdom.* Putting a year or two between you and graduate school will only make you more mature, thoughtful, and experienced before your next academic chapter—all traits that will help you make good use of your studies.

- *You might avoid making a mistake.* Too many students seriously ask themselves, "What am I doing here?" in the midst of graduate studies. Walking, rather than running, to graduate school will give you time to reflect on and test the decision, talk to more people, and make sure it is the right path for you.

- *You'll have a stronger application to a better graduate school.* With more experience, you'll be able to create a stronger application, gather more recommendations, and spend more time studying for any required entrance exams. The result is that you'll increase your chance of getting into the most competitive and suitable programs. Higher qualifying exam scores also will help with financial aid applications.

- *You can focus on skills.* You can devote yourself full-time to developing a very specific (and potentially marketable) skill that you can use for the rest of your life. An obvious example is living and working in a country to become fluent in a second language.

- *You can build a network.* You can make contacts to individuals and organizations who might help you when you get out of graduate school.

There are many reasons that going directly to graduate school might be the right choice for you. However, more often than not, students err on the side of moving too quickly to more studies. Carefully weigh the opportunities involved with taking time off before you commit to a timeline. ∎

Robert F. Ashcraft, PhD, is a former volunteer senior policy adviser to the American Red Cross National Office of Volunteers. He also served the organization in various salaried staff roles in three chapters as director of youth and community volunteer services, manager of human resources, and executive director. Robert earned a BA in broadcast communications, an MA Ed. in human relations and behavior, and a PhD in educational leadership and policy studies.

TOP 10 TIPS
FOR PLANNING YOUR COURSE OF STUDY AND ACTION

by **Kala M. Stroup**

President • American Humanics • www.humanics.org

There are almost as many ways to prepare for a career in the nonprofit sector as there are types of careers in the sector. If you are still a student, your campus and its community offer abundant resources from which you can develop knowledge, skills, and experiences that, combined with your personal passion, will make you a very attractive candidate when you enter the job market. The trick, however, is to identify and take advantage of the opportunities that are right for you and your professional goals.

American Humanics is a nonprofit organization that works to educate, prepare, and certify professionals to lead and strengthen nonprofit organizations (you can read more about American Humanics on pages 281–282). While American Humanics focuses on undergraduate students, our philosophy applies to students at any level of education—from high school all the way up to doctoral candidates working on a PhD—who are interested in working for a nonprofit organization.

Whenever I talk with students who are eager to know how to develop the best course of study to achieve their professional goals, I emphasize "the other stuff" beyond their coursework. Make no mistake: your classes are vital. Selecting and excelling in those that are appropriate for your area of interest is a key part of your education. But just as important, you must develop a rich body of experiences that enables you to apply your education to the real world.

These experiences—combined with your coursework—will allow you to fine-tune the skills and competencies necessary to help advance the mission of the organization where you will work one day. Volunteering, internships, and other extracurricular activities are just as important as doing well in rigorous, carefully selected classes.

Here's my Top 10 list of recommendations for a course of study (and course of action) to prepare for a meaningful career in the nonprofit sector.

1. Develop your expertise. Think about the issue areas that you are passionate about and enroll (and excel) in classes that will build your knowledge in those fields. For example, if you care about human rights, you might find yourself taking political science classes. If it's the environment, you might be camped out in the ecology department. A desire to teach could lead you to an education or sociology concentration. A love of international development might send you down a public policy track. Any of a number of majors is likely to support your professional interest. The key is to carefully plan your course of study and actively and thoughtfully attain the knowledge you want. And be sure to always "go the extra mile"; for example, make a habit of reading appropriate publications that will allow you to stay up to date on developments in your field, even if this reading isn't assigned in your classes.

But remember: A major is an academic field of inquiry—it does not determine what career you must pursue. Of course you'll want to be thoughtful about your academic focus and have it reinforce the professional direction you think you want to take. But prospective employers are as interested in what you have done as in what you have studied. Just think about your résumé as a good example: only a small section of it is devoted to your degree; the rest is about your volunteer, internship, and work experiences.

2. Build your competencies. Nonprofit sector practitioners and scholars have identified a set of competencies that are critical for successful employees of the sector. Some competencies are related to personal and professional development,

others focus on very specific skills. American Humanics incorporates these competencies into the curricula we offer on college campuses with our certificate program, but everyone interested in becoming a nonprofit sector leader would benefit from having these skills and knowledge:

- fundraising principles and practices
- the historical and philosophical foundations of the nonprofit sector and how it differs from the for-profit sector
- youth and adult development
- nonprofit sector accounting and financial processes
- human resource development and management, including volunteer management
- nonprofit sector marketing and event planning
- community building
- new technologies related to reaching others
- ethics
- the formation of public policy

Coursework is only one avenue for achieving these and other necessary competencies. A wide array of on-the-job and student association activities can assist students in developing

(continued on page 192) 191

(continued from page 191)

and strengthening their knowledge, skills, leadership abilities, and understanding of the nonprofit sector. Your job is to learn about the skills and knowledge you need, secure them, and then communicate to a prospective employer that you have them.

3. Get involved. Build a well-rounded program that includes great courses in your major and interesting electives, as well as meaningful extracurricular activities. As soon as possible, start researching and reaching out to organizations where you might like to volunteer, intern, or work while in school. Think strategically about how you will spend your time and how the different facets of your life will complement one another so that you are preparing yourself for the career—and life—you want. Take advantage of your own membership in the YMCA, 4-H, Junior Achievement, Scouts, or your church youth group, and leverage those experiences to help you achieve your professional goals.

4. Get advice. The single greatest resource your campus offers is its human resources. As you explore what classes to take, what major to choose, what clubs and projects to participate in, and what internships might be helpful, reach out to those around you for advice and contacts. Academic advisors, faculty members, deans, career services professionals, service learning program directors, and so many others offer expertise in certain fields and are eager to help you navigate the academic and extracurricular offerings your campus has. And don't forget about upper class students! Their firsthand experiences are invaluable.

5. Get more advice. That is, cast as wide a net as possible. Even if you feel you've reached out to an impressive list of contacts in your area of study and field of professional interest, push yourself to expand your net. Personal contacts are vital in finding a job. Think beyond your campus. Reach out to professionals in your community, volunteers you've worked with, family members, and friends-of-friends. Engage them in what you are studying and the work you are doing. Stay in touch with them through periodic e-mails, telephone calls, and in-person coffee breaks so that they are part of your personal community and support network when you begin job seeking. The best advice often comes from someone who is in the position you would like to hold.

6. Get an internship. Professions such as medicine, social work, dentistry, accounting, and teaching have a long history of faculty members and practitioners working collaboratively to connect students to internships, clinical work, residencies, student teaching assignments, and other practical experiences that prepare them for the profession. If the field you're interested in doesn't make internships as readily available, you still must seek them out. Applying your coursework and living the daily routine of the professional through a well-managed internship will allow you to learn concrete skills that are vital to a complete educational experience. (See "Interning," pages 201–205 for more information.)

7. *If possible, take advantage of the American Humanics (AH) program.* The American Humanics certificate in nonprofit management and leadership is a program founded in experiential education and offered at nearly seventy-five colleges and universities nationwide. If it's available on your campus, enroll. (See pages 281–282 for more information on AH.) If the American Humanics program doesn't exist on your campus, explore what other nonprofit sector-related tracks might already be in place. Otherwise, work with an academic advisor to build your own program that delivers the knowledge and experiences you need.

8. *Participate in a year-of-service (or summer-of-service) program.* It's vital that you pursue meaningful internship opportunities in the nonprofit sector, and you can arrange these on your own while you're in school or immediately after. However, a number of excellent, more formal channels also exist for year-long service experiences, if you're interested in taking time off either during or after your academic studies. Many of the programs are funded through the AmeriCorps program of the U.S. government's Corporation for National and Community Service. Spend some time on the AmeriCorps website (www.americorps.org) to learn more about the various programs. Another large selection of service programs is organized through faith-based organizations. You can identify these and other programs with the help of your career center staff, the library, or with online research.

9. *Communicate effectively.* It won't matter what skills, competencies, and experiences you've acquired if you can't communicate these to a potential employer. Spend time on all of your communication tools to make them as professional—and persuasive—as possible and to ensure that they reflect all of your strengths. Ask friends and colleagues to review your cover letters and résumé; incorporate the feedback they give you. A reader shouldn't find one typo in any of your materials—employers look for a reason to put a résumé on the "discard" stack, and sloppy writing will get you there quickly. Think about how you want to talk about your experiences and describe your passion for an organization's mission and practice interviewing. Follow up promptly with thank-you letters and immediately pursue any leads you get.

(continued on page 194)

(continued from page 193)

10. Have fun! There's a lot to the words of writer Maya Angelou: "You can only become truly accomplished at something you love. Don't make money your goal. Instead, pursue the things you love doing, and then do them so well that people can't take their eyes off you." Take classes, create internships, and find jobs that you love. Pursue them with such joy and dedication that those around you can't take their eyes off you. When you collapse into bed at the end of the day, feel happy and proud of all that you accomplished. If you're unhappy, make the job better or switch jobs. Be good at what you do, and love doing it. ∎

Kala M. Stroup has served as president of American Humanics since 2002. Previously, Kala spent more than four decades as a leader in higher education, holding such positions as Missouri commissioner of higher education, president of Southeast Missouri State University and of Murray State University (Kentucky), and vice president for academic affairs at Emporia State University (Kansas). Kala holds a liberal arts BA degree, an MS in educational psychology, and a PhD in speech communication.

Volunteering

If you are interested in a career in the nonprofit sector, it's likely that you already have volunteered extensively. Your commitment to public service is not just a professional calling, it probably comes from an even deeper place inside of you. Before you were legally allowed to work, you may have been donating your time to a nonprofit organization in your community. If so, know that your demonstrated belief in giving back to your community is a critical piece of who you are and that it is information you will want to communicate on your résumé and to a potential employer. Volunteering is an excellent way to prepare for a career in the nonprofit sector; the work you have already done will make a difference.

But regardless of whether or not you have volunteered extensively in your past, now that you are pursuing a nonprofit sector career it's time to be deliberate about your volunteer activities. Volunteering at organizations of interest to you and that work on issues you care about is a must. Volunteering allows you to develop skills and knowledge. It can help you develop your leadership ability. It offers an insider's look at the range of jobs and career paths within an organization. It connects you to staff members and board members who will become part of your network and can help you find employment. And it demonstrates passion for a mission that potential employers want to see.

The range of volunteer opportunities is endless, even in the smallest community. Your top priority should be to find an organization you believe in and one that will make good use of your time and talents. You'll also want to consider the nature of the work you want to do. Do you want to deliver services directly to clients (e.g., work in a soup kitchen) or would you rather be part of the administrative and management processes of the organization (e.g., help develop a website)? Reflect on your professional goals and where your advisors have suggested you might have holes in your résumé. What type of volunteer opportunity will allow you to contribute in a meaningful way to the organization, and also help you gain the experience you need?

Once you have some idea about the type of organization you'd like to volunteer for, and the type of work you would like to do, be honest about your time commitment and other obligations. Are you willing to guarantee regular weekly hours to the organization, or do you want to show up for work on weekends, or only when you have time?

Finding a meaningful volunteer opportunity takes time. It's not enough simply to show up at the doorstep of an organization you've identified as doing good work. You need to ensure that the organization knows how to manage volunteers and will make good use of your time and talents.

It should be a win-win situation where the organization and its clients benefit from your energy, and where you gain experiences and knowledge about that organization and the field.

As you think about places to volunteer, you might first consider organizations and programs that have been meaningful in your own life. Did you take classes or take advantage of services sponsored by a local nonprofit organization? Was the experience a positive one? These groups might be places that you believe in and would feel good about giving back to with your time. Other places to consider include

- nonprofit organizations working in your field of interest
- service clubs on campus
- alumni associations
- schools
- local affiliates of national clubs
- programs connected to your place of worship

Use the networking strategies described in the "Effective Networking" section, pages 226–233, to talk with people about the volunteer work they enjoy. Identify a handful of possible opportunities and then research them to make sure you'll feel good about the time you plan to devote to the organization.

MELISSA SCHULZ
Volunteer Services Administrator

Age: 37

Education: BA, communications

Years at current organization: 5

Years in current position: 5

First job out of college: Current position

First job in nonprofit sector: Visitor services at a children's museum

Family Violence Prevention Services, Inc.

www.fvps.org

Mission: Family Violence Prevention Services works to break the cycle of family violence and to strengthen families by providing the necessary tools for self-sufficiency through the delivery of emergency shelter, transitional housing, education, effective parenting, and early intervention with children and youth.

Operating budget: $4 million

Number of employees: 77

Number of employees who report to you: More than 60 individual volunteers and several community groups

Q&A

Q: Informally, describe your career track.
A: I was working at the Alamo and going to school, got married, and then worked with my husband in insurance claims while I finished my last two years of college. During college I participated in the American Humanics (www.humanics.org) certification program that prepares students for nonprofit sector careers. As part of the program, you must complete an internship requirement; I worked in the community relations department of the San Antonio Children's Shelter, as well as

the development department of the San Antonio Symphony. These experiences helped me secure my current position upon graduation.

Q: What do you know now that you wish you had known when you were first job hunting?
A: Volunteer work or community service makes any résumé shine brighter. You need to identify opportunities that will make you—and your application—stand out to a prospective employer.

Q: Describe a representative work day.
A: I recruit, screen, train, and place new volunteers. I give public speeches, presentations, and tours, and I staff United Way and community health fairs to recruit more volunteers. I work with the president/CEO and board members on annual fundraisers and help coordinate other community-sponsored events and media relations. I attend professional business meetings, church meetings, and community group meetings to speak about the work of the organization or accept donations. A significant part of my day is spent answering inquiries on everything from volunteering to donations or requests for guest speakers. In between this, I schedule screening interviews with individuals and community groups, prepare marketing materials for volunteers to distribute, and plan events for the agency. About 40 percent of my time is spent out of the office at fairs, working alongside a volunteer group, making presentations, or attending meetings.

Q: What misconceptions do people have about your job? What's the reality?
A: A basic misconception is that Volunteer Services Administration (VSA) is a hard job with low pay. The reality is that VSA is challenging and rewarding but not "hard" *if* you are organized, pay attention to detail, are flexible, and are able to stay on top of things. The pay is midrange depending on the region of the country.

Q: What do you love about your work?
A: I love the agency's mission, involvement in my community, and working with people who value the gift of themselves. Volunteers are precious people.

Q: What advice would you give to someone interested in a career similar to yours?
A: My advice is "Go for it!" Working with volunteers is a tremendously rewarding experience. However, you have to be willing to manage people and conduct administrative work as well. Take extra classes in administration, management, or human resources.

Q: What resources might help someone interested in your field and job function?
A: For information on domestic violence work in Texas, visit the websites of Family Violence Prevention Services (www.fvps.org) and the Texas Council on Family Violence (www.tcfv.org); for national information see the National Coalition Against Domestic Violence (www.ncadv.org). For information on managing volunteers, start with ServiceLeader.org (www.serviceleader.org) and Energize, Inc. (www.energizeinc.com).

Q: What do you look for when hiring a new employee?
A: I look for a commitment to our organization's mission, flexibility, good communication skills, and no hidden agendas.

SERVING ON A BOARD OF DIRECTORS

Q&A with **Susan Meier**

Vice President of Consulting and Training • BoardSource • www.boardsource.org

All nonprofit organizations are governed by a board of directors. Board members, in partnership with the chief executive, help lead an organization and provide stewardship of its resources. Serving on a nonprofit board of directors is a volunteer opportunity that can be highly rewarding. However, board service is a serious personal commitment, not just an honorary position within an organization.

Q: What is a board of directors?
A: A board of directors is the legal and responsible entity for the organization. The board has a fiduciary duty to govern the nonprofit. The board as a body is accountable to the organization's beneficiaries, funders, community, and the general public. Board members are usually unpaid volunteers who are donating their time and talent to advance the mission of an organization.

Q: What's the difference between a non-profit and for-profit board of directors?
A: In principle, both nonprofit and for-profit boards have the same governance purpose, just the focus varies. For-profit corporate boards are accountable to shareholders. Nonprofit boards are accountable to the organization's constituents and the general public. The for-profit mission, as the term already indicates, is to make a profit for the owners. Naturally, the bottom line also matters to nonprofit boards but the main concern is to remain true to the organization's primary purpose—its mission—whether that is helping those who suffer or beautifying the neighborhood. For-profit board members are usually compensated for their work, whereas nonprofit board members generally serve as volunteers and are not supposed to personally benefit from their affiliation with the organization.

Q: What's the role of a nonprofit board?
A: Nonprofit boards have three primary roles: they guard the mission and set the direction for the organization. They ensure resources are adequate to enable the organization to carry out its programs and services. And they provide oversight over the affairs of the organization. To achieve all this, they delegate the daily operations to a chief executive and support his or her work without micromanagement.

Individual board members attend board meetings, work on committees, and use their particular expertise and experience to help the board make sound decisions. When appropriate, they serve as special advisors to the chief executive in the fields of communications, fundraising, program development, and so forth.

Q: How much time is required to be a board member?

A: It depends. The time required of an individual board member to participate in board work depends on how many board members share the workload, how the board is structured (committee assignments, meeting frequency), what specific expectations are placed on board members (fundraising, leadership duties), and what issues and events need the board's attention at any given moment. Naturally, time commitment also depends on the investment the board member is willing to make.

Q: Are nonprofit organizations really interested in recruiting young professionals to their boards?

A: Smart, forward-thinking, strategic organizations recognize the value of having a diverse board of directors with members who have a range of backgrounds, areas of expertise, and perspectives. Unfortunately, not all organizations have this commitment. You'll want to investigate the organizations you're interested in, and try to determine whether they are open to having young voices on their boards. Organizations serving youth and populations of different ethnicities tend to demonstrate a greater commitment to diversifying their boards, and might be the best places to start.

Q: How do board members benefit from the volunteer experience?

A: Serving on a board allows you to contribute time and talent to an organization and to participate firsthand in giving back to your community. As a board member you have an opportunity to gain leadership experience. Professionally, the service can be a great networking and knowledge-building experience. And, finally, the experience allows you to enjoy the company of interesting individuals while working together to achieve a mission that is important to you.

(continued on page 200)

(continued from page 199)

Q: What type of organization has the best boards of directors?

A: Committed leadership makes a successful organization. Strong, high-functioning, and efficient organizations—whatever their mission, scope, or size is—tend to have motivated boards that work in close partnership with the chief executive. The board and the chief executive in these organizations share the organization's vision, know the boundaries of their own roles, and work diligently to achieve the mutually agreed-upon goals.

Q: What type of person makes a good board member?

A: A good board member is passionate and informed about the mission of the organization, dependable when it comes to meetings and commitment of time, willing to make a personal contribution and to raise monies, well-connected within the community, and a professional team player.

Q: How can someone find a board position?

A: First of all, remember that this search is a two-way street. You must feel comfortable about the organization and its board and this board should not accept you just because you express an interest in joining and there is a vacancy. You want the board to ensure that your talents are needed and will be used. Start by identifying organizations where you would like to serve, do your due diligence research, and meet with the chief executive and board members to talk about your interest and the skills you can offer. Ask many questions and expect the organizational representatives to grill you too. At the end, if there is a meeting of the minds, join the board and become the exemplary board member you intended to be. ∎

Prior to joining BoardSource in 2004, Susan Meier served as vice president, chapter services, for Prevent Child Abuse America, where she developed a state chapter credentialing program for the organization's forty-state chapter network. Susan is a current board member of The LemonAid Fund.

Interning

A well-managed, focused, challenging, professional internship is one of the best ways to prepare for a nonprofit sector career. Like meaningful volunteer work, interning allows you to develop skills and real-world work experiences, network with people in the field, and learn more about an organization and its issues. In addition, you might be able to receive college credits and even a stipend for your internship. Plus, many organizations say that interns are a prime source for building their pipeline of talent. Your internship potentially could turn into a full-time position, should you prove yourself and be interested.

Internships are short-term work experiences that emphasize hands-on learning. They provide context for what you have learned as a student, and allow you to make practical sense of ideas that may previously have only been theoretical. An internship allows you to apply your academic work to a professional setting and in doing so explore certain career opportunities. Ideally, an internship results in a win-win situation for the intern and host organization. The nonprofit organization provides a learning laboratory, management, resources, and performance evaluation for the intern. In return, the intern contributes to the real work of the organization and thereby helps advance its mission.

A nonprofit sector internship allows you to

- explore your career interests while working in a professional nonprofit sector setting

- build knowledge about the nonprofit sector and its interaction with the public through the direct services it provides and other work it performs

- understand the structure and functions of a given nonprofit organization, including its mission, programs, policies, financial base and administrative structure, and method of service delivery

- examine the short- and long-term goals of the organization

- acquire specific skills and experiences that will enhance your value to a potential nonprofit sector employer

- study leadership models that will prepare you for a career in the sector

- transfer classroom learning into practice

An internship may take place concurrently with your academic term, during a summer break, or a semester or year off.

The most successful internship experiences occur when both the student and host organization are strong and highly functioning. Successful interns are goal oriented, have a strong work ethic, are professional, and are eager to learn and advance. Successful host organizations place a high value on interns and dedicate the necessary resources and

the dilemma of the unpaid internship

While many nonprofit organizations pay competitive stipends to their interns, the sector is famous for its unpaid positions. If you're a college student looking to intern, it's likely that you would like to—or must—receive a stipend to help cover your tuition or offset your living expenses. If you can't get paid with a nonprofit sector internship, you may be tempted to find a position with a for-profit company. If this is the case, you miss out on a potentially valuable learning experience and the launch of a meaningful nonprofit sector career, and the nonprofit sector loses the prospect of a talented and passionate addition to its workforce.

In truth, you deserve to be paid for the work you perform, and nonprofit organizations need to be encouraged to raise the necessary resources to compensate their student workers. So how should you handle the dilemma of an unpaid internship?

If it is not possible for you to accept an unpaid internship, then put extra energy into identifying opportunities that are paid. You might have to cast a wider net and be more tenacious in your networking. If, however, you're somewhat flexible on compensation, pursue both unpaid and paid leads, and ask questions about compensation as early as appropriate. You might consider accepting an unpaid position but propose that you write into your job description some fundraising work to raise your own stipend, as well as one for the next intern the organization hires. The organization might find this an attractive and creative proposition, and it would be a great learning opportunity for you.

You also should explore grants available through your campus or in your community that you can apply for independently. Use your network of advisors to learn about programs, foundations, and individual benefactors who might underwrite your internship. And finally, don't let the organization off the hook. If you convince a senior manager that you are going to add value to the organization, you might find that they can carve out a reasonable stipend from their budget.

supervisory time to managing them. These organizations set clearly defined and realistic goals for interns. As a student seeking an internship, you'll want to position yourself as a great potential asset to an organization, but you'll also want to ensure that the organization will be an asset to you and your career. Be discriminating in your search.

Identifying prospective organizations

Landing a great internship involves many of the same components of the hunt for a full-time job, so be sure to read Chapter 5 as you embark on your internship search. Internship-hunting requires planning and time. You need to know what you want and be deliberate in your efforts to get it. To begin, consider these questions:

- What are your interests?

- What are your skills?

- Is there a particular ethnic group, community, or social problem that you want to work for?

- What do you want to gain by interning?

- Where do you want to be based? What time period and hours are you available to work?

- Who do you know who can help you secure a meaningful internship?

Zero in on the type of organization you want to work for and the nature of the work you would like to do. Be clear in what you can offer and what you require from the experience. Start your search early and undertake thorough research on the organizations you will pursue. Tap all resources you can think of to help you in your search, including

- campus career development center, service learning programs, and internship centers

- professors

- classmates

- personal contacts and past professional contacts

- the Internet

- traditional print services, such as newspapers and internship guides

- school alumni network

As you work your network of contacts, remember that you are trying to find not just an appropriate internship, but the best possible internship. This means that you want a strong and healthy host organization. Ask questions about the resources and management of potential organizations, and determine if they have a good track record in working with interns.

Your research should help you narrow down potential organizations to a "Top 5" or "Top 10" list of targets. Your list of top prospects should include organizations that have a history of hiring interns or a solid commitment to building a new internship program. They should be organizations working in your field of interest and with a geographical base that is suitable for you. You'll want to gather more extensive background information on these target organizations, such as

- mission and philosophy

- reputation in the community

- services provided to constituents

- leadership and agency background

- internship opportunities and application process

- internship roles, training methods, and compensation and benefits

- performance review process and expectations

If your research raises any red flags, don't ignore them. If upon further investigation they prove to be legitimate concerns, drop the organization from your list. Your time is too precious to waste on an organization that won't make good use of it.

Securing and starting the internship

Once you've identified organizations that could host an intern or specific internship spots to apply for, it's time to start your outreach efforts. The strategies to use are the same as in applying for a full-time staff position (see Chapter 5). You need to

- identify the best point of contact

- submit a persuasive cover letter, flawless résumé, and any other collateral materials requested

- follow up with telephone calls or e-mails as appropriate

- land an interview, and sell yourself in it as well as ask targeted questions

- write a follow-up letter following the interview

- leverage your network to make calls supporting your application

- try to get any offer in writing, and respond to it in writing as well

Many nonprofit sector managers feel overextended, having to juggle multiple responsibilities. Often they are working on fascinating projects and are desperate for additional help, but they don't know how to delegate tasks and are inexperienced managers. One way to protect yourself and help get an internship off on the right foot is to establish clearly defined expectations and responsibilities from the start. An offer in writing accompanied by a formal job description helps do this.

If the organization hasn't extended an offer in writing, put your acceptance in a letter. Detail as many of the terms of the agreement as you can, including naming your supervisor and specifying work hours and any vacation days, compensation, evaluation process, and an overview of your specific duties, as well as any unusual requirements. You also may want to identify what you hope to receive at the conclusion of your internship (e.g., a written evaluation, a completed school form, and a letter of recommendation should they be pleased with your performance).

If the organization is unable to provide a job description, offer to write one for them, either in advance of your start date or as part of your initial responsibilities. Talk with the individual you'll be reporting to about your responsibilities, and ask for permission to communicate with other members of the department. Learn about the organization's goals for the time period you'll be on site and how you might help. Craft a job description that reflects the organization's needs and your own objectives for the internship. Remember that most people in a nonprofit organization wear many hats, and you may be called on to perform other duties beyond those in your job description. Make sure the description sets rigorous but realistic goals for your tenure.

On the job—making good use of your internship

The active job seeker will find the best internships and full-time positions. Likewise, the most active and engaged worker will make the best use of the work experience. It should go without saying that you will give 100 percent to your internship, and approach it professionally and enthusiastically. But it will pay if you go the extra mile and dedicate yourself to learning as much as you can about the issues and programs you're focusing on.

If you're not challenged by the work or are feeling underutilized, identify unmet needs and propose additional work that you can take on. Figure out who are your most interesting and hardest-working colleagues, build relationships with them, and ask whether you can assist with their projects. Do extra reading and make yourself a resource to your colleagues by sharing relevant newspaper clips or newly released reports.

Be intentional about the knowledge you want to gain and the skills you want to build, and make sure you are achieving your goals. Also think strategically about work that you can include in a professional portfolio. Try to contribute to or, better, take the lead on at least a few projects that result in concrete deliverables, such as a report, press release, or a foundation grant proposal. Put these materials in your portfolio so you can share them with prospective employers in the future.

Check in with your manager periodically, even if a meeting hasn't been scheduled. Share updates on your progress and ask for feedback on your work. Be open to constructive criticism and apply it.

As your internship draws to a close, make sure that your supervisor is aware of your departure. Do what you can to make the transition run smoothly. Consider preparing a written memo that updates your manager (and colleagues, if appropriate) on the status of your projects and offers notes about next steps required. Meet with your supervisor for a final time, and provide candid feedback on the experience. If it has been a successful experience, ask for a general letter of recommendation to include in your portfolio. Be sure to thank the organization's leadership and your colleagues for the experience and their support—and hopefully mentorship—of you.

INTERNSHIPS "PAY" IN MULTIPLE WAYS

by **Marilyn Mackes**

Executive Director • National Association of Colleges and Employers (NACE) • www.naceweb.org

Internships offer college student many benefits, including a shot at a full-time job.

The National Association of Colleges and Employers' latest survey of recruiting practices found that employers offered full-time jobs to nearly two out of three of their interns; and more than 70 percent of those offers were accepted. Nearly half of the interns came on board as full-time hires. Overall, employers reported that nearly 31 percent of all their new college graduate hires from the Class of 2006 came from their own internship program.

Employers see their internship programs as an effective way of identifying and connecting with talent. These programs allow employers and interns to test each other and determine how well they fit. And even if the internship doesn't result in a job offer, the experience boosts a student's chances of securing employment elsewhere. Although employers said that nearly 31 percent of their new college hires came from their own internship program, they also reported that 62 percent had internship experience. Employers prize relevant work experience even if the student served an internship with another organization. ■

NACE connects more than 5,200 college career services professionals at nearly 2,000 college and universities nationwide, and more than 3,000 human resources professionals focused on college relations and recruiting. Marilyn Mackes previously served as executive director of career services and corporate relations at Lehigh University (Bethlehem, PA). She holds a PhD and an MA in English.

creating a professional portfolio

Many employers request examples of past work in their hiring processes. Since every employer wants to recruit adept writers regardless of whether it's a communications position, writing samples are the most common request. While academic papers may demonstrate strong research and writing skills, they are often not what an employer wants. Employers need to know that you can communicate with the public, not just with your professor. Creating a professional portfolio as soon as possible—and building it throughout the early part of your career—offers a significant boost to your application for any future job. Internships offer the perfect opportunity to develop a few materials for your portfolio.

A professional portfolio includes examples of your work. As you develop an area of expertise, your portfolio will reflect that focus: a fundraising professional will feature letters of inquiry and successful grants; a graphic designer may highlight a revamped website and the invitations that promoted a special event; and a communications associate might showcase press releases and the resulting media coverage. An advocate might include a campaign plan, a human resources professional might share an employee handbook, and a research director might include a policy brief. Your first portfolio may not demonstrate a specific area of expertise, and that is fine. It is simply helpful to have a few stellar examples of work done outside of the classroom that you can show to a prospective employer.

Even if your internship or first job doesn't require it, see if you can take the lead on a few work products that are particularly suitable for a portfolio. Examples of appropriate portfolio materials include

- internal communications, such as a policy or program memo
- external communications, such as a newsletter article targeted to constituents
- press releases, media advisories, or public service announcements
- letters of inquiry and grant proposals
- a revised website, with examples of the "before" and "after" interface
- collateral materials to support a special event or campaign (such as a program script, talking points on a policy issue, or strategy memo)

Experience preparing and disseminating these types of materials is attractive to almost all prospective nonprofit sector employers, whether you are applying for a program, communications, or development position. Nonprofit organizations want to recruit candidates who know how to communicate persuasively and professionally, and who can demonstrate the impact that their communications had in advancing an organization's mission or smooth internal operations.

Sharon Williams
Teen Membership and Program Specialist

Age: 41

Education: BA, elementary education; MA, nonprofit management; JD

Years at current organization: 5

Years in current position: 5

First job out of college: Assistant school-age director for a local YMCA chapter

First job in nonprofit sector: As above

YMCA of the USA

www.ymca.net

Mission: YMCA of the USA is the national resource office for America's 2,594 YMCAs, collectively the nation's largest community service organization and largest provider of child care. YMCAs work to meet the health and human service needs of 20.1 million men, women, and children in 10,000 communities in the United States. YMCAs are at the heart of community life across the country: 42 million families and 72 million households are located within three miles of a YMCA.

Operating budget: $90 million

Number of employees: More than 300

Number of employees who report to you: None

Q & A

Q: Informally, describe your career track.
A: I worked with the YMCA of Greater New York for thirteen years, starting as an assistant school-age director and then as the youth and teen director. After three years in that position, I moved on to become the director of a center dedicated to youth work, and then ultimately as the association director of youth and teen services. During this period I took advantage of numerous professional development opportunities

(including trainings, seminars, and higher education experiences) to remain focused and up to date on the youth work field.

Q: What do you know now that you wish you had known when you were first job hunting?
A: I know now that the first job you obtain does not have to determine your ultimate career. It is merely a stepping-stone to get you to where you want to go in the future.

Q: Describe a representative work day.
A: I provide local YMCAs that serve and work with teens the best resources, the most up-to-date information, and the most comprehensive training opportunities that will help them prepare teens to journey down the path to becoming productive adults. My days are filled in talking directly to YMCA staff members regarding their work with teens—suggesting how they can improve their program mix and what they might do to enhance their skills. Other tasks include writing training curriculum, responding to e-mails, and general project administration.

Q: What misconceptions do people have about your job? What's the reality?
A: People believe that all the traveling (visiting YMCA locations around the country) involved in working at a job such as mine in a national organization is exciting and adventurous. In reality, the travel is a challenge. Although I enjoy my site visits and meeting so many people who are part of the Y family, because I am always on the go, I cannot spend a lot of quality time in one YMCA location.

Q: What do you love about your work?
A: I love having the ability to assist staff in making a difference in the lives of the youth and teens they work with. My nonprofit experience has also afforded me the flexibility to pursue personal interests and the support to enhance my skills.

Q: What advice would you give to someone interested in a career similar to yours?
A: If you are going into the nonprofit sector, remember that it is only slightly different from the for-profit sector. The desire to make broad distinctions between the two worlds will frustrate you. A nonprofit must operate with the business-like mindset just as any for-profit entity does; the real distinction is that in nonprofits you usually serve others and in a for-profit entity you sell products to others.

Q: What resources might help someone interested in your field and job function?
A: To learn more about the work of the YMCA, visit our website (www.ymca.net). The youth development field is broad and has many good resources, including the National Youth Development Information Center (www.nydic.org), the National Human Services Assembly (www.nassembly.org), and Youth Service America (www.ysa.org).

Q: What do you look for when hiring a new employee?
A: I look for individuals with the necessary knowledge and skill sets and who have a positive attitude and passion for the work.

Other extracurricular activities

Volunteering and interning are substantial, usually longer-term extracurricular activities that are covered in their own sections (pages 194 and 201, respectively). With these, you commit to an organization and develop a relationship with it, and, ideally, assume concrete responsibilities. But campuses and communities offer an endless array of other extracurricular activities that can help you develop skills and leadership experience to prepare for a nonprofit sector career. These activities can involve long-term relationships and yield many of the benefits of the best internship experiences. Or, they can be discrete, one-day-only volunteer activities that offer you a glimpse of an organization and its activities and help you network in your field.

If you're a student, you're probably overwhelmed by the number of options your campus offers. There are sports teams, clubs of every type, newspapers and perhaps a radio station, political groups, arts and cultural programs, and the list goes on. If you have extra time, fill it with some new activities that allow you to "test the waters" of an organization or field of interest. If you're already involved with extracurricular activities you enjoy, stick with them. Either way, make your involvement count. Assume a leadership role, make recommendations for a new or improved activity, or take ownership of a specific project. Dedicate your time in a way that will have an impact on the organization, for the people it serves, and for your own career development.

Mentoring

Having a great mentor can be the difference between building a good nonprofit sector career and establishing a great one. This may sound like hyperbole, but it's not. Mentors literally change lives. Not everyone is lucky enough to find one, but everyone should try.

A mentor is a professional advisor, coach, trusted ally, and confidant. The best mentors usually work in your general field and understand the nature of the work you do. They tend to be more senior professionals who are more experienced and perhaps more settled in their own careers.

A mentor can provide counsel on virtually all aspects of your professional life, from issues as technical as negotiating a compensation package to ones that tap into core values, such as work-life balance. A mentor will offer advice on your career path and new job opportunities, and many mentors will share their own professional contacts with you. A mentor is part of your inner circle, working to support you and help you succeed and be happy.

Many people find their first great mentor on the job—it might be a boss or a colleague you meet at your workplace. As such, a mentor might not be in place to help you launch your nonprofit sector career. But not necessarily. Think about cultivating a mentor as you network to find a job. Stay in touch with particularly helpful and supportive individuals, maintain close communications with them, and nurture the relationship. A cup of coffee lined up during your job search might, in a year or two, evolve into a mentoring relationship that enriches your life for decades.

And don't forget that you, too, are capable of changing lives, not just in the work you do in the nonprofit sector, but in the relationships you build. Regardless of your age, you can serve as a mentor. Commit to sharing your knowledge and experiences with someone next in line. If you're impressed with a student or young professional, make the effort to build a deeper relationship. Make yourself available for conversations and advice. Be a role model and source of support for those who will serve as tomorrow's leaders. Help pass the torch.

Professional development opportunities

No matter what point you are at in your career, enrolling in select professional development opportunities throughout the year can offer a significant boost to your career and give you a chance to "recharge your batteries." Participating in seminars, workshops, conferences, and other issue- or skill-specific training and leadership programs allows you to

- stay up to date on developments in your field
- make new contacts and network
- strengthen specific skills

- gain a credential that you can add to your résumé
- take a break from your day-to-day job to reflect on the work you do

Charge yourself with seeking out at least two meaningful opportunities each year.

To identify appropriate opportunities, ask your network of contacts as well as your colleagues and supervisor at work. Join membership associations associated with your targeted job function and scan their publications for relevant programs. Read trade publications and journals, join appropriate listservs, and connect with your alumni association. If a nonprofit sector support center exists in your community, monitor its offerings.

In addition, a number of organizations provide nonprofit sector-related professional development opportunities, either at the national level or through regional or local affiliates. Here are some of the top organizations in the field:

- **Alliance for Nonprofit Management** is a professional association of individuals and organizations devoted to improving the management and governance capacity of nonprofit organizations. It creates a learning community through its annual conference, year-round online networking programs, and many other events. Review the Alliance's calendar of offerings and decide whether membership might be worthwhile for you. (www.allianceonline.org)

- **The Foundation Center** works to strengthen the nonprofit sector by advancing knowledge about philanthropy in the United States. It operates regional libraries and local Cooperating Collections nationwide and offers many programs focused on grant writing, fundraising, management, and other aspects of the philanthropic world. (For more information, see "The Foundation Center's Libraries," page 221.) (www.foundationcenter.org)

- **National Council of Nonprofit Associations (NCNA)** is a network of state and regional nonprofit associations serving more than 20,000 members in forty-one states and the District of Columbia. The state associations organize a wide range of programs and conferences to provide training programs and networking opportunities for their members. Brown bag series help build specific communities—for example, bringing together communications professionals, executive directors, or minority leaders in the sector. Many associations operate a job and internship site. Some associations offer student memberships. Visit the NCNA website to find out whether a state association exists near you and, if one does, explore all of its resources. NCNA is also the convening organization for the Nonprofit Congress (www.nonprofitcongress.org), which works to unite nonprofit organizations and strengthen the charitable sector. (www.ncna.org)

Year-of-service programs

If you're thinking about a possible lifetime of service with a career in the nonprofit sector, what does it mean to perform a year of service?

A *year of service* typically refers to programs that place individuals or groups of people in service projects for ten- to twelve-month periods. Some involve an intermediary placement agency that connects the participant with an independent host organization. Other agencies oversee their programs directly. Many programs offer some limited benefits, such as stipends, health insurance, housing, or educational awards.

These one-year programs may have some educational, age, or experience requirements; it depends on the program. They often appeal to recent college graduates who are looking for a meaningful and rigorous service experience as they contemplate a career in the nonprofit sector or take time off before graduate school; however, many programs also attract a wide range of participants at various points in their lives.

A large percentage of year-of-service programs are connected to AmeriCorps, a program that falls under the U.S. government's Corporation for National and Community Service. More than 70,000 Americans serve at more than 3,000 local, state, and national organizations each year through AmeriCorps. The work covers all kinds of service, from building affordable housing to mentoring youth.

BRINGING BACK THE BROWN BAG

A note from **Audrey R. Alvarado**

Executive Director • National Council of Nonprofit Associations (NCNA) • www.ncna.org

When it comes to career and professional development, I am a big believer in the brown bag. These are convenings—sometimes called "brown bags," but not always—that bring together small groups of individuals to discuss a given topic. The basic idea is that you bring your own sandwich and sit around a table and talk.

Brown bags are organized everywhere: on a campus, at your local library, and in the conference rooms of an organization. They bring together people around an issue (e.g., global warming), or a job function (e.g., chief financial officer), or a community (e.g., African Americans working in human services). People might gather in response to a breaking news story, the release of a report, or a crisis in the office. Or the brown bag may have been planned months in advance, to share "best practices" in a given discipline (conducting field research, for example). An expert might be invited to speak for part of the meeting, or not.

Regardless of who is meeting or why, a brown bag offers an intimate setting to learn, share ideas, and network. Usually less formal than a workshop or conference (and always less expensive), people don't stand on ceremony. The events are not highly structured—they're really just a BYO lunch for people interested in a topic. And yet participants tend to find the nonprofit sector's brown bags extraordinarily beneficial. You get information, you share ideas, you trade business cards. NCNA's state associations have found them to be very successful. If you're working to launch a career in the nonprofit sector, take advantage of brown bags (or the equivalent) on your campus or in your community. It's a surefire way to learn more about the work you want to do and to connect to leaders who can help. ∎

Prior to her appointment at NCNA, Audrey R. Alvarado served as the associate dean for student and external affairs at the University of Colorado at Denver Graduate School of Public Affairs. She was executive director of the Latin American Research and Service Agency (Denver) and program director of the Hispanic Office of Planning and Evaluation's Talent Search Program (Boston).

Public Allies

one example of a year-of-service program

www.publicallies.org

The Public Allies AmeriCorps program is one example of a year-of-service experience. Public Allies is changing the face and practice of leadership in communities across the country by building an effective pipeline for young adults to begin careers in nonprofit and community leadership and promoting leadership styles well suited for our changing times. Their signature AmeriCorps program has three main components:

- recruiting young adults, ages 18 to 30, from diverse backgrounds (67 percent are people of color, 60 percent women, 50 percent college graduates, and 15 percent LGBT) who have an interest in working for community and social change

- placing allies at nonprofit organizations in their communities where they serve four days a week to expand and improve services in areas such as youth development, public health, economic development, the environment, and more

- developing allies personally and professionally through a rigorous leadership development program that blends weekly skills training, team building, coaching, and critical reflection

The Public Allies curriculum is based on the idea that the next generation of leaders should look like America will look, connect across cultures, facilitate collaborative action, recognize all of a community's assets, commit to self-development and be accountable for results. The program works: more than 80 percent of its 2,200 graduates have continued to work in the nonprofit and public sectors with high rates of volunteerism and activism.

Allies receive a stipend of between $1,250 and $1,800 per month (depending on the community), health insurance, child care, interest-free student loan deferment, and a postservice education award of $4,725 that can be used to pay off past student loans or future education. Public Allies currently serves fifteen communities across the country and plans to double its size over the next five years.

Esteban Ramos is a Public Allies alumnus and is currently associate executive director of Fresh Youth Initiatives (FYI). See his profile on pages 114–115.

AmeriCorps participants receive a Segal Ameri-Corps Education Award to help cover the cost of their education.

To learn more about the AmeriCorps program—as well as related initiatives such as Volunteers in Service to America (VISTA) and the National Civilian Community Corps (NCCC)—spend time at the comprehensive website of the Corporation for National and Community Service (www.nationalservice.gov). Once you have solid background information, find individuals in your network who have firsthand experiences with the programs to determine whether an AmeriCorps "year of service" would be right for you.

Other year-of-service programs are sponsored through private nonprofit organizations, including many faith-based organizations. To create a list of programs that might be a match for you, start at the Action Without Borders/Idealist website (www.idealist.org), and visit their "Year of Service Programs" section.

If the year-of-service model sounds appealing, you might also consider similar programs of shorter or longer duration. If you're still in school, explore "summer of service" and "alternative spring break" (such as Break Away, www.alternativebreaks.org) programs. If you might be interested in a multiyear commitment, and especially one overseas, you might consider the Peace Corps (www.peacecorps.gov).

In a Nutshell . . .

You now have a better understanding of who you are, how and where you want to live, what you care about, and the work you would like to do. You have taken classes and worked at internships, volunteer opportunities, and jobs to gain the preparation you need. You even may have identified additional training and educational opportunities that you plan to pursue later on that will help you cultivate your career. You've reflected on your skills and experiences, established the types of positions you are qualified for, and begun to zero in on the types of nonprofit organizations where you would like to work. If so, you are ready for Chapter 5, and the concrete tips and strategies it offers to find appropriate openings, create a strong application package, and land a great job in the nonprofit sector.

five

LANDING A GREAT JOB
IN THE *nonprofit* SECTOR

So now it is time to roll up your sleeves and actually get a great job in the nonprofit sector. But how? No doubt you already have heard the adage, "Finding a job is a job." And it's true. Many of the characteristics that lead to success in the workplace will lead to success in the job hunt. You need to approach the nuts and bolts of job hunting as a disciplined, demanding, virtually all-consuming undertaking. It is best to follow the "six P's" of a successful job search: be persuasive, prepared, professional, prompt, persistent, and positive.

1. Be **persuasive** in communicating your goals. You can't convince your contacts that you deserve their help in your job search (or a potential employer that you deserve a job) unless you can clearly and persuasively articulate your professional goals. And you won't be able to find a job unless you have an idea of what you are looking for.

Be focused and directed. Be clear about where you want to live, what you want to do, and the type of organization you want to work for. Put thought into your long-term career goals. It's okay if they change, but have a current vision of where you want to head. Yes, you should be open to opportunities you might not have considered and flexible in your search. But knowing—and being able to communicate persuasively—what you want is the vital first step. It allows you to refine your search and be effective and efficient in your outreach. Plus, having direction is very attractive in the eyes of potential employers and individuals in your network of advisors. (Refer to the section "Understanding Yourself," pages 168–182, if you need to brush up on what you want.)

2. Be **prepared** in your research. Hopefully you will have taken coursework and have had internships or jobs in your field of interest. You're approaching your job search with an existing arsenal of knowledge and experience. But being truly prepared for the job hunt is an ongoing responsibility. You need to be reading continually and staying up to date with the latest developments in your field. Every informational meeting or formal job interview requires hours of preparation. It's your job to learn everything you can about the organization in advance of an interview and arrive with demonstrable knowledge, targeted questions, and ideas appropriate for that specific job. All of this takes time and attention.

3. Be **professional** in your outreach and networking. You need an orderly workspace in your home from which you will conduct your job search. You need well-maintained files with accurate logs of the calls you make and e-mails and letters you send, and you need to track the responses you receive. You need a quiet space where you can make uninterrupted telephone calls and write thoughtful letters. Your written communications all must be up to business standards, persuasive and thoughtful, and without a single typo. Approach in-person meetings with the care they deserve, even if you are just meeting someone for a cup of coffee. Your attire should be appropriate to the setting.

4. Be **prompt** in your follow-up. There's no good excuse for tardy (or, worse, nonexistent) follow-up to informational meetings and job interviews. Always send an e-mail or letter of thanks for an individual's time within twenty-four hours of a meeting. If you get leads to other individuals for advice or potential job openings, use your thank-you letter to state that you will be contacting them, and then do so immediately. If you see an announcement for a position of interest, don't delay. Apply as quickly as you can prepare a strong application package.

5. Be **persistent** in your desire to achieve your goal. Job hunting is often discouraging, occasionally baffling, and always exhausting. There will be days when you want to throw in the towel and go back to that restaurant job that helped you pay for college. There will be times when you won't land an interview for a position that you are perfectly qualified for, but then you'll be recruited for something totally out of your area of expertise. A close family friend won't return multiple messages you leave, despite his effusive promises of help. It takes time and patience to find a job. You need to pursue your contacts steadfastly and write (and mail) one cover letter after another. Be prepared to spend many months on the job hunt.

6. Be **positive** in your attitude. Although it can be discouraging, have fun with your job search. Approach every hour you spend on the Internet researching an organization, every informational meeting you arrange, every letter you write, and every interview you land as an opportunity. Appreciate the time and insights you receive from professionals in your field and share with them your own good energy and fresh perspective on the issues you care about. Spend more time celebrating each new connection than mourning every rejection letter. Stay positive in your public meetings—it's best not to complain about a past job or boss, as that raises a red flag for a potential employer. And stay positive in your personal life as well. Treat yourself to the things that help you relax and take the time necessary to periodically recharge yourself. Maintain strong connections to your friends and family and reach out to them for support and encouragement. Job hunting is tough; be good to yourself in the process.

The "six P's" are the backdrop for your search and the characteristics that will help you succeed when you apply them to the nuts and bolts of the job hunt. Your actual search will involve a strategy that is tailored to your specific situation, style, and goal. However, it's likely that any job search will depend on sound research, effective networking, targeted search strategies, persuasive cover letters, a stellar résumé, deal-closing interviews, and appropriate follow-up and negotiation. Here are some tips on how to use each of these tools to your advantage.

Sound Research

Conducting sound research builds your knowledge and is connected to every aspect of the job hunt, from networking to interviewing. A very savvy and persistent researcher will be the job seeker who hears first about a great job opening and has already identified the individuals who can help him or her gain entrée to it.

Job seekers need to research organizations, individuals, job openings, issues, policy developments, books—the list goes on and on. You have already conducted significant research as a student, through appropriate courses, internships, and extracurricular activities. Now you need to apply that knowledge (and your research skills) to your own career development and specific job hunt.

What to research

Use as a backdrop to your research what you already know about yourself, your interest areas and skills, your professional goals, and the organizations that you've been connected to. Now it's time to hone in on all of these areas and make sure that you can answer key questions relevant to them.

- **Your field of interest.** Are you conflicted about whether to pursue one field or another, and would a deeper understanding of the issues help you refine your goals? Do you know enough about your field, from historical underpinnings to the most recent policy developments? If a recent conversation with an expert in the field pointed out gaps in your knowledge, recognize them and address them.

- **Possible career paths.** Do you have long-term goals about the work you would like to do, and an awareness of the possible career paths that could lead you there? Many career paths in the nonprofit sector are circular—there isn't a clear point A-to-point B-to-point C linear progression of how to advance. Have you explored what people who hold your dream job did in order to get where they are? Have you identified common threads to some career paths? Can you see how one entry-level position might lead to a position more directly aligned with what you want to do?

- **Appropriate employers.** Have you identified the organizations working on your issues? Do you understand differences in mission and strategy among them? Do you know about the size and structure of organizations and their funding streams, and what types are more appealing to you? Have you learned about the executive directors and senior staff members who lead your targeted groups and about their reputation in the field? Have you established where organizations are based and whether you can and want to live in those cities?

- **Specific job functions.** Are you clear on the specific job functions that match your skills and experiences and that you would like to pursue? This is not the task of researching specific

positions that are vacant. Rather, your charge is to truly investigate a type of job—what it means to be a program director or a development associate at an organization. You learn this by talking to people.

If you can't answer all of these questions with clarity and direction, you need to do more research. But how?

How to research

While the Internet might seem to offer one-stop shopping, don't depend on it for all of your research needs. It's a great and powerful tool and you'll use it endlessly in your job hunt; but it is not the be-all and end-all. If you don't get away from your computer and out into the world, you'll seriously hamper your ability to land a job. You need to use your network of people, libraries, periodicals, public events, and career services offices (as well as the Internet) to conduct your research, build your knowledge, clarify your goals, make connections, and get that job.

- **Your network.** The value and art of networking are discussed in detail in the section that follows ("Effective Networking," pages 226–233), but keep in mind that your contacts in the field are a valuable source of information. Use them in your research efforts. They will give you more honest, more practical, and more up-to-date information than any Internet search or guidebook will yield. Identify people to talk to and reach out to them with enthusiasm and curiosity. Tap them for information on all aspects of your job search. Be prepared to learn from them. When you hear good advice, follow it. When you receive great leads, pursue them.

- **Library time.** If you're a serious job seeker and committed researcher, your local public library should soon recognize your face. (And if you still have access to your college library, use it as well.) Just spending time in a library helps you avoid the distraction of e-mail and telephone calls and forces you to devote focused time to career development. Libraries provide books, magazines, and journals that cover your field. Many libraries have "job corners" with resources specific to the job hunt. Good reference librarians are invaluable resources; they can point you toward new resources and creative research strategies as you try to find out more about people and organizations appropriate to your career goals. Ask reference librarians for help.

- **Targeted subscriptions.** You'll be able to read most if not all of the important periodicals in your field by regularly visiting your library. However, if a magazine or journal is particularly relevant to your work, now is a good time to invest in a subscription. Having guaranteed access to the publication—delivered to your mailbox—will help ensure that you're up to speed with the latest developments and issues and, as such, properly positioned to be a well-informed networker and interviewee.

the Foundation Center's libraries

The Foundation Center is a nonprofit organization dedicated to strengthening the nonprofit sector by advancing knowledge about philanthropy in the United States. It operates five regional libraries and learning centers—in New York City, Atlanta, Cleveland, San Francisco, and Washington, DC—that are open to the public. These special libraries are wonderful spots to spend an afternoon researching aspects of the nonprofit sector, and their staff members are particularly knowledgeable about the sector. The center offers courses and programs (in person and online) on various aspects of fundraising, which are excellent professional development opportunities for anyone interested in a career in the nonprofit sector (and make a great addition to your résumé). The Foundation Center also operates more than three hundred Cooperating Collections, which are information centers housed in local libraries, community foundations, and other nonprofit resource centers that contain core collections of the Foundation Center. If you don't have access to one of the five regional libraries, visit the Foundation Center's website (www.foundationcenter.org) to see whether a Cooperating Collection is based near you.

But don't focus only on issue-specific periodicals. Explore periodicals that cover the nonprofit sector as a whole, such as the *Chronicle of Philanthropy* and the *NonProfit Times,* to name just two. And be informed about your community and world generally. To be an attractive candidate, you need to be knowledgeable on the news of the day and current political debates. Read a local and national daily newspaper every morning.

- **Public events.** If you're out of school you may think you have lost access to interesting lectures and other educational events that helped you learn about your field. However, you will probably be surprised at the quantity of public programs that your community offers. Stay apprised of events sponsored by your local colleges, alumni association, performing arts spaces, galleries, libraries, church groups, and other nonprofit organizations. Attend conferences and public meetings on policy issues relevant to your work. Accept every dinner and cocktail party invitation; you never know who will be seated next to you.

Keep your engagement calendar packed with events, attend them, and stick around for any receptions that follow the programs. If attendees wear name tags, wear one with pride, and use the event to practice your networking skills. Talk about your past work and be frank about your current job search. Challenge yourself to learn as much as you can about the people you meet and to find any connections they may have to what you want to do.

the Craigslist Foundation's Nonprofit Boot Camp

Held bicoastally each year, the Craigslist Foundation Nonprofit Boot Camp is an all-day smorgasbord of workshops, roundtables, keynote addresses, booths, and networking. Appropriate both for nonprofit sector veterans and newbies, the conferences turn out an impressive collection of local and national organizations. Just by browsing the convention hall, participants can get an idea of who's working in what areas, as well as the organizations supporting the sector overall. Early birds can sign up for free one-on-one career coaching, and the keynote addresses and workshops identify important themes in the sector. The bonus? The boot camp costs less than $100 and includes an organic lunch and eco-friendly water bottle. Bring your business cards. For more information, visit www.craigslistfoundation.org.

- **Career services offices.** Some students and recent alumni believe their college office of career services can't help them in a nonprofit sector job search. They're wrong. For starters, many attributes of a successful job search translate across sectors. You need strong cover letters, perfect résumés, and polished interviewing skills whether you are pursuing a for-profit, government, or nonprofit sector job. Career centers know how to help you prepare for the job hunt. In addition, many centers have staff members with sector-specific expertise, so be sure to inquire if your center has a nonprofit sector "pro" on staff.

  Career counselors can provide feedback on your materials, connect you to professors and administrators with knowledge of your field, suggest community leaders to reach out to, and show you Internet and print resources that may help you identify specific vacancies. Career centers also sponsor programs ranging from résumé writing workshops to career fairs. Take advantage of all of them. If an initial meeting at your career center seems unproductive, give the office (or a different staff member) another chance. Determine what the career center does well and take advantage of it.

- **Internet searches.** While you shouldn't depend exclusively on the Internet, there's no denying it is a wonderful research tool in the job search. Online news coverage can provide information on your field of interest and will feature organizations and experts you can try to integrate into your network. Your local library may have a web presence that allows you to research their collection, including periodicals, online.

Organizations that support specific job functions (e.g., SHRM, the Society for Human Resource Management, www.shrm.org) have websites that can educate you about a given discipline. Umbrella organizations that support groups of organizations in a geographic region (e.g., NCNA, the National Council of Nonprofit Associations, www.ncna.org) can help you identify nonprofit organizations in your community; and those that support organizations around a specific issue area can help you identify nonprofit organizations in your field.

Most nonprofit organizations have their own websites offering abundant information on their mission, programs, staff, media coverage, advocacy agenda, funders, and board of directors. Many post their annual reports, which provide a comprehensive review of the organization's previous year's activities and should be read in advance of any meeting or job interview. You can learn about organizations a group collaborates with (through coalition work or discrete partnerships), and thereby find links to other potential employers in your field. A staff member's bio or résumé, if posted online, will tell you about career paths and also point to other organizations where you might be interested in working.

Shash Yázhí
Spirit in Motion Director

Age: 36

Education: High school diploma

Years at current organization: 5

Years in current position: 4

First job out of school: Community organizer at an indigenous people's advocacy organization

First job in nonprofit sector: As above

Movement Strategy Center

www.movementstrategy.org

Mission: Movement Strategy Center (MSC) is committed to advancing the next generation of leaders for a sustainable progressive movement. We are building local, regional, and national networks of young activists across issues, constituencies, and geographies. We are helping activists to develop the skills, culture, analysis, and vision to work together in broad, cohesive alliances—with a strong emphasis on the leadership of base-building groups working to address the needs of young people, low-income communities, and communities of color.

Operating budget: $975,000

Number of employees: 12

Number of employees who report to you: 2, administrative assistants

Q&A

Q: Informally, describe your career track.
A: I was raised on the Diné reservation in New Mexico by my grandparents, who taught me the importance of living in harmony with Mother Earth. Traditional ceremonies were passed down to me through my ancestors, and I have implemented many of these practices in my work with

individuals who wish to create internal healing and balance in their lives. For the last fourteen years I worked as a community organizer on issues ranging from indigenous sovereignty to racial equity in schools. My passion is intergenerational work with a focus on youth organizing. I now apply my experiences and commitment to spirit work and organizing work at the Movement Strategy Center as their first Spirit in Motion Fellow.

Q: What do you know now that you wish you had known when you were first job hunting?
A: I realize the importance of creating and realizing your own talents and setting personal goals that you can then work to integrate into your professional life.

Q: Describe a representative work day.
A: I direct the Spirit in Motion project that supports the integration of spirit and health on an individual, organizational, and community level to create a stronger, more sustainable movement for social justice. We sponsor workshops, seminars, gatherings, and ceremonies. One of our goals is to create a buzz in the movement community around self-wellness. My days are full and varied, but generally involve travel, meetings, and other outreach and organizing efforts to build alliances and create a shared vision around our work.

Q: What misconceptions do people have about your job? What's the reality?
A: People often don't understand how hard it is to manage so many competing energies. It's a delicate dance to encourage activists to stop connecting around the angel of burnout and instead come together around spirit, healing, transition, and transformation.

Q: What do you love about your work?
A: I feel blessed to have the position that I have, that I support a movement for social justice that I believe in so strongly. I feel spiritually settled by doing the work I was meant to conduct in this universe.

Q: What advice would you give to someone interested in a career similar to yours?
A: It is important to balance all aspects of your life in order to be fully present in your work and healthy in your life. So much of nonprofit sector work involves energy of the heart and a desire to give to the community, but it's vital to remember who we are and how we are connected to the community, and to take care of our spirit as well.

Q: What resources might help someone interested in your field and job function?
A: For information on youth organizing, visit the Movement Strategy Center's website (www.movementstrategy.org), as well as Youth In Focus (www.youthinfocus.net) and the Youth Media Council (www.youthmediacouncil.org). Some other organizations working on sustaining the spiritual life of activists are Tools for Change (http://toolsforchange.org), Center for Contemplative Mind in Society (www.contemplativemind.org), and Stone Circles (www.stonecircles.org).

Q: What do you look for when hiring a new employee?
A: I look for experience, passion for our mission, and the ability to work independently and with a team.

225

research dos and don'ts

DO . . .

- make a conscious effort to continue your learning every day, even when your formal education is complete

- reach out to people to learn about issues, organizations, and different career paths

- attend as many relevant public events as possible

- take notes—if it's not appropriate to take notes at a specific event, be sure to record the names of new contacts, ideas, and other leads as soon as you leave

- keep reading—be a "media junkie" and peruse newspapers and listen to the radio

- get out of your house—the best research is often conducted out in the world, not in front of a computer

Do NOT . . .

- arrive for an informational meeting or job interview unprepared or underinformed— and certainly not late

- depend only on the Internet for research

- dismiss your college career center's ability to help

- trust everything you read on the Internet— check your sources carefully

Effective Networking

Networking is possibly the single most important strategy in the job hunt. Networking—and the informational meetings that are a key part of networking—will help you learn about career paths, organizations working in your field, and specific job openings. Networking will enable you to continuously expand your circle of contacts so that more and more people are available to you for advice, specific leads, help getting your foot in the door at organizations, and to advocate on your behalf. Networking keeps you up to date with developments in your field. Networking provides opportunities for you to test your ideas and continue your education. Most importantly, networking often leads directly to a job.

While networking is important for government and business jobs, it is particularly vital in the nonprofit sector. Many nonprofit sector employers consider their staff a "family" and quite consciously consider whether a candidate will fit into their team. For this reason, they value and depend on word-of-mouth referrals from their colleagues in the field. If you have someone making calls on your behalf, your application will receive a tremendous boost. Nonprofit sector leaders are hungry for candidates who come to them recommended by someone they trust.

Don't be shy

It's challenging for many people to pick up the phone and ask for a favor. To network successfully, you need to be willing to ask for an expert's time, and believe you're worthy of it. Remind yourself that most people like to talk about themselves. After all, it's the subject they know the best. Nonprofit sector professionals are passionate about their work and, although they're often very busy, most enjoy having the opportunity to reflect on their programs and organizations. Plus, most leaders have had someone help them along the way, and they appreciate having the chance to extend the favor to the next generation of talent. If you're a savvy and professional networker, you'll make your contacts feel good about any time they spend with you and create a win-win situation.

Write it down

The best way to start networking is with pen and paper. Peruse your hard-copy and electronic address books. Tap your brain to create a list (in writing) of everyone you might call as you embark on your search. Be clear about the fields and job functions you are interested in and then identify relevant people you know who you can talk to. Be sure to include

- friends
- family members
- family friends
- professors
- employers
- classmates

When you think you've exhausted your list, challenge yourself to identify a dozen more names:

- friends-of-friends who you met only once or twice, but who are connected to your field of interest
- people you met through your place of worship
- your supervisor when you volunteered just for a summer
- a parent's college classmate who you always thought had your dream job
- your long-lost relative doing fascinating work abroad

Networking requires not only identifying the people you know, but also the organizations that you are interested in. Many of the organizations that you'll want to reach out to will be covered by your list of contacts. But some will not. List those organizations that you want to explore but where you don't have a point of entry yet. You'll ask your network of advisors for referrals to individuals at these organizations.

At this point your list may need some sorting. For example, if you are exploring opportunities in a number of cities, you may want to group your contacts geographically. If you have two very different fields of interest, you should group people and organizations by issue area. Or, if you have expertise in rather divergent skill sets, you may make groups around job functions. Finally, if your list is rather long, you may want to separate contacts into "A" and "B" lists and concentrate your attention first on individuals you think will be the most helpful.

Gather and confirm contact information

Your notebook should be starting to overflow with names of organizations and individuals. But before you pick up the phone, make sure you gather and verify contact information. For every individual on your list, confirm the following:

- full name and how to spell it
- current job title
- organization name
- organization address
- telephone, with extension
- e-mail address

If you can do this via the Internet, great. (Be advised, however, that some websites are not updated as frequently as they should be.) Otherwise, pick up the phone and call the receptionist at the individual's organization. Your call might go like this:

> "Hi, my name is _____ and I was referred to [*Name of Contact*] by one of her colleagues, [*Name of Person Referring*]. I'd like to send her a letter, and wanted to confirm that she is still [*Title You Believe She Holds*]. Is this correct? Also, can you give me her e-mail address? And, does she have a direct-dial number or extension?"

If you need to confirm your contact's mailing address, do so during this call.

Set aside your coffee budget

If you live in the city where you are job hunting, you'll want to try to secure as many in-person meetings as possible. (If not, you'll do the majority of your networking via telephone.) You'll want to offer to meet your contacts for coffee or a drink at a café very convenient to their office or home, and ideally you'll be prepared to treat them. You can also offer to meet at their offices, of course. Set aside the money you'll need for transportation to your meetings and to cover the costs of modest snacks.

The "one-two" punch: telephone and e-mail

And now it is time to begin. Pick up the telephone and start calling your contacts. What you say will depend on who the contact is and how you know the person, as well as your own personal communication style. But regardless of any of these variables, all of your calls should be focused, clear, direct, friendly, and brief.

You're calling to ask for an informational meeting, or to schedule a time to talk by telephone. Mention the contact who referred you or, if they are your direct contact, remind them who you are and how they know you. Err on the side of assuming they will not remember who you are and help trigger their memory. Then tell them that you're beginning a job hunt and explain how their work is directly relevant to what you want to pursue. Ask if they would be willing to meet with you for twenty minutes for an informational meeting. You may find that, "May I buy you a cup of coffee sometime next week?" works very well. It also might help if you stress that you are not asking them for a job, but rather that you hope to "pick their brain" about the field, and to learn more about their work and experiences. A little flattery also never hurts; be clear that you are impressed by what they do (provided you know enough about their work to say so).

Your goal is to schedule a meeting. However, you should be prepared to have a conversation at that moment if the individual replies, "I am too busy over the next few weeks to meet, but I am happy to speak with you for a few minutes right now. Fire away!"

With many of your calls, you're likely to get voice mail. Leave a brief, clear message explaining why you're calling and slowly state your telephone number twice. Let your contact know that you will also follow up by e-mail, in case that's a more convenient method for communication.

Use e-mail to follow up on your voice mail messages, but keep it focused on scheduling the meeting. A follow-up e-mail might look something like this:

Dear Ms. Smith:

As per my voice mail message just now, I am contacting you on the referral of Mark Luke. I am beginning a job search in the field of human rights, and Mark knows of my experience working on refugee issues. He suggested that you would be a terrific resource for me as I explore opportunities in this field in Washington, DC. Might you be available to meet with me for 20 minutes—just for an informational meeting—so that I could learn more about your background and work? I'd be happy to come to your office, or buy you a coffee at a place convenient to you. My telephone number is 202-555-1212, and I also check e-mail regularly. If you are available to meet, please let me know if I may send you my résumé in advance.

I look forward to the possibility of meeting with you. Thank you for your consideration.

Sincerely,
Jane Brown

Do not use an e-mail to ask for advice. It's extraordinarily labor intensive for someone to offer guidance in writing, and especially in response to a vague electronic inquiry. The only exception is if you have a very specific question and your contact has requested communication by e-mail.

a note about cell phones

Those television commercials are no joke: cell phones often produce bad connections and frequently lead to dropped calls. Try to avoid doing any outreach from your cell, even to make an appointment. And definitely do not conduct an informational conversation via cell. If you must use the cell for scheduling purposes or if it is the only telephone available to you, make sure you are in a quiet place with a stable connection. It is inappropriate to make a call to or take a call from a contact while you are walking, driving, or doing anything else that would prevent you from focusing and taking good notes, or that could add noise to the line. Nothing is more frustrating to a busy professional than to be in the process of providing a lead and having to shout, "Can you hear me? Can you hear me?" or to be cut off in mid-sentence. Do everything you can to prevent this from happening.

a note about e-mails

E-mail is a terrific way to network and a convenient tool for communicating with your contacts. In fact, it may be the preferred method for more logistical communications for many of the individuals you approach. But just because e-mail is convenient does not mean it should be informal. Apply the same standards to every e-mail you send as you would any professional communication. Use salutations (e.g., "Dear Mr. Smith") just as you would in a business letter. Pay close attention to spelling, formatting, and punctuation: there is no excuse for typos, paragraphs should be separated by line breaks, and sentences should be appropriately punctuated. Unfortunately, e-mails have become increasingly sloppy as we use them more frequently and more casually, but this doesn't mean you shouldn't set your own high standards. Don't send them from your phone. Prepare them with care. Avoid smiley faces, other emoticons, or superfluous graphics. Remember, this may be your first impression with a contact or potential employer. Make it a good one.

Telephone calls and e-mails are often not returned, which is frustrating. Don't hesitate to leave three or four messages in the space of two weeks—but keep them brief, friendly, and professional. At a certain point, however, you need to cross off an unresponsive person from your list. You might try that contact again in a month or so, or ask another contact to place a call on your behalf, but you shouldn't relentlessly pursue an elusive lead.

Prepare for and then hold the informational meeting

The informational meetings that are part of networking require almost as much preparation as formal job interviews. In advance, you want to learn as much as you can about the individual with whom you're meeting and the organization where he or she works. If the person came to you through a referral, ask your source for background information. Use the Internet to learn about the organization and the contact's specific program area and job function. Some organizations post senior staff members' biographies online and, if they do, those are "must reads." Be aware of any recent media coverage the organization has received. Read annual reports. If you have identified other staff members or board members at the contact's organization whom you would like to meet, note their names so you can ask for a referral to them, if appropriate. Also identify other organizations where you're looking for entrée, and ask the contact for leads to them, if they're in the same field. (Be sure to ask, "May I use your name when I contact this person?" And make a note of the response.)

At the meeting, you'll want to give an overview of your background, clearly state your interest in the contact's field, and show your appreciation for his or her career. You may have sent your résumé in advance, otherwise be sure to share a copy at the meeting. Highlight the experiences that are particularly relevant to this meeting, provide an overview of what you believe you are good at, and share your enthusiasm for the field. But don't spend too long talking about yourself—limit your introductory remarks to just a few minutes.

Even if you are passionate about many diverse issues, focus your comments on your interest in *this person's* specific area and try to appear as directed as possible. This is not the time to talk through your indecision; this is the time to hone in on the subject where your contact has expertise. Tell the person why you wanted to talk to him or her, and then start asking questions. Listen carefully to the answers so that you can ask appropriate follow-up questions and direct the conversation in a way that is helpful to you. Remember, *you* asked for the meeting, and it is your job to make the conversation flow and be beneficial to you.

The questions you might ask are limitless. Think strategically about how you should use the time, especially considering you probably only have twenty minutes or so. Keep the conversation on point while maintaining a relaxed and open demeanor. Your questions might focus in on some aspect of some of the following areas:

- the contact's career path—how she or he ended up where she or he is

- the nature of the work she or he does and a typical day

- the skills and experiences she or he depends on (and looks for in colleagues or new hires)

- the structure of the organization and how one advances in it

- where the jobs are and any specific positions she or he's aware of in the field

- other people you might contact (or, better, background on specific individuals you ask about)

- advice for adjustments you might make to your résumé, tips for your cover letters

Reserve a few minutes for slightly more heady and less practical discussion. Ask about how a recent policy development will affect the field, for example. Or explore your contact's contributions to a report her organization just released. Find a way to leave the meeting with deeper knowledge in your contact's area of expertise.

Take notes, especially if the contact proves to be a wealth of information and generous in sharing additional referrals. Make sure you capture the names of individuals and organizations referenced. Don't hesitate to ask for the complete name of an organization referred to by an acronym. Note anything the contact offers to do on your behalf, and, likewise, any specific recommendations on actions you should take.

what is an informational meeting?

An informational meeting is an in-person or telephone conversation with a nonprofit sector professional to learn about his or her job, organization, and field. You schedule meetings with individuals at organizations irrespective of whether a job opening exists at their organization (indeed, you are more likely to land one if they don't currently have any openings, since it is then clear the meeting is just for exploratory purposes). Leaders will agree to meet upon the request of someone in your network, but also just based on a "cold call" from you—because your telephone call or letter persuaded them of your passion for their field and they're happy to devote a half-hour to mentoring. Informational meetings are opportunities to get advice on your job search. You might ask for specific tips on your cover letters or résumé. You might ask about job openings in the field or connections to other individuals who might help in your search. Holding as many appropriate informational meetings as possible is a vital strategy in landing a job and in advancing your career.

Be respectful of the individual's time and end the meeting punctually, unless you pick up cues that it is okay to extend it. When it is time to leave, make eye contact, shake hands, say that the meeting was extraordinarily helpful, and offer a hearty thank-you. Ask if you may stay in touch.

Follow up with a letter and pursue all leads

Immediately after an informational meeting, draft a thank-you letter. The letter should be type-written and on business paper, not a note card. If you choose to use e-mail, still approach it as a professional business communication and format it accordingly. Repeat your thanks and reference aspects of the meeting that were particularly helpful. Be explicit in your appreciation of the contact's offer to make calls on your behalf; that is, use the thank-you letter as an opportunity to remind him what he promised. Likewise, tell him what leads you will pursue and then pursue them promptly. If you referenced an article or a report in your conversation that was new to your contact, include a copy in your thank-you letter. Go the extra mile.

If this contact refers you to individuals with whom you eventually meet—or, better, if she helps you land an interview or job—be sure to let her know. It seems obvious, but you would be surprised just how many job seekers don't extend basic courtesies. Any successful referral warrants another thank-you note (or e-mail) to the initial contact, letting her know that you connected and appreciated the referral.

networking dos and don'ts

DO . . .

- cast a wide net and create as large a network as possible

- keep careful notes and document the date and time of calls placed

- follow up promptly on every lead

- prepare for your meetings by thoroughly researching individuals and organizations

- write polished letters and e-mails

- say "thank you" for people's time and help

Do NOT . . .

- send an e-mail asking for advice via e-mail

- use a cell phone if you can avoid it

- arrive late for appointments, and never cancel one unless it's a real emergency

- expect your contact to guide the conversation—be the "host": ask questions

- communicate indecision in your professional goals—discuss options, but show direction, focus, and passion for a specific area

- be overly modest—this is a time to articulate your strengths and experiences

- speak negatively about past employers or jobs—be honest, but find the silver lining for even the most trying experience

CHRISTOPHER MURRAY, LMSW
Project Coordinator and Counselor

Age: 40

Education: BA, theatre; MSW

Years at current organization: 4

Years in current position: 1

First job out of college: Singing cocktail waiter, yikes!

First job in nonprofit sector: Marketing associate/literary associate for a theatre company

The Lesbian, Gay, Bisexual & Transgender Community Center

www.gaycenter.org

Mission: The Lesbian, Gay, Bisexual & Transgender Community Center provides a home for the birth, nurture, and celebration of our organizations, institutions, and culture; cares for our individuals and groups in need; educates the public and our community; and empowers our individuals and groups to achieve their fullest potential.

Operating budget: $6.5 million

Number of employees: 72

Number of employees who report to you: 1 staff member and 1 intern, plus volunteers

Q & A

Q: Informally, describe your career track.
A: I came to New York City after college to pursue a career in the theatre but transitioned into a social service career. I most recently worked for a health care training organization while I studied for my master's in social work and then began working at the LGBT Center.

Q: What do you know now that you wish you had known when you were first job hunting?
A: I wish I had a clearer sense of the benefits of more formal mentoring relationships early on in my career. I also wish I was clearer on how valuable asking detailed questions of people who know about a job can be.

Q: Describe a representative work day.
A: I am a counselor in a mental health program at a gay center, working with people on issues related to drug and alcohol use, coming out, HIV, and gender identity issues. I also work on special topics like methamphetamine abuse and tobacco addiction. On a typical day, I see an average of five clients per day for forty-five-minute sessions. In between, I work on everything else I have to do: creating workshops, developing and conducting trainings, doing outreach, engaging in policy efforts, or screening walk-in or phone clients.

Q: What misconceptions do people have about your job? What's the reality?
A: People think that identity-based organizations shouldn't have the same challenges or problems that all nonprofits have. They think an organization that is for a particular kind of people should function better, so they hold it to a higher standard. Maybe they should.

Q: What do you love about your work?
A: I love my community and working with people who are trying to make their lives better. I like being so integrated into my community by working at a place where 6,000 people walk through the doors each week to come to one of 300 groups or 90 twelve-step meetings—or even a dance!

Q: What advice would you give to someone interested in a career similar to yours?
A: Take advantage of specialized education, whether a social work degree or something else. It gives you an expertise and a framework for what you do, and it increases the likelihood you'll get paid better and be more respected.

Q: What resources might help someone interested in your field and job function?
A: If you're in New York, visit CityLimits.org (www.citylimits.org) for job listings. Then get on the mailing list for the Center's monthly free newsletter, *Center Happenings,* which describes everything we do and that goes on here and that is mailed to more than 50,000 households in the New York area. For social work information, explore the National Association of Social Workers (www.naswdc.org), *Psychotherapy Networker* magazine (www.psychotherapynetworker.org), and The National Association of LGBT Community Centers (www.lgbtcenters.org).

Q: What do you look for when hiring a new employee?
A: Someone smart and with clear qualifications; someone who represents the diversity of the community we serve; and someone who has a sensibility that is client-centered, compassionate, and curious.

NETWORKING IN THE E-AGE

Q&A with **Reid Hoffman**

Founder • LinkedIn • www.linkedin.com

Q: What do professional networking sites offer a job seeker?

A: Online networks such as LinkedIn offer access to quality connections within organizations. It is a resource that can help you identify job openings, research organizations, and find contacts at organizations you're interested in. You're able to leverage your personal contacts—and the contacts of your contacts—to make professional referrals on your behalf. And it's also a two-way street: you're set up online so that headhunters and other recruiters can find you as well.

Q: What makes for successful e-networking in the job hunt?

A: It's important to prepare a compelling profile—and one that is created specifically for the web form. Don't cut-and-paste your print résumé for your online presence. Rather, adapt it appropriately so it suits the electronic medium, and expand it from there. Take advantage of the format and be both creative and professional. If you're using LinkedIn, new users should claim their personal URLs as soon as they join, and get that page up and running.

Q: How many contacts should you start with?

A: It's best to establish twenty to thirty connections to launch your e-networking. Otherwise you won't have enough visibility on the network.

Q: What if someone doesn't have that many contacts?

A: Most people are surprised by how many professional contacts they actually have. Even if it's early in your career, you have professors, key family members and friends, and individuals who managed you as a volunteer, intern, or employee. And once you get up and running, you'll be pleasantly shocked to see just how many people your friends know.

Q: What type of information should be included in a profile?

A: When using a network to job hunt, be careful and strategic about the information you post. Remember, this is not a social network. Be professional. Put your best foot forward. Don't hesitate to include your interests and passions when appropriate, but approach the profile as an executive bio and only include information you would like a potential employer to see. Use the space to promote your skills, experiences, and other credentials that will make you an attractive employee. And be concise. Make sure you have a summary section that captures readers' attention quickly.

Q: Can e-savvy job seekers do all of their job hunting online?

A: Absolutely not. A networking site should be considered only one job-search strategy of many. The Internet can help you find new connections and maintain relationships, but nothing replaces interacting with people in the real world. If you spend time on your profile it can communicate elements of your personality, a great deal about your experience, and insights about what you would offer a potential employer. But to convey your passion, and to motivate someone to help you find a job—or better, to offer you one—you need to meet that person face-to-face.

Q: Any special tips for the nonprofit sector job seeker using the Internet?

A: Nonprofits care a lot about personal referrals. At LinkedIn, your profile can feature recommendations. People interested in public service might use this function to highlight written endorsements from professors or nonprofit sector leaders in their field. Have your references concentrate on specific skills or personality traits. Also, be thoughtful about the key words you use in your profile so that organizations with vacancies that fit your experience are likely to find you if they're searching the site. And finally, make sure you use the advanced search option to hone in on an industry—such as "nonprofit"—and to research specific nonprofit organizations and their key staff.

Q: Any final thoughts?

A: Even if you first enter e-networking for your job hunt, don't stop networking once you accept an offer. Networking is critical at every stage of your career. As you advance, your network will only become more powerful and be able to do more for you and the organizations, issues, and individuals you care about. So, in other words, stay linked in! ∎

Reid Hoffman founded LinkedIn in 2003 and currently serves as chairman and president of products for the company. The LinkedIn network includes more than 12 million experienced professionals from around the world, representing 150 industries.

Targeted Search Strategies

As you search for specific job vacancies, the operative word for your approach should be "targeted." You want to identify and implement search strategies that allow you to hone in on openings in your target issue area and job function. And you want to localize your search to a specific geographic region. The openings you uncover also should match your skill sets, level of experience, and salary requirements. Pursuing leads that don't match your core criteria wastes time, energy, and your precious contacts whom you will ask to serve as references.

In general, the more targeted the search strategy the fewer positions you'll uncover. But these positions are apt to be the most suitable for you. As such, it is worth the investment of time to get that one golden lead. And then it is worth the extra time it takes to prepare a targeted application package for that specific job.

The broadest search strategies—for example, Internet searches with open-ended criteria plugged in—will yield the most hits, but you'll need to sort through the leads carefully to identify postings that are a true match for you. It does not make sense to send out hundreds of résumés in the hopes that one will stick. People rarely land jobs this way, and certainly not good ones. When using the broader strategies, do what you can to refine and localize them. The Appendix lists specific websites and other resources that provide nonprofit sector job postings.

Ranked in order from the most targeted to the broadest, here are search strategies that you will want to consider:

- research that leads to direct employer contact
- networking
- executive recruiters
- career and job fairs
- newspaper advertisements
- websites and Internet searches
- listservs
- résumé banks

You may employ some or all of these search strategies. But make sure you don't invest too much time in the seemingly easiest approaches. If you're shy about networking, for example, you may find Internet searching and posting your résumé online the most appealing routes. But you'll be doing yourself and your career a real disservice if you don't also "pound the pavement" and try the more personal strategies as well.

- **Research that leads to direct employer contact.** The research discussed in the previous section ("Sound Research," pages 219–223) will help you develop a list of dozens of organizations where you are interested in working. You should regularly monitor the websites of these organizations so that you become aware of any job openings as soon as they are posted online. These organizations should also be on your radar screen as you review other job resources, as not every organization posts their positions online. The goal is to identify vacancies of interest to you and that you are qualified for, and then contact the employing organization directly.

- **Networking.** Networking also is discussed in the previous section ("Effective Networking," pages 226–233). It's vital that, as you communicate with individuals in your ever-growing network, you ask them about any existing or forthcoming vacancies that they are aware of. You'll want to ask them about specific organizations where they might have leads and if they are aware of any job openings on the horizon. Insider information—of an upcoming maternity leave, family relocation, firing, or new foundation grant that will expand programs, to name just a handful of examples—can give you early access to a position. If someone in your network provides the lead to a position, that contact might also help you get your foot in the door to pursue it.

- **Executive recruiters.** Executive recruiters—often known as headhunters—work to fill specific positions on behalf of a client organization. These positions are usually senior-level posts (e.g., presidents or executive directors, senior vice presidents, and senior development directors).

While working with executive recruiters is a very targeted strategy (since a headhunter recruits only for a particular position), it is also a passive strategy: you have to hope a recruiter comes to you. If one does, great. However, unless you are at the executive director level or a seasoned development professional, it makes little sense to try to secure an interview with a headhunter for exploratory purposes. It would be quite a long shot that you're a match for the select positions a headhunter is currently pursuing.

Having made these disclaimers, however, it's worth noting that executive recruiting agencies specializing in nonprofit sector positions are multiplying. If you have significant professional experience—especially in senior management, administration, or directing development programs—you might reach out to some agencies and determine for yourself whether building a relationship with them would be worthwhile.

- **Career and job fairs.** Career fairs bring together prospective employers in a region for a one-day recruitment and informational event. Some college campuses organize nonprofit sector-specific career and job fairs, either independently or in partnership with other schools (and some nonprofit organizations may participate in more traditional for-profit career fairs as well). Idealist.org/Action Without Borders (www.idealist.org) and many state chapters of the National Council of Nonprofit Associations (www.ncna.org) also host career events.

THE ELEVATOR PITCH

by **Kerri Day Keller**

Director of Career and Employment Services • Kansas State University • www.k-state.edu/ces

As a job seeker, you need a concise, compelling "elevator pitch" that delivers your personal marketing message in the two or three minutes you would have if caught in an elevator with a potential employer. It's the message you'll use when describing your background at an informational meeting or when introducing yourself to someone new in your network. In the time it takes to ride to the top floor of a high-rise, you need to be able to speak smartly and persuasively about your background, experiences, focus, and career goals. And for individuals interested in nonprofit sector careers, you need to take your pitch one step further—you have to communicate passion.

The elevator pitch takes time to prepare and can be challenging to deliver. You need to communicate key information thoughtfully and not sound rushed. You need to strike the right balance between humility and confidence. You need to convey passion without appearing immature. You need to look your subject in the eye as you talk.

Start out by developing a ten-second sound bite:

"Hi, I'm _____. I'm excited to be graduating this year from _____. Over the course of my college career, I have developed experience in _____ and I'm looking for an opportunity to _____."

For your two- to three-minute elevator pitch, add to your sound bite by briefly describing why you are attending an event, who you are visiting at an agency, or what you have been doing in regards to your job search:

"I was researching information online today and ran across an interesting article about Doctors Without Borders. Did you know that _____?"

Stockpile questions you could use to end your pitch so that it forces your listener to respond and engage, and leads more smoothly into a conversation:

"How did you get into your area of work?" "What do you wish you had known when you graduated from college?"

Spend time thinking about the message you want to convey. Remember, voice tone and body language are critical to accurately conveying your message. They can frequently trump your message's content so make sure your voice, body, and message are all in sync. Practice your pitch with friends and family members, or in the shower. Two minutes go by more quickly than you might think. ∎

Kerri Day Keller has been the director of Career and Employment Services at Kansas State University since 2003. Prior to that, she worked in career services at University of North Carolina–Asheville, Northwest Missouri State, Denison University (Granville, Ohio), and Indiana State University. Her interest in nonprofit sector careers developed during her undergraduate studies in social work, volunteer experience with a women's shelter, and a faith-based commitment to social justice issues.

If your campus (or one nearby) is hosting a career fair, you should participate. Fairs allow you to build your network of individuals and organizations and learn about specific opportunities currently or becoming available. Many of these events include skill-building workshops on résumé writing and interviewing, such as those delivered across the country by Commongood Careers (www.cgcareers.org). Career booths are staffed by individuals with substantive knowledge about their organizations and their fields and who can tell you about the skills and experiences they seek in new recruits. At the booths you can test your "elevator pitch"— the pithy, powerful two-minute description of yourself, your experiences, and your career goals that you should be prepared to deliver if you find yourself in an elevator with the executive director of an organization in your field. (See Kerri Day Keller's advice at left for details on how to prepare your elevator pitch.)

Some organizations say they don't have the capacity to send staff to career fairs, so you're more likely to find the larger nonprofit organizations at these events, as these are the organizations with dedicated human resources staff members and recruitment budget dollars. Other organizations participate to find unpaid (or underpaid) interns and don't have full-time professional vacancies. If you attend a fair and don't find an open position that's a match, don't despair.

Use career fairs as an opportunity to learn something new—about an organization, their programs, or the salaries they pay, for example. Introduce yourself to as many people as appropriate and circulate copies of your résumé. Gather names to build your network. Find out whether the staff members attending know of organizations not represented at the fair that you should perhaps contact.

- **Newspaper advertisements.** If you are committed to living in a specific town or city, you should be reading the local paper regularly, as well as perusing its online edition. Local papers provide valuable news and information on policy, people, and organizations working in your field. And of course, the paper's classified section lists specific job postings. In the print editions, they're listed by job function, so you'll need to scan the entire section to find nonprofit sector positions that match your skill sets. A paper's online edition might allow you to conduct a more advanced search and select by industry, job type, or even specific company or organization. Not all organizations post jobs in both a paper's print and online, so you'll want to review both.

Some organizations avoid posting their vacancies in a newspaper or through Internet sites because these methods generate too many applications and they don't have the capacity to review them. Although you need to make your application stand out regardless of how a position is advertised, when responding to a newspaper posting it's particularly important. You might be competing against literally hundreds of other applications. Spend extra time tailoring your cover letter perfectly to that job and organization. Tap your network to see whether anyone is connected to the organization and can make a call flagging your application.

- **Websites and Internet searches.** The Internet provides a seemingly endless array of websites that post job openings. In turn, these sites allow you to search an equally endless array of jobs located throughout the world. Some of the best sites—and ones that are nonprofit sector-specific—are listed in the Appendix. A few issue-specific jobs sites are listed in Chapter 2, following each subsector Spotlight.

Because the Internet is such an endless resource, however, you need to find a way to manage and leverage it for your specific needs. At the start of your job search, spend time reviewing and identifying suitable sites. Determine which sites attract your category of potential employer and job function, and confirm that these sites represent the geographic region you want. Become adept at navigating your targeted sites and concentrate only on these, otherwise you'll become overwhelmed. Experiment with different search terms for "key words" and other core categories that the sites employ, and figure out which uncover vacancies that match your level of experience, skills, and fields and interest.

Monitor and limit the time you spend on the Internet. Don't let Internet searching distract you from more personal, direct outreach. Remind yourself that many organizations do not post their positions online. If you only search electronically, you are likely to miss out on many terrific opportunities.

Only apply for positions that truly match your criteria and that you are qualified for. As with newspaper advertisements and other very public search strategies, remember just how many applicants you will be competing against and dedicate the extra effort to creating a stellar application for the positions that are truly a match.

- **Listservs**. Listservs or electronic newsletters distributed via e-mail to subscribers exist for almost every field and job function and often post vacancies. In addition, many nonprofit sector job websites operate listservs for their registrants that notify you of job postings matching your criteria.

  The Appendix features some nonprofit jobs websites that offer listservs. Research and subscribe to other listservs appropriate for your career goals and monitor them regularly. Ask all of your contacts what listservs they subscribe to and join those if you are able. When you are researching organizations online, check whether their websites post information about listservs they operate and subscribe if appropriate. Think creatively about the types of lists you could join—consider community groups, nonprofit organizations and coalitions, alumni associations, young professional networks, your college career center, the local newspaper and other publications, and other organizations and entities that might publish electronic newsletters.

- **Résumé banks.** Résumé banks, job banks, or job boards are websites where recruitment agencies and employers post job openings and can view the résumés posted by job seekers. Many are massive, with thousands of postings covering a broad geographic area. Using them—or being used by them—often feels like a long, slow fishing expedition. Job seekers can while away countless hours finding jobs for which they're not qualified, based in cities where they have no intention of living. Headhunters often troll these sites for résumés, looking for new clients for their fee-based job placement services. Rogue marketing agencies also sweep job sites gathering e-mail addresses and telephone numbers that they use for unwelcome—or worse, fraudulent—solicitations.

If you want to use a résumé bank, do so cautiously. With the largest sites, target and localize your search as much as possible. Better yet, try to identify niche job boards that specialize in your issue area or job function. Always confirm that a posting is current—check the date stamp and certainly don't apply for a position more than a few weeks old unless you first confirm it is still open. Concentrate on postings that offer complete information on the job and organization, as well as those where you apply directly to the employer.

Persuasive Cover Letters

In your job search you are likely to write dozens of cover letters that will accompany your résumé. You'll write cover letters to

- build your network and request informational meetings

- inquire about possible job openings and request that your résumé be kept on file

- apply for specific positions

The cover letter is perhaps the single most important tool in your communications arsenal. It personalizes your résumé and "pitches" your candidacy to a potential employer, for a specific job. Your cover letter allows you to

- communicate your passion for the mission of a specific organization and your qualifications for a given position

- provide context for your résumé, by elaborating on highlights of your experience

- leverage your network of contacts by mentioning a leader who referred you

- explain "red flags" in your résumé (e.g., a gap in employment or a major career switch)

- demonstrate strong writing skills

Every cover letter must be personally crafted for each communication. (A generic cover letter is a surefire strategy for putting yourself on the "reject" pile.) You may recycle the core of your letters, but generally you should allocate a couple of hours to preparing a personalized piece.

You must thoroughly research the organization and the open position before you write your letter. It's also helpful if you know something about the person the position reports to, the organization's other leadership, and its key funders. This information could inform how you craft your letter.

When applying for a vacant position, your written cover letter should

- be addressed to an individual whenever possible (not "Dear Director of Human Resources")

- start with a clear statement of why you are writing and, if appropriate, who referred you

- communicate your interest in the position and your passion for the organization's mission

- focus on highlights of your experience and skills that have been tailored to the posting
- convey something about your work ethic and team spirit
- state clearly how and when you will follow up
- contain no typographical or grammatical errors
- consist of three or four tight paragraphs and fit on one page (or two pages at most)

As touched on above, a cover letter for a nonprofit sector position or informational meeting request needs to do more than most letters accompanying for-profit job applications. In the nonprofit arena, it's critical that you emphasize both your qualifications for the position and your commitment to the organization's mission. Given the nonprofit sector's need for multitaskers, you may decide to convey your familiarity with wearing multiple hats in a professional setting. You might also consider highlighting any communications and development experience no matter what position you're applying for, since the ability to effectively communicate and raise funds is prized by every nonprofit organization. Nonprofit sector leaders often believe a new hire is joining their "family," so be prepared to demonstrate that you're a team player in addition to your ability to work independently and with minimal direct supervision.

Take the time to share draft cover letters with contacts in your network. Solicit and then incorporate feedback so that your final cover letter is as strong as possible. Keep it up to date. If after a few concentrated weeks of outreach your cover letters don't produce results, start fresh and recraft your letter. If a position is a match for your qualifications but you can't land an interview, it's possible your cover letter or résumé is to blame.

A Stellar Résumé

While your cover letter might be your most vital communication tool, your résumé is your most central. This core document details your career objective, work experience, academic background, and skills.

The purpose of your résumé is to win an interview or secure an informational meeting. It must contain an honest accounting of who you are and what you have accomplished, and it must be error free. It also must be designed and formatted flawlessly so that it is pleasing to the eye and easy to read. The layout and design really do matter, so if you don't have a strong graphic sense, ask for help from someone who does.

Opinions abound as to how to format a résumé and what information should go where. Many resources are dedicated exclusively to the preparation of résumés, and you might consult with these to see the range of thought on the subject and which format makes the most sense for you.

Regardless of which approach you take, your résumé should tell a story—your professional story. In the nonprofit sector, it's particularly important that even the youngest professionals frame their experiences in a way that shows continuity of work, a focus on a specific issue area, the development of clear skills, and a progression of leadership responsibilities. If you've pursued two or more significantly different career paths—and if you are undecided on the type of position you want—then you might have two or more versions of your résumé where you emphasize different aspects of your background.

Many recent graduates put their education information at the top of their résumé. By doing so,

electronic and text-only résumés

After you have prepared your perfect résumé in a hard copy format, you will want to convert it into an electronic or text-only edition. Such a version is mandatory if you are sending your résumé in the body of an e-mail or using it to cut and paste content to an online application, for example.

In a nutshell, electronic résumés have absolutely no formatting. Layout and design are not important (and, in fact, cause problems). Remove all underlining, bullets, italic, and bold text. Delete any autoformatted items such as em dashes and smart quotes (i.e., replace a long dash "—" with two hyphens "--" and curly quotation marks " " with straight ones " "). Take out all tabs and columns and instead divide sections only by line breaks (paragraph marks), with the entire document left justified. Use a sans serif font such as **Arial** in 12-point.

Depending on the job function and type of organization you are interested in, you may find it necessary to create a "keyword" résumé in an electronic format. These text-only or scannable résumés emphasize specific nouns or phrases that an employer (or computer) may search for when scanning résumés housed in a stored electronic database. The keywords include job titles, skills, responsibilities, industry terminology, and education and certification. Keyword résumés are more common in the for-profit sector, especially in the high-tech arena.

Once you have completely removed all the formatting, cut and paste the new text-only document into an e-mail and send it to yourself as a test. If any formatting glitches come through, correct them.

you're highlighting your academic life over your professional life. Ideally, you have enough work and internship experience that you can lead with these—your academic credentials can be at the bottom of your résumé. You can't hide the fact that you are a recent graduate, but you want a potential employer to focus first on what you have done, not what you have studied.

The basic approach to a strong résumé is apt to be the same whether you're applying for a business, government, or nonprofit sector position. However, a nonprofit sector résumé needs to communicate some additional elements. As touched on throughout this book, nonprofit sector employers want to see commitment to their mission. As you describe your skills and accomplishments, convey your knowledge in and passion for a specified field.

In addition, you might choose to highlight certain skills in a separate section. Applicants often mention computer skills and proficiency in certain software applications. But unless such qualifications are truly relevant to the position, don't spend much time on them. In our current age, it goes without saying (one hopes) that you're proficient with a computer. Instead, focus on the skills that nonprofit organizations seek, irrespective of the specific vacancy. If you have fundraising and development experience, say so. List any workshops you've completed on grant writing or media strategies. State your communication and editing skills, and if you are bilingual, say so.

As with your cover letter, circulate your draft résumé to your advisors. Make sure someone in your network is a stickler for detail, and ask that person to edit your document carefully. If you still have access to your college's office of career services, ask a staff member there for feedback. During informational meetings, encourage your contacts to offer their thoughts on your résumé. Find a graphic designer to give her opinions on the style and format of your résumé.

Deal-Closing Interviews

Your research, networking, cover letter, and résumé worked and you have landed an interview. Congratulations! Now it's time to try to seal the deal. The interview is your opportunity to show the face and personality that lie behind your paper trail. It is a time to elaborate on your experiences in response to the interviewer's questions, communicate your commitment to the organization's mission, ask thoughtful and focused questions about the job and organization, and sell yourself. It is your chance to demonstrate your personality, critical thinking ability, professionalism, work ethic, passion, and good humor. The interview is your opportunity to prove that you are the candidate for that job.

An organization's hiring process may consist of one interview or a series of them. A human resources professional may conduct a preliminary screening interview that you must pass before you can meet directly with the supervisor for the vacant position. Interviews may be conducted one-on-one or in a group setting with a number of staff members. Regardless of the format, interviews require serious preparation.

As discussed earlier, you must thoroughly research the organization before applying for a position and attending an interview. Employ all research tools—including your network—to learn as much as you can about the organization, its senior staff members, and the position. Learn about the personality and personal interests of the hiring director. Gain a deep understanding of the skills and experiences the organization is seeking. Think about how you will articulate highlights of your background, and how you will handle a question about your weaknesses.

Be prepared with excellent questions about the organization and the specific department where you would work. Ask pointed questions about the nature of the position, and use your questions—and the answers you receive—to further sell yourself. While preparation is vital, be flexible and able to respond to the flow of the conversation. Listen carefully during the interview so that you think of appropriate questions on the spot.

If you have holes in your résumé, think carefully about how you will address them if asked (or

perhaps address them proactively). In some areas, remind yourself that less is more. If you have a clear, honest explanation for a gap in employment, for example, say it, and then stop. You don't need to go into an in-depth explanation.

If you have gripes about a past employer, keep them to yourself. No matter how justified you may be in your feelings, a potential employer doesn't want to hear about your past problems, and you don't want to risk the chance of coming off as a difficult employee. Rehearse answers to the most difficult questions with a friend or family member. Keep those answers brief. If the conversation pauses, don't rush to fill it with unnecessary information; rather, redirect the flow to a related question that you have.

Make eye contact throughout the interview. If necessary, take notes, but take them quickly and look up as much as possible. Try to determine the organization's timeline for filling the position and get a sense of when you are likely to hear back from them. Consider asking whether you may stay in touch with the interviewer and follow up in a given period of time if the anticipated deadline has passed. End the meeting with a hearty handshake, a smile, and an enthusiastic "thank-you."

Appropriate Follow-up and Negotiation

You've made it this far. Your hard work paid off, and you landed an interview for a position that is a great match for you and your qualifications. You nailed the interview. It only seems fair that you now should get to sit back and relax.

Unfortunately, the process—and your role in it—is not yet over. You need to deliver strong follow-up to the interview and be prepared to act if you don't hear from the organization within a reasonable time. You also need to think carefully about how you will respond to an offer once you receive one.

The following two sections cover what to do while waiting for an offer, as well as what to do once you receive one.

Waiting for an offer

Mail a follow-up letter or send a formal e-mail within a day of an interview. If you are still interested in the position, restate your interest and briefly recap your most relevant credentials. Thank the interviewer for his or her time and emphasize again your passion for the work and mission of the organization. Include at least one item that distinguishes your letter from a generic follow-up communication. Consider highlighting something that you learned during the meeting that served to increase your enthusiasm for the position, or perhaps mention additional research you did following the interview on a specific program area and your impressions of it.

If during your conversation you mentioned an article, expert, or other resource that was of interest to the interviewer, provide details on that reference as a courtesy. If the interviewer asked for more information, a writing sample, or references, provide those. Even if nothing in particular was requested, you may decide it is appropriate to voluntarily submit some additional materials or the name of a past employer who could support your application.

a note on handwritten notes

Some job seekers (and career coaches) believe a handwritten follow-up card adds a personal touch to the recruitment process. And indeed, some prospective employers find such notes appealing. Others, however, find them sweet but unprofessional. Don't risk it. Save the personal note writing for thank-you's and updates to close friends, family members, and other people in your network's inner circle. Keep the rest of your communications—those that reach out to new contacts for your network, request informational meetings, apply for jobs, and thank interviewers for their time—professional. Type all of these outreach efforts on business stationery. Apply the personal touch just to your signature.

If the interviewer pointed out an area where your application seemed weak, see whether you can address that. Communicate the right mix of enthusiasm for the position and willingness to make an extra effort in your follow-up without seeming overly eager. Above all, be prompt and professional in your communications.

Have a plan for how you will continue to follow up if you don't hear back within a reasonable amount of time. Ideally, you will have learned during the interview the organization's timeline for reviewing applications, checking references, scheduling follow-up interviews, and making an offer. You may have gotten a sense of the interviewer's receptiveness to receiving follow-up calls from you. And you may also have determined how organized, efficient, and professional the organization is likely to be in the process and adjusted your expectations accordingly.

Once your deadline for hearing back has passed, launch your follow-up plan. Keep in mind Lisa Brown Morton's advice on how to handle this difficult situation (see "How to Handle 'Deafening Silence,'" pages 251–252) and try not to get too discouraged. You might place a call or send another letter, or have a member of your network call on your behalf. You might attend an event sponsored by the organization or find another way to stay connected to it. Be tenacious but calm, and persevere as long as it seems appropriate.

benefits beyond salary

Be sure to think about compensation beyond your salary. Some of the benefits that might be included in your package—and which you should consider—are

- medical insurance
- dental insurance
- vision care
- life insurance
- vacation
- holidays
- sick leave/personal days
- 401(k) plans
- pension plans
- tuition reimbursement
- overtime and comp time
- parking, commuting, and mobile phone fee reimbursements
- expense reimbursement

Determine which of these are most important to you and determine if the offer concerning them is adequate. If not, approach any negotiation around your job offer with a clear understanding of your goals and any flexibility you have. Work hard to learn where your employer has the ability to adjust the offer.

HOW TO HANDLE "DEAFENING SILENCE"
OR WHAT NOT TO DO WHEN FACED WITH BAD HIRING BEHAVIOR

by **Lisa Brown Morton**

President and CEO • Nonprofit HR Solutions • www.nonprofithr.com

You've done everything right. You crafted a strong résumé and perfect cover letter. You networked and identified positions that match your skill sets. You landed an interview and prepared admirably for it. You showed up on time, dressed professionally, were articulate, and asked great questions. The interviewer seemed to like you. You promptly sent a follow-up letter. And then …

Nada. Zilch. Nothing.

When a prospective employer drops the ball—or worse, behaves unprofessionally—at any point in the recruitment process, it's frustrating at best. Candidates deserve to be treated with the same respect that they show a potential employer. Interviewers should be punctual for appointments, and ask only appropriate and legal questions. Ideally, employers follow up with all applicants within a reasonable time, but certainly with everyone who made it to the interview stage.

Unfortunately, this doesn't always happen. Organizations are frequently understaffed and many don't have dedicated human resources professionals. Some may not even be aware of the mistakes they make or the bad image they project. However, while this may explain the behavior, it doesn't excuse it. If bad behavior happens to you, there are a number of reactions and actions to avoid.

- **Don't take it personally.** The behavior reflects on the organization, its processes, and its management—not on you or your qualifications.

- **Don't make it universal.** The vast majority of nonprofit organizations strive for a professional and smooth recruitment process. One or two bad experiences should not turn you off of a nonprofit sector career.

- **Don't overreact.** Consider just how bad the behavior was and see whether you can understand what went wrong. Was the organization in the throes of a crisis, in the middle of a move, or operating with a short staff? Might the behavior have been an anomaly, and is it possible that the organization really is a great place to work?

- **Don't underreact.** No matter how hungry you are for a job, don't dismiss your intuition or the evidence. If you were treated poorly and you can't attribute it to one person's bad day, move on. You will hurt yourself and your career if you take a job at a poorly run organization or have to report to a weak manager.

(continued on page 252)

(continued from page 251)

- **Don't assume you're powerless.** During an interview, get the interviewer's business card and confirm the organization's anticipated hiring timeline. Ask if you may follow up, and do so if you haven't heard. If egregiously inappropriate questions were asked during an interview, consider alerting the organization's human resources or executive director—it's a risk, but they may welcome the feedback so they can make their practices better.

No one wants to be treated poorly, especially when you're in the vulnerable position of job hunting. But don't lose sight of the forest for the trees. The nonprofit sector is filled with talented, professional, and passionate individuals doing great work at stellar organizations. Bad apples exist everywhere, and mistakes are made—especially in the HR function. If you have a negative experience, learn from it. And remember it. Once you land the job you dream of, use that experience to help your organization become an even better place to work.

Lisa Brown Morton founded Nonprofit HR Solutions to provide human resources consulting services to nonprofit organizations. Previously, Lisa worked as director of human resources and administration for the American Symphony Orchestra League. Lisa volunteers extensively and serves on the board of directors of the DC Rape Crisis Center.

Once you receive an offer, use the advice presented in the next section ("Responding to an offer," below). If declined, use the experience to your advantage. If you believe the organization was impressed by you and your application, regard its key point people as new additions to your network. Send another note thanking them for their consideration of your application and informing them that you would like to stay in touch. Keep apprised of their work. If their organization has a newsletter, ask to receive it. If they have a listserv, ask to put yourself on it. Stay connected to the organization and the leaders whom you have gotten to know. Don't let them forget you or what they liked about you.

Responding to an offer

Good news! You've received an offer. The first thing to do is congratulate yourself. Take time to reflect on what you accomplished, for the journey was probably not an easy one. Your research, networking, application, and interviewing were effective. An organization—presumably one where you would like to work—wants you to be part of its team. Allow yourself to feel proud and recognize your achievement.

It's extraordinarily helpful to be prepared when you receive an offer. In the best cases, you discussed the compensation package in advance of receiving the call, as well as all of the most important details about the job. You established that the organization would be a good place to work and has adequate resources, the job is a match for your career goals, and the offer is acceptable to you. In these situations, there are few surprises or unknowns, and you can simply extend enthusiastic thanks and ask for a certain amount of time to respond.

Otherwise, you should think through the unanswered questions you have in advance of receiving an offer. You did the necessary research to speak with confidence about the job and your value. When the call comes in, lead with grace. Communicate pleasure and appreciation for the invitation. Then ask for details. Follow up with the specific questions you have about the package.

Some of the details you may want to confirm include monetary items, such as salary, anticipated increases and the schedule for reviews, benefits, overtime, comp time, relocation assistance, and coverage of expenses. Other details are nonmonetary (see "Benefits Beyond Salary," page 250, for a list of some items to consider), such as your title, training and educational opportunities, access to technology, and travel assignments. As Deepak Malhotra stresses in "Negotiating with Aplomb" (pages 256–260), be sure to think beyond just salary. Determine the issues that are most vital to you, and make sure to get the information you need about those in particular. And remember, with a nonprofit sector position it's as important that you assess the merits of the job as the merits of the organization.

Once you have the information you need, ask whether you can expect to receive the offer in writing (as you should) and for time to respond. If you receive a written offer—and even if you don't—acknowledge it in writing and confirm that you will respond by the deadline. Then weigh your options.

Hopefully, you will be in a position where you do not have to accept the first offer you receive. You can reflect on all aspects of the job and organization to determine whether it meets your goals for your next career move. The issues you should consider are discussed throughout this book, from the nature of the work to the mission of the organization. You'll consider where the organization is based; how well the job taps into your skills and strengths; the organization's culture, size, reputation, and financial security; who you will report to; and the package they offer you.

If you're unsure about the job and the offer you received, this is a good time to return to the most trusted members of your network. Talk through your excitement as well as your concerns. Discuss how this offer compares to other offers you have, your current job, or staying unemployed and continuing to search. Get guidance on additional questions you should ask. On your own, decide whether there are issues that are "deal breakers" and then prioritize secondary issues as "nice but not necessary" versus "important." Weigh what you have been offered with what you want and have carefully determined that you deserve.

BYRON HATCH
Associate Director of Membership Services

Age: 31

Education: BBA, accounting; JD

Years at current organization: 2

Years in current position: 1

First job out of college: State tax consultant for an accounting firm

First job in nonprofit sector: Current position

National Collegiate Athletic Association

www.ncaa.org

Mission: The NCAA's core purpose is to govern competition in a fair, safe, equitable, and sportsman-like manner, and to integrate intercollegiate athletics into higher education so that the educational experience of the student-athlete is paramount. The association shares a belief in and commitment to the collegiate model of athletics in which students participate as an avocation, balancing their academic, social, and athletic experiences.

Operating budget: $564 million

Number of employees: 400

Number of employees who report to you: 2, coordinator of membership services and a part-time membership services associate

Q&A

Q: Informally, describe your career track.
A: I began in the for-profit sector as a tax consultant for an international Big 5 accounting firm. After three years as a tax consultant, I realized I wanted a career in intercollegiate athletics. It was a major shift, and I could not secure interviews because I lacked experience. I started networking, and an associate athletics director suggested I volunteer in the athletics department of an NCAA member institution, which I did. Six months

later, I attended an NCAA job fair, where I introduced myself to the president of the organization and then immediately followed up with an e-mail. He helped me secure an interview in the membership services department at the NCAA, and I landed the job.

Q: What do you know now that you wish you had known when you were first job hunting?
A: I wish I had known the real value of networking and experience in your chosen field. Get your foot in the door—through volunteering, interning, or entry-level work—so you can then demonstrate knowledge and experience.

Q: Describe a representative work day.
A: I serve as the NCAA's main point person on issues surrounding student-athletes who possess a learning disability and are not initially eligible for NCAA athletics participation because they do not qualify academically. I serve as a liaison to the Committee on Athletics Certification. I provide written and verbal interpretations of NCAA legislation and serve as a member of the membership services hiring team. In a typical day I might participate in a number of meetings addressing the eligibility of student-athletes or the work of an NCAA committee. I may be scheduled for shifts to handle telephone inquiries from the general public and athletics staff at NCAA member institutions and conferences.

Q: What misconceptions do people have about your job? What's the reality?
A: People often believe the NCAA does not set as its priority the well-being of students. In fact, our mission—and what drives the people who work here—is the "student-athlete first" philosophy.

Our objective is to help prepare student-athletes for life beyond college.

Q: What do you love about your work?
A: I love that I get to work with such talented individuals who are so dedicated to their jobs. I feel blessed that I have the opportunity to make a positive impact on intercollegiate athletics on a daily basis.

Q: What advice would you give to someone interested in a career similar to yours?
A: First, gather as much information as you can about the field and the nonprofit sector before launching your search. Reach out to people with experience in jobs you are interested in and learn what specific careers entail.

Q: What resources might help someone interested in your field and job function?
A: I would recommend such organizations (and their websites) as the National Association of College Directors of Athletics (NACDA) (http://nacda.cstv.com), National Association of Collegiate Women Athletic Administrators (NACWAA) (www.nacwaa.org), Sports Lawyers Association (SLA) (www.sportslaw.org), and Black Coaches & Administrators (BCA) (http://bcasports.cstv.com), as well as the NCAA conferences and website.

Q: What do you look for when hiring a new employee?
A: Experience in the field and in the specific job function (or directly transferable skills). Communication skills, education, and an understanding of the NCAA. The ability to multitask, balance work and life, and participate in a team setting.

NEGOTIATING WITH APLOMB

Q&A with **Deepak Malhotra**

Coauthor, *Negotiation Genius* [40]

Q: Is negotiation really a science and not an art?

A: Negotiation is a process at least as old as human existence. Any time you have a situation with two or more people having different interests or perspectives who need to reach an agreement, you're in the domain of negotiation. Since we've all been negotiating since a very young age, we often don't think about it systematically or scientifically. But there is tremendous new knowledge on how people interact, create value, influence others, and manage satisfaction. We now know there are proven strategies, principles, and techniques you can employ that will advance your position.

Q: Does everyone have it in them to be a "genius negotiator"?

A: When we think of geniuses, we focus on the Einsteins and Mozarts of the world, and conclude that their level of performance is out of reach. With negotiation, it's not so true. The two raw elements for successful negotiation are being open to and interested in the perspective of other people, and being able to reflect thoughtfully about the situation you are in. Virtually everyone has these capabilities, and thus the ability to succeed at the bargaining table.

Q: In your book, you talk about "investigative negotiation." What can a negotiator learn from *Law and Order*?

A: If a detective approached a crime scene assuming he had all the answers from the get-go, we'd have a lot of bungled investigations. Your gut instinct is to assume you know what is going on (or who is guilty). When you enter a negotiation, you need to put aside your assumptions and learn as much as you can about the people and their interests. What's really at play here? What are the hot button issues? Where is there flexibility? What do they need from me? How can I bring value to them?

Q: Does all of this investigation take place during the actual negotiation?

A: Absolutely not. Advance investigation is critical. For example, in a job search, you should learn as much about the organization as possible. Talk to current and former employees, visit a career placement office, and conduct research regarding what the job entails and how much flexibility there is in your role and your compensation. Be aware of your assumptions and gather information that will support or refute them. A lot of the action in a negotiation happens before you get to the bargaining table. The earlier you start, the better positioned you are when it comes time to negotiate.

United Nations ambassador Lakhdar Brahimi is credited with superb negotiation skills in Afghanistan and elsewhere. When asked how he prepared, he recalled advice he once received: "You go somewhere and you try to understand that country *because one day you may need to negotiate with that country.*" I love this perspective. The best negotiators prepare for as many eventualities as far in advance as possible and not just when the real or metaphorical bombs start falling. They think on a macrolevel about their interests and the nature of success, and work to gain trust and establish the setting for open communications well before they find themselves in the hot seat.

Q: How is building trust particularly important in a job negotiation?

A: Job negotiations are special in many ways, but a key factor is that you will be working with the people with whom you are negotiating. It's not like buying a car or a house, where the players are

out of your life soon after the negotiation concludes. It's important to keep your negotiations positive when you're dealing with your work. Always define your task as having two objectives: to manage your outcomes and manage their satisfaction. If you negotiate effectively, you can have a good deal and a good relationship; if you rely entirely on gut instinct, you might end up with neither.

Q: What are the biggest mistakes people make when approaching a negotiation?

A: The top mistake is that people don't prepare enough—or at all. They neglect to consider all of their interests, or they narrowly define them. Second, they tend to talk too much and ask too few questions. They fail to grasp the situation as perceived by others and fail to identify constraints that will get in the way of what they want. If you want a good job offer, you really need to understand both what you want and all of the issues that stand in your way. Avoid being too focused on one issue (such as salary); define your interests more broadly. If you do, you will give the other side more ways of satisfying your needs and you

(continued on page 258)

(continued from page 257)

will avoid talking yourself into a corner because you've made extreme demands for something they simply cannot give.

Q: How, specifically, can you negotiate a higher salary than what has been offered?

A: To begin with, it's critical to remember it's not just about salary, it's about the entire compensation package and job offer. My advice for making the whole package as strong as possible is best explained through four different—and increasingly persuasive—approaches you might take to an offer.

Approach 1: You just ask for a higher salary and see what they say.

Approach 2: You ask for a higher salary and restate the value you bring to the organization.

Approach 3: You ask for a higher salary, restate your value, share research that justifies your number, and open up the conversation for discussion.

Approach 4: You do all of the above, but instead of focusing only on a higher salary, you create a dialogue around your other interests (e.g., other ways they can sweeten the deal for you). This might be more advancement opportunities, better projects, or a flexible schedule, for example.

The fourth approach offers you the most. You justify your request by talking about your value and legitimize your justification with evidence. But you also offer flexibility and openness, which puts you in the most powerful bargaining position.

Q. Do you have any special negotiation tips for the nonprofit sector job seeker?

A: I have stressed that for any job seeker, salary should be considered only one issue of many. With nonprofits, it's particularly true. Approach any negotiation thinking carefully about the full range of benefits and opportunities available.

Often, there's less precedent regarding compensation for a particular job in the nonprofit sector, so smart negotiation is even more vital. Nonprofit jobs are often quite unique. They are usually specific to a given issue, to an organization's approach, and to the people filling them. A Fortune 500 company does so much hiring that they're apt to follow a boilerplate process in recruiting and extending offers. But a nonprofit may not be following much precedent, and could have more flexibility than you realize.

Q: How should a job seeker approach the dreaded "What's your salary range?" question?

A: Understand the data out there, and be very clear in your own mind about your bottom line. Based on your research regarding similar jobs, the organization itself, and your own background, ask yourself, "What is the highest number I can justify?" As you present your figure, also share the value you bring. For example, you might say, "Let me share some data with you and aspects of my background that are unique." Do you speak and write fluently in another language? Do you have a relevant specialized degree? Use this moment to reinforce your qualifications.

Sometimes, the job seeker doesn't have good information on the employer's parameters. In these situations, don't cut yourself short. You may decide not to offer a figure at this point, and instead discuss the whole package and try to learn more about the zone of possibilities. You might very confidently and respectfully say, "I'd love to have that discussion. But first, it may help us both if I share with you more about what I bring to the organization, and you share with me more about what the organization needs and values. I don't want you to pay too much or too little, so maybe we can start out working together to figure out how best I can maximize the value I bring to your organization."

Q: What if a job seeker has only one offer, and is bargaining from a position of weakness?

A: First, you often can choose the information you want to share and how you frame it. Second, if you are asked directly, don't fabricate nonexistent job offers. People lie when they are unprepared for a tough question and think they will lose power. Be confident and tell the truth. For example, there is nothing wrong with the following response: "I have just started interviewing and am not entertaining any other offers at the moment. This puts me in a good position to concentrate on your organization and this position, both of which I am very interested in." Use your response to redirect the conversation to the value you bring and the research you have on what you are worth.

In addition, if you have very little leverage, consider one seemingly counterintuitive approach to negotiating your job offer. First, accept the offer with enthusiasm and clear commitment. Then tell your future boss, "I'm going to accept this offer regardless, because I am extremely passionate about the work we will be doing. However, I would like to explore any possibility of improving the offer." This can send a strong signal that you are not trying to play the power game (which is good if you have no power), but are simply

(continued on page 260)

(continued from page 259)

interested in working together to figure out what is most fair. Present your rationale for what you believe you deserve and, again, the value you bring to the organization.

Q: Is there a way to practice good negotiation?

A: Most negotiation courses in business and law schools revolve around role-playing and simulations. In our book, we offer lots of advice and strategies, but you need to figure out which ones will work best for you and how to apply them to your own situations. Role-playing can help in this area. It involves other people so you can get objective feedback on your strengths and weaknesses. Prepare a scenario that requires a job-related negotiation. Ask a friend to act the other side, and then play out the conversation different ways—when the negotiator is aggressive, conciliatory, distracted, or unprofessional. Hone your arguments, anticipate reactions, ask questions, and practice responding to tough and simple questions alike. In the process, you're apt to learn more about what you want and the best approach for achieving it.

Q: Are there situations when you shouldn't negotiate at all?

A: I think our negotiation book may be unique in that it actually addresses when you shouldn't negotiate. In general, people can and probably should negotiate more often—and more systematically—than they do. But some people over-negotiate. You shouldn't "nickel and dime" someone just to score a win. In the process, you could ruin an important relationship. Also, consider the timing. Right *now* is not always the best time to negotiate. For example, if you've been invited for a site visit following a job offer, that's a time to learn more about the organization, its people, and the work they do. Don't start negotiating in the first hour of your visit, or you'll risk sending the wrong signal about what you value most.

Deepak Malhotra is an associate professor in the Negotiations, Organizations, and Markets Unit at the Harvard Business School. He teaches negotiation in the MBA program and various executive programs, including the Advanced Management Program. Deepak's research focuses on negotiation strategy, trust development, international and ethnic dispute resolution, and competitive escalation. For more on *Negotiation Genius*, visit www.NegotiationGenius.com.

If you decide you need to negotiate the offer, do so thoughtfully and systematically. Read carefully Deepak Malhotra's interview ("Negotiating with Aplomb," pages 256–260), establish clarity on your goals and note where there is "wiggle room," and role-play the expected negotiation. End the negotiation with enthusiasm and a restatement of your interest in the organization and position, and let them know that you will follow up immediately.

In a Nutshell . . .

This chapter has reminded you of the characteristics a person brings to a successful job search. You've charged yourself to be persuasive, prepared, professional, prompt, persistent, and positive in your outreach efforts. You've considered the research, networking, and targeted search strategies you must employ to identify appropriate openings, and you've started working on the cover letters and résumé that will highlight your qualifications and get your application noticed. You've practiced interviewing and negotiating. You know what to do to find and land a job. As important, you know who you are and what you want, and you are prepared and motivated to launch a meaningful career in the nonprofit sector.

The information in the Appendix ahead will direct you to some of the top websites and other resources connected to nonprofit sector careers. They can provide more information on the nonprofit sector and careers in it, as well as specific jobs available at the time you are conducting your search. But a successful job hunt depends on very specialized research, developed around an individual's areas of interest and expertise as well as work and life priorities. Use these resources as a starting place, but quickly identify the best resources for who you are and what you want in your next professional chapter—and then concentrate on those.

CLOSING THOUGHTS

Finding a great job is a major undertaking. Building a meaningful and rewarding career is a lifelong commitment. Tackling the complexities, challenges, and exhilarating opportunities of work in the nonprofit sector is an investment of time and passion that can yield profoundly rich rewards.

You undoubtedly have friends who delight at the closing of a deal and others who measure success by the size of their paycheck. You probably also know many people who approach their jobs simply as the part of their lives that pays the bills and takes their time from 9 to 5.

If you're considering a nonprofit sector career, it's likely that you see your life of meaning as connected to public service. You're committed to finding work that "makes a difference," that contributes to some aspect of the health and welfare of people or our planet.

You're fortunate if this is your calling. Meaningful work is a gift to yourself. Building a career that helps advance your concept of what is good and establishing a life that is meaningful to you will carry into your senior years. Lucky the person who crawls into bed at night and feels great about his or her day at the office. And what a joy that with nonprofit sector work, a "day at the office" is usually anything but.

Today, the nonprofit sector is more vibrant than ever. There is a place for you at a healthy, effective, and stable nonprofit organization. There is work for you that taps into your experiences, leverages your skills, and speaks to your passion. And there is a career for you that will allow you to pay rent, support a family, take vacations, and even retire one day.

Reading this book is just one small part of building that career, but it's an important step. By taking time to focus on your goals, you've recognized the work and commitment required to realize them. It is this thoughtfulness and determination that makes a successful job seeker and a great addition to the nonprofit sector's workforce.

APPENDIX: RESOURCES

The following job search resources can assist in implementing the strategies discussed in the book. Though some overlap exists, the resources are organized into five categories:

- nonprofit jobs websites
- nonprofit career books and jobs directories
- periodicals focused on the nonprofit sector
- academic programs
- resources for more information

These lists of resources certainly are not exhaustive. They highlight some of the materials out there that could complement this book in a nonprofit sector job search. As a job seeker, you need to do your own research specific to the field, type of job, and organizations that interest you.

Nonprofit Jobs Websites

A growing number of websites specialize in nonprofit sector jobs and careers. A few are listed here. In addition, select subsector-specific jobs sites are noted in Chapter 2. Spend time with these and similar sites. Determine which seem to be the most appropriate for you and yield promising results in test searches that you conduct.

In addition, conduct research online to develop your own list of city-specific, issue-specific, and job-function-specific jobs websites that you should monitor, as well as national job sites that are not nonprofit specific but that represent well nonprofit sector employment opportunities. And of course, monitor the websites of individual organizations on your target list so you are aware of new positions as soon as they are posted.

Many of the sites listed below also provide valuable information on the nonprofit sector and careers in it. Some operate career- and job-related listservs. Be sure to subscribe to the ones appropriate for you.

In addition, many of the comprehensive jobs sites such as Yahoo! HotJobs (http://hotjobs.yahoo.com), Monster (www.monster.com),

CareerJournal.com (www.careerjournal.com), and many others now have fairly substantial nonprofit sector representation.

Bridgestar
www.bridgestar.org

Chronicle of Philanthropy/
Philanthropy Careers
www.philanthropy.com/jobs

Commongood Careers
www.cgcareers.org

Idealist.org/Action Without Borders
www.idealist.org

Nonprofit Career Network
www.nonprofitcareer.com

nonprofitJOBMARKET.org
www.nonprofitjobmarket.org

NonprofitOyster.com
www.nonprofitoyster.com

Opportunity Knocks
www.opportunityknocks.org

Society for Nonprofit Organizations
www.snpo.org/nonprofitcareers

OneWorld United States (OneWorld.net)
http://us.oneworld.net/job/list/professional

work4agoodcause.com
www.work4agoodcause.com

WorkforNonprofits.org
www.workfornonprofits.org

Young Nonprofit Professionals Network
www.ynpn.org/CareerCenter

Nonprofit Career Books and Jobs Directories

Countless resources are dedicated to the job hunt and career counseling. The following books are specific to careers in the nonprofit sector. If you want to add to your library beyond this nonprofit career guide, be sure to review the book you are considering at a library before purchasing. Although only titles released since 2000 are included in this list, you might find that some of them are outdated. Some function more like directories than guidebooks and may be of limited use to you in your search.

In addition, if you think you need particular help with networking, résumé writing, or interviewing, abundant resources specific to those areas are available, so be sure to tap into them.

100 Best Nonprofits to Work For
by Leslie Hamilton and Robert Tragert (Stamford, CT: Arco/Thomson Learning, 2000).

150 Best Jobs for a Better World
by Laurence Shatkin (Indianapolis, IN: JIST Publishing, 2008)

Be Bold: Create a Career with Impact
by Cheryl L. Dorsey, Lara Galinsky,
Don Cheadle, and John Prendergast
(New York: Echoing Green, 2006).

Career Opportunities in the Nonprofit Sector
by Jennifer Bobrow Burns
(New York: Checkmark Books, 2006).

Careers for Good Samaritans & Other
Humanitarian Types
by Marjorie Eberts and Margaret Gisler
(New York: McGraw-Hill, 2006).

Careers in Nonprofits and Government Agencies
by WetFeet (San Francisco: WetFeet, Inc.,
2008).

Change Your Career: Transitioning to the
Nonprofit Sector
by Laura Gassner Otting (New York: Kaplan,
2007).

From Making a Profit to Making a Difference:
How to Launch Your New Career
in Nonprofits
by Richard M. King (River Forest, IL:
Planning/Communications, 2000).

A Guide to Careers in Community Development
by Paul C. Brophy and Alice Shabecoff
(Washington, DC: Island Press, 2001).

The Harvard Business School Guide to Careers
in the Nonprofit Sector
by Stephanie Lowell (Boston: Harvard
Business School, 2000).

The Idealist Guide to Nonprofit Careers
by Meg Busse and Steven Pascal-Joiner
(Action Without Borders, 2007). Available at
http://www.idealist.org/en/career/guide/
index.html.

Search: Winning Strategies to Get Your Next Job
in the Nonprofit World
by Larry Slesinger (Glen Echo, MD:
Piemonte Press, 2004).

Periodicals Focused on the Nonprofit Sector

The following periodicals are a sample of publications that focus on the nonprofit sector. Some lean more toward the academic, others the practical. Read these resources in your local library (or online, when available). Identify the periodicals that cover your issue area of interest and determine which you should subscribe to while job searching and beyond. And of course always read a national and local newspaper daily, especially when making a career move. You are hoping to have many informational meetings and need to be up to date on the news of the day.

The Chronicle of Philanthropy
www.philanthropy.com

Nonprofit and Voluntary Sector Quarterly
www.arnova.org

Nonprofit Management and Leadership
www.case.edu/mandelcenter/nml/

Nonprofit Online News
http://news.gilbert.org

The Nonprofit Quarterly
www.nonprofitquarterly.org

The NonProfit Times
www.nptimes.com

Nonprofit World
www.snpo.org/publications/nonprofitworld.php

Academic Programs

College campuses that offer the American Humanics certificate preparing students for non-profit sector careers are listed on the American Humanics website (www.humanics.org). Click the "Academic Partners" button.

Researcher Roseanne Mirabella in the Department of Political Science at Seton Hall University created a comprehensive database of university-based programs in nonprofit education (http://tltc.shu.edu/npo/query.php). The database includes undergraduate, graduate, for-credit, noncredit, and continuing education programs in nonprofit management and related subjects.

Resources for More Information

To get a more in-depth understanding of the nonprofit sector, spend some time in that section of your library. You might start by looking at books and research papers by Peter Drucker, David Hammack, Paul Light, Steven Ott, and Lester Salamon, among others. And be sure to spend time with *The Nonprofit Almanac 2008* (The Urban Institute Press) for the most up-to-date information on the sector.

To learn more about the nonprofit sector and specific organizations in it, check out the resources listed below.

Alliance for Nonprofit Management
www.allianceonline.org

Association for Research on Nonprofit Organizations and Voluntary Action
www.arnova.org

Foundation Center
www.foundationcenter.org

GuideStar
www.guidestar.org

Independent Sector
www.independentsector.org

National Council of Nonprofit Associations
www.ncna.org

Nonprofit Sector Workforce Coalition
www.humanics.org

ENDNOTES

1 Roger A. Lohmann, "And Lettuce Is Nonanimal: Toward a Positive Economics of Voluntary Action," *Nonprofit and Voluntary Sector Quarterly* 17, no. 4 (1989): 367–83.

2 To learn more about the legal and tax-related classification, visit the Internal Revenue Service's website at www.irs.gov (accessed January 7, 2008).

3 Nonprofit organizations with annual revenue less than $5,000 are not required to register with the IRS. So small voluntary associations such as parent-teacher associations and neighborhood groups are absent from IRS registration lists and therefore underrepresented in data.

4 Independent Sector, "Value of Volunteer Time" (2006); available at www.independentsector.org/programs/research/volunteer_time.html (accessed January 7, 2008).

5 Peter F. Drucker, *Managing the Non-Profit Organization: Principles and Practices* (New York: HarperCollins Publishers, 1992), 3.

6 Based on expenditure, 501(c)(3)'s can spend up to 20 percent of their exempt purpose budget (up to $1 million) on legislative lobbying.

Based on the "substantial part" test, 501(c)(3)'s may only lobby so long as those activities do not constitute a substantial part of the charity's activities. However, "substantial" has not been fully defined. For more information about laws governing lobbying, visit the websites of the Alliance for Justice (www.afj.org) and the Center for Lobbying in the Public Interest (www.clpi.org).

7 Unless noted otherwise, data in this chapter as well as in Chapter 2 are drawn from Kennard T. Wing, Thomas H. Pollak, Amy Blackwood, and Linda M. Lampkin, *The Nonprofit Almanac 2008* (Washington, DC: The Urban Institute Press, forthcoming); and Thomas H. Pollack and Amy Blackwood, *The Nonprofit Sector in Brief: Facts and Figures from the Nonprofit Almanac 2007* (Washington, D.C.: National Center for Charitable Statistics at the Urban Institute); available at www.urban.org.

8 Lester M. Salamon and S. Wojciech Sokolowski, "Employment in America's Charities: A Profile," Nonprofit Employment Bulletin Number 26 (The Johns Hopkins Center for Civil Society Studies, 2006).

9 Based on 2006 World Bank data for total GDP worldwide, the U.S. nonprofit sector's revenue would represent the eighth largest economy in the world, ahead of Canada, Spain, Brazil, and Russia, and behind Italy. For World Bank data, see http://siteresources.worldbank.org/DATASTATISTICS/Resources/GDP.pdf (accessed January 7, 2008).

10 Data reflect growth rates of organizations from 1993 to 2003. From the Urban Institute's National Center for Charitable Statistics and the Census Bureau, as reported in "Where the New Charities Are: Gains in 50 Big Metropolitan Areas," *The Chronicle of Philanthropy* (January 6, 2005); available at http://www.philanthropy.com/premium/articles/v17/i06/where.htm (accessed January 30, 2008).

11 Data from *Giving USA*, as reported in Holly Hall, "Donations by Americans reached $295-billion in 2006," *The Chronicle of Philanthropy* (June 28, 2007), available at http://www.philanthropy.com/free/articles/v19/i18/18002701.htm (accessed January 11, 2008).

12 Steven Lawrence, Algernon Austin, and Reina Mukai, *Foundation Growth and Giving Estimates: Current Outlook* 2007 ed. (New York: Foundation Center).

13 Paul Light, "The Content of Their Character: The State of the Nonprofit Workforce," *Nonprofit Quarterly* (Fall 2002): 6–27.

14 Mike Allison and Jude Kaye, "Characteristics of Nonprofit Organizations," in Sue Bennett, *The Accidental Techie* (Saint Paul, MN: Fieldstone Alliance, 2005), 149–53.

15 Thomas Tierney, *The Nonprofit Sector's Leadership Deficit* (Boston: The Bridgespan Group, 2006).

16 Jeanne Bell, Richard Moyers, and Timothy Wolfred, *Daring to Lead 2006: A National Study of Nonprofit Executive Leadership* (San Francisco: CompassPoint Nonprofit Services, 2006).

17 Paige Hull Teegarden, *Nonprofit Executive Leadership and Transitions Survey 2004* (Silver Spring, MD: Managance Consulting and the Annie E. Casey Foundation, 2004). http://www.aecf.org/upload/PublicationFiles/executive_transition_survey_report2004.pdf.

18 A. Gordon, "Turnover Nears For Top Leaders of Nonprofits: Generational Change Approaches in City," *New York Sun* (October 23, 2003): 1.

19 *2007 GuideStar Nonprofit Compensation Report* (Williamsburg, VA: Philanthropic Research, Inc. [GuideStar], 2007). All salary information in this section is from the GuideStar report.

20 These figures reflect all positions reported for each category. Some of the median salaries may look high because for many smaller organizations, only the CEO's compensation is reported on Form 990, on which these data are based. Either no one else in the organization is compensated, or no other employees make more than $50,000, and therefore their compensation is not reported.

21 U.S. Census Bureau, "Minority Population Tops 100 Million," press release, May 17, 2007; available at http://www.census.gov/Press-Release/www/releases/archives/population/010048.html (accessed January 11, 2008).

22 Francie Ostrower, "Nonprofit Governance in the United States," (Washington, DC: The Urban Institute, 2007).

23 Lester Salamon, "The Nonprofit Workforce Crisis: Real or Imagined?" (Baltimore: Johns Hopkins Center for Civil Society Studies, Listening Post Project, 2007).

24 Girl Scouts of the United States of America, "The Architecture of Inclusion," (2007): 8; available at http://www.girlscouts.org/who_we_are/leadership/the_architecture_of_inclusion.pdf (accessed January 11, 2008).

25 Contributing writer Kelly Nuxoll researched and wrote each of the nine subsector Spotlights in this chapter. For more information on Kelly, see the Acknowledgments.

26 Margaret Wyszomirski, "Arts and Culture," in Lester M. Salamon, *The State of Nonprofit America* (Washington, DC: Brookings Institution Press, 2002), 205.

27 Daniel Goleman, Richard E. Boyatzis, and Annie McKee, *Primal Leadership: Realizing the Power of Emotional Intelligence* (Boston: Harvard Business School Press, 2002); Harry Beckwith, *Selling the Invisible: A Field Guide to Modern Marketing* (New York: Warner Books, 1997); Stephen R. Covey, *The Seven Habits of Highly Effective People: Restoring the Character Ethic* (New York: Simon and Schuster, 1989).

28 National Coalition on Health Care, Health Insurance Cost: Facts on the Cost of Health Care, available at www.nchc.org/facts/cost.shtml (accessed January 11, 2008).

29 Bureau of Labor Statistics, U.S. Department of Labor, *Career Guide to Industries, 2008–09 Edition*, Health Care, available at www.bls.gov/oco/cg/cgs035.htm (accessed December 18, 2007).

30 Ibid.

31 Community chests and similar organizations may be categorized in the subsector public or societal benefit.

32 Shepard Forman and Abby Stoddard, "International Assistance," in Salamon, *The State of Nonprofit America,* 261.

33 Lester M. Salamon, *America's Nonprofit Sector: A Primer* (New York: The Foundation Center, 1999).

34 Anthony Mancuso, *How to Form a Nonprofit Corporation*, 5th ed. (Berkeley: Nolo, 2002).

35 Rosalind Wiseman, *Queen Bees & Wannabes: Helping Your Daughter Survive Cliques, Gossip, Boyfriends, and Other Realities of Adolescence* (New York: Crown Publishers, 2002); Larry Brendtro, Martin Brokenleg, and Steve Van Bockern, *Reclaiming Youth at Risk: Our Hope for the Future*, rev. ed. (Bloomington, IN: Solution Tree, 2002); Jonathan Kozol, *Savage Inequalities: Children in America's Schools* (New York: Crown Pub., 1991).

36 Jeanne Bell and Elizabeth Schaffer, *Financial Leadership for Nonprofit Executives: Guiding Your Organization to Long-term Success* (Saint Paul, MN: Fieldstone Alliance, 2005).

37 Ed Michaels, Helen Handfield-Jones, and Beth Axelrod, *The War for Talent* (Boston: Harvard Business School Press, 2001); Michael Watkins, *The First 90 Days: Critical Success Strategies for New Leaders at All Levels* (Boston: Harvard Business School Press, 2003); James C. Collins, *Good to Great: Why Some Companies Make the Leap—and Others Don't* (New York: HarperBusiness, 2001).

38 *U.S. News & World Report's* special report, "Best Careers 2008"; available at http://www.usnews.com/features/business/best-careers/best-careers-2008.html (accessed January 30, 2008).

39 Ronald T. Takaki, *A Different Mirror: A History of Multicultural America* (Boston : Little, Brown & Co., 1993); Samuel F. Yette, *The Choice: The Issue of Black Survival in America* (Silver Spring, MD: Cottage Books, 1996); Howard Zinn and Anthony Arnove, *Voices of a People's History of the United States* (New York: Seven Stories Press, 2004).

40 Deepak Malhotra and Max H. Bazerman, *Negotiation Genius: How to Overcome Obstacles and Achieve Brilliant Results at the Bargaining Table and Beyond* (New York: Bantam Dell, 2007).

Notes from page 281, About American Humanics

41 Data for 2005 (most current available) from *Nonprofit Almanac 2008*.

42 As of the second quarter of 2004, as reported in Lester M. Salamon and S. Wojciech Sokolowski, "Employment in America's Charities: A Profile," Nonprofit Employment Bulletin Number 26 (The Johns Hopkins Center for Civil Society Studies, 2006).

43 Based on World Bank data for the year 2006 of world GDPs, the U.S. nonprofit sector's revenue would represent the eighth largest economy in the world, ahead of Canada, Spain, Brazil, and Russia, and behind Italy. For World Bank data, see http://siteresources.worldbank.org/DATASTATISTICS/Resources/GDP.pdf (accessed January 4, 2008).

INDEX

ABOUT AMERICAN HUMANICS, INC.

www.humanics.org

The nonprofit sector is growing at a faster rate than ever. There are now more than 1.4 million registered nonprofits in the United States.[41] These organizations employ more than 12.9 million people, along with the equivalent of 4.7 million full-time volunteers.[42] Together, they generate annual revenue of approximately $1.6 trillion dollars—by some estimates, the eighth largest economy in the world.[43]

Nonprofit organizations' leadership needs are increasing as fast as—if not faster than—the sector itself. Who are the next generation of nonprofit sector leaders, and how will they prepare for the challenges of leading the nonprofit organization of the future?

American Humanics (AH) is a national alliance that brings together nonprofit organizations, universities, and community partners to educate, prepare, and certify future nonprofit sector leaders. The AH program is offered on seventy-five U.S. college campuses. Students pursuing the American Humanics certificate on these campuses benefit from being part of a network of experts with national perspectives on workforce issues unique to the nonprofit sector.

The annual AH Management/Leadership Institute (AHMI) convenes AH students, alumni, and faculty from across the country to participate in three days of workshops, plenary sessions, case studies, professional development, and keynote addresses by nationally recognized experts in nonprofit sector management and leadership. AHMI includes nonprofit sector placement services, as well as workshops for office of career services professionals to expand their knowledge and expertise in nonprofit sector employment.

AH initiated the Nonprofit Sector Workforce Coalition in 2006 as part of its Initiative for Nonprofit Sector Careers. The coalition is a growing alliance of academic institutions, foundations, corporations, and more than fifty national nonprofit organizations working collaboratively to address the most pressing issues related to establishing the next generation of nonprofit sector professionals. Current coalition strategies address workforce diversity, the impact of student debt on nonprofit sector internships and young professionals' career choices, and a national campaign to promote nonprofit sector careers.

As more students come to college with the desire to "make a difference," American Humanics is the only national organization addressing the growing need for dedicated and experienced entry-level professional employees to lead and manage nonprofit organizations. In the United States, 87 percent of all undergraduate nonprofit studies, courses, and programs are offered through AH-affiliated universities. These programs also are accessed by young professionals returning to college with the goal of switching to the nonprofit sector from their current line of work.

The nonprofit sector is clearly a growth industry that offers promising careers to individuals committed to community service. For more information on the American Humanics certificate in nonprofit management and leadership, or to contact one of the seventy-five AH-affiliated colleges and universities, visit www.humanics.org or call 800-343-6466.

Contacting American Humanics:
American Humanics
1100 Walnut Street, Suite 1900
Kansas City, MO 64106
800-343-6466 or 816-561-6415
www.humanics.org
careerguide@humanics.org

American Humanics NextGen Leaders

In 2007, American Humanics introduced the Next Generation Nonprofit Sector Leaders (NextGen Leaders) program. This competitive internship stipend program supports a racially, ethnically, and economically diverse group of college students having demonstrated leadership potential as they complete the requirements for AH certification in nonprofit management and leadership. The goal is to help talented and passionate young people pursue nonprofit sector careers.

Through 2012, one thousand American Humanics students will be awarded a NextGen internship stipend of up to $4,500 each. NextGen Leaders also receive access to and support from a mentorship network of nonprofit and philanthropic leaders.

The NextGen Leaders stipend is funded by the W.K. Kellogg Foundation. For more information, visit the American Humanics website at www.humanics.org.

ABOUT THE AUTHOR

SHELLY CRYER is the founder of the Initiative for Nonprofit Sector Careers, a research and advocacy project begun in 2002 and now housed at American Humanics. The project launched the national Nonprofit Sector Workforce Coalition and through this and other programs works to cultivate a skilled, prepared, and diverse next generation of nonprofit sector leadership. Shelly's initial research was funded by The Forbes Funds and conducted in partnership with New York University's Wagner Graduate School of Public Service.

For the past seventeen years, Shelly has worked as an independent consultant to nonprofit organizations, designing and implementing strategic media and public education campaigns, conducting research, and assisting with development efforts. She focuses on women's rights, public health, and international affairs, and has spent significant time working for coalitions of nongovernmental organizations that have collaborated around major UN initiatives. Shelly worked on the Beijing Women's Conference, the Cairo Population Conference, and with the Coalition for an International Criminal Court, among other campaigns.

Shelly served as an adjunct professor at Columbia University and Baruch College of the City University of New York, teaching graduate courses on the media, policy, and nonprofit organizations.

Prior to working as a consultant, Shelly served as research associate for the Feminist Majority Foundation, where she helped launch a national "Rock for Choice" benefit concert series and organize a diverse coalition of community leaders to investigate violence in Los Angeles. She also conducted campaign work in Oregon and Utah for the American Civil Liberties Union Reproductive Freedom Project. She began her professional life as a journalist in Colorado, covering public policy and the arts for a weekly newspaper and hosting a radio show for the regional public station . . . and paying rent by waiting tables and adjusting ski bindings at Crested Butte mountain.

Shelly received a Master of International Affairs, with a concentration in public health, from Columbia University's School of International and Public Affairs (SIPA) in 1997. She received a Bachelor of Arts degree in English from Duke University in 1989. She is married to Michael Stern, music director of the Kansas City Symphony and founder of the IRIS orchestra based in Memphis. They and their daughter divide their time between New York City and Kansas City, Missouri.

donation of proceeds

The author is donating a percentage of the royalties she receives from the sale of this book to three organizations working to make college more accessible to traditionally underrepresented populations: the American Indian College Fund, the Hispanic Scholarship Fund, and the United Negro College Fund. Organizations such as these, in partnership with organizations such as American Humanics, are helping to ensure that our country's future leaders—including leaders for the nonprofit sector—truly reflect our country's population.

For more information on these organizations, visit their websites at www.collegefund.org, www.hsf.net, and www.uncf.org.